And the Blood Cried Out

"AND THE BLOOD CRIED OUT"

A Prosecutor's Spellbinding Account of the Power of DNA

HARLAN LEVY

BasicBooks
A Division of HarperCollins*Publishers*

Copyright © 1996 by Harlan Levy.
Published by BasicBooks,
A Division of HarperCollins Publishers, Inc.

Designed by Laura Lindgren

Library of Congress Cataloging-in-Publication Data

Levy, Harlan.
    And the blood cried out : a prosecutor's spellbinding account of the
power of DNA / Harlan Levy.—1st ed.
        p. cm.
    Includes bibliographical references and index.
    ISBN 0–465–01704–5
    1. DNA fingerprinting—United States. 2. Evidence, Expert—United
States. 3. Trials (Murder)—United States. I. Title.
    KF9666.5.L48   1996
    345.73'067—dc20   96–10385

96 97 98 99 00 ❖/HC 10 9 8 7 6 5 4 3 2

CONTENTS

1
Getting to Homicide   1

2
Breakthrough   17

3
The Trouble with DNA   33

4
Inside the Central Park Jogger Trial   59

5
The Triumph of DNA   87

6
Vitriol   105

7
Manhunt   125

8
Sudden Insight: The World Trade Center
Bombing and Beyond   137

9
O. J. Simpson: What the Blood Really
Showed   157

10
The Power of DNA   189

vi   CONTENTS

Acknowledgments   *201*
Notes and Sources   *203*
Index   *215*

And the Blood Cried Out

1 GETTING TO HOMICIDE

HOMICIDE DETECTIVE MIKE SHEEHAN was frustrated. The suspect, Matias ("Tony") Reyes, had confessed to two of the serial rapes when interviewed earlier by a different detective, but homicide was another matter. When a related murder was raised, a homicide the detectives believed had been committed by the same man who committed the rapes, the suspect was obstinate in his denials, unequivocal and unwavering.

The only hope of building a homicide case lay in continuing to work Reyes until he confessed. The detective knew what to do. He had done it many times before, and, while the specifics change, the rules of the game remain the same.

Detectives know that the strategies and approaches they use to elicit confessions from suspects are built upon very simple but broad underlying principles. This is true from homicide cases to rape and robbery cases.

The first objective is to cause the suspect to abandon all hope that he can walk away from this one. The detective tells the suspect how much evidence the police have against him. There are the witnesses who have identified him. There is the victim's property or the weapon that was found in the suspect's pocket. The detective asks the suspect how he can explain these things, and tries to make the suspect think that the only available course of action is to confess.

And, when he feels trapped, when he believes he will have to explain these things to the detective but cannot face doing so because he has no explanation that can possibly save him from the terrible fate he now faces, the detective will offer him a little grace. It may simply be the grace of a confession. Most killers, like most other people, are raised with morality and religion, and some irreducible core of moral feeling or guilt usually survives even among those who resort to the most grievous of crimes. A person who has just committed an awful act may feel a tremendous need to confess. He may also be feeling that nearly universal impulse simply to talk about a traumatic experience he has just been through, even if he is the principal architect of his trauma.

It seldom occurs, though, that the suspect confuses the detective with a priest, therapist, or friend—any one of whom can dispense absolution—and confesses outright. In most cases, the detective tries to have the suspect take a first step toward an eventual confession by offering the grace of an excuse. This serves the detective's purposes, because the suspect's assertion that the act was not as bad as it may seem to outsiders concedes that an act requiring an explanation has in fact occurred. The smart detective will encourage his suspect to start down this road by offering him a menu of excuses to choose from. There may be, the detective will tell the suspect, many alternative explanations for what happened. Was it an accident? Did he intend only to frighten the victim? Maybe it was self-defense? Did the deceased deserve to die because he had done some terrible injury to the suspect or to a third party?

The detective will make it clear that as things now stand it looks bad for the suspect and he, the detective, is the only one who can make sure the world gets to hear the suspect's side of things. The relationship is a peculiar one, for the detective seeks both to intimidate and to charm the suspect. The Miranda warnings, advising the suspect that he need not talk, will have been read with the verbal equivalent of a wink, in a tone and cadence suggesting that all in the room know that this is simply a formal legal nicety to be gotten past before they get down to business. Now that the real business has begun, the sympathetic and purportedly gullible detective offers the suspect a chance to put one over on him by explaining the terrible situation in a way that will make the suspect seem much less the monster than everyone now believes him to be. Above all, the detective seeks to get the suspect to "put himself in it," to say, "Yeah, I killed the guy, but there was a reason for it." The detective knows that the world will hear the reason as the lame excuse that it is, but keeps any hint of censure or even skepticism out of his voice, for he understands that his own initial acceptance of the suspect's excuse is often an essential element in getting the suspect to agree to dictate and sign a full confession.

While the homicide detective would go through this process later that night, Bruno Francisi, the sex crimes detective who had already gotten Matias Reyes to admit to the rapes, had taken another tack. An eighteen-year veteran of the New York City Police Department, Francisi was a member of the Manhattan Sex Crimes Squad. He was well dressed, trim, dark haired with a mustache, direct, smart. Everything about him inspired confidence. Francisi had investigated many of the most notorious and sensational sex crimes in Manhattan. He was the detective in the Sex Crimes Bureau who handled the "pattern cases." These involve tracking and finding miscreants who repeatedly commit similar crimes. The crimes may be linked by a common location or by a trademark signature, like stealing the victim's shoes or committing some highly distinctive and seemingly senseless assault.

The trademark of the big pattern case in the summer of 1989 was much less amusing than a shoe fetish. The East Side Slasher tried to blind his victims. His motive was simple and not altogether senseless from the criminal's perspective. He did not want them to be able to identify him. A blind victim would not be able to pick him out of a lineup or point to him in court.

His clarity of purpose was apparent from his startling and chilling words as well as from his hideous acts. "I have to kill you or I have to blind you," he told one victim. "Your eyes or your life," he said to another. During the summer of 1989 three women were raped and stabbed in or about their eyes. One died. The others were severely injured but survived with their sight. All three rapes took place on Manhattan's Upper East Side.

Detective Francisi had been called on the afternoon of Saturday, August 5, 1989. It was his day off, and he was at home. Francisi had been working this pattern all summer, and now he was told that there had been another Upper East Side rape. On the chance that it was related to the earlier rapes, he hurriedly dressed and set off for work. Forty-five minutes after receiving the call, Francisi was at the Nineteenth Precinct. Quickly, he learned the details of the latest rape.

Just two hours earlier, a man had raped twenty-three-year-old Elizabeth Reynolds. Reynolds, a young professional, was returning home when a man followed her into her apartment building. He walked up the stairs and listened at each floor for the elevator to open, tracking Reynolds to her floor. At the third floor, he furtively watched and noted which apartment she entered. As soon as she was inside and had closed the door, he rang the doorbell.

Having come in only a minute before, Reynolds was caught off guard and opened the door. The man pushed his way into the apartment and told Reynolds that he would shoot her unless she was quiet. His hand was in his pocket as if he were holding a gun. He ordered Reynolds to take off her clothes. He raped her in the shower; then he raped her on the bed.

The man told Reynolds that he would have to tie her up or kill her. As he walked about the apartment, he became somewhat distracted, and Reynolds raced to the door. She fled the apartment with a towel wrapped around her body, ran down the stairs, found the doorman, and told him what had happened.

The doorman and another man grabbed the rapist in the lobby. They called the police, who came and arrested the man. The police then asked Reynolds to take a look at the person they were holding. Reynolds walked by and told the police, "That's him."

The man who raped Reynolds never had a chance to try to blind her. Perhaps he was looking for a knife with which to do it as he wandered about the apartment distractedly. When she ran, she was escaping from a crime in progress, one that had not yet reached the point at which the criminal got to leave his signature. But while this case lacked the slasher's signature, Francisi spotted some other similarities to the pattern cases he was working. One of the prior rapes had also taken place in the shower. The general description of the rapist was the same, and the rapes all took place on the Upper East Side.

As soon as the arresting officer completed the case paperwork at the precinct, Francisi personally took custody of the suspect. He put Matias Reyes in a car and took him across town through Central Park. Their destination was Francisi's office in the Sex Crimes Squad on the Upper West Side. Reyes did not know where they were going because Francisi did not tell him. The detective figured it would be better if it came as a surprise. That would give Reyes less time to compose his thoughts and more of a jolt when he found out where they were.

Arriving at the squad, Francisi told Reyes they were at Sex Crimes. He said that he wanted to interview Reyes about the arrest today and some other investigations he was conducting.

"I didn't touch that girl," said Reyes, talking about that day's rape.

"Tony, just be quiet," said Francisi. "I want you to listen to a tape."

The tape was from an earlier crime. On another awful afternoon weeks earlier, on July 19, 1989, at 3:30 P.M., a man had followed another young woman into her apartment building. He was able to enter with impunity; workers were fixing the front door, and it was open and unsecured. The man tagged along after the young woman into the building.

The victim that day was twenty-year-old Katherine Davis, a student living with her parents on Madison Avenue. Davis walked up the stairs, and the man walked up after her. When Davis reached the fifth floor, he continued walking up the stairs. Immediately, though, he doubled back and accosted his victim in the hallway outside the door to her parents' apartment.

The man pointed a knife at her and took Davis inside. He raped Davis three times, including an anal rape. Before leaving, he tied her hands and ankles together with a television cord and placed her on the floor.

"I have to kill you or I have to blind you," he said. Davis replied that her choice was to give up her sight rather than her life. She pled with her attacker to place a cloth over her eyes when he stabbed her, so that she would feel less pain. He agreed and did place a cloth over her eyes. Then he hit her repeatedly in each eye with a sharp object.

As the man prepared to leave Davis bound, bleeding, and gagged with a telephone cord, he told her that he would call her an ambulance. And, strangely, he was true to his word. Minutes after leaving the apartment, the rapist called 911 and gave them Davis's address and apartment number. At the same corner where he engaged in this errand of mercy, he used Davis's bank card and the code he had demanded from her to steal $300 from her account.

This extraordinary call, like all 911 calls, was on tape. As part of his investigation of the Davis rape, Francisi had obtained a copy of the tape from the Communications Division of the Police Department at One Police Plaza, and had listened to it. On the Saturday of the Reynolds rape, when Francisi spoke to Reyes, he immediately recognized Reyes's voice. This was the tape Francisi now played.

Reyes became very quiet. He put his head down a little and started to sob.

"I'm fucked," said Reyes.

"Tony, do you recognize that voice?" asked Francisi.

"Yes, it's me," said Reyes.

"Tony, tell me the truth," said Francisi.

And Reyes admitted the Katherine Davis rape and all its details.

Then, said Reyes, he was downtown today and decided to do it again. Francisi asked for the details of that day's incident.

But, all of a sudden, Reyes backed off. He denied the latest rape. "What would my grandmother think if she found out?" he asked.

Look, said Francisi, the facts are as they are. You were arrested. You were identified. You saw the girl confront you today. You had her property on you.

And, once again, Reyes admitted to rape.

But to Reyes, murder was another matter.

The murder that Francisi believed to be part of the same pattern had shocked a city immune to shock, a city in which Jack the Ripper with his handful of murders of anonymous prostitutes would be a small time player. The only account of the crime came from the victim's small children.

The children said that a stranger had gained entrance to their apartment and asked for money. Their mother, visibly upset, placed the children in another room and locked the door. The words and sounds the children heard from the next room were terrifying. Their mother cried, "Don't kill me," and the stranger shouted, "I'll take out your eyes or the kids' eyes." The children cowered in the next room, listening to their mother's screams as she was raped and then stabbed to death. Her wounds included wounds to her eyes.

When Detective Mike Sheehan was brought in to question Reyes about the homicide, he had no hard evidence with which he could confront him. He had nothing to work with but his skill at what he did for a living, and some considerable charm. The rare ability to turn on the charm for a low-life who has raped someone just hours earlier is an important part of a successful detective's arsenal.

No detective was more skilled at turning on the charm than Mike Sheehan, who would later become a television newsman covering the police beat. As a detective, as a person, Sheehan was pure insinuation and seduction. Fortunately, he exercised his considerable powers on the right side of the law. He was a brilliant investigator and an extraordinarily gifted interrogator. He had been the detective on the "preppie murder" in Central Park of Jennifer Levin by Robert Chambers. In fact, Sheehan was a natural actor; he played his own boss in the television movie about the Chambers case, and a fight promoter in *Rocky IV*. He bragged of having dated Lauren Hutton. He was every inch the promoter, the storyteller, the joker, the charmer.

That night, his winks and his skill were directed toward gaining a confession to murder from Matias Reyes.

Sheehan first took a turn with Reyes after he had confessed the rapes to Francisi. Sheehan introduced himself, extending his hand to Reyes as if they were two guys meeting for the first time under normal circumstances. Then he interviewed Reyes from 9:00 to 10:30 P.M.

Reyes had just been fingerprinted. Sheehan explained that these were not ordinary fingerprints that had been taken but "major case prints." Ordinary fingerprints are limited to the five fingers of each hand, but major case prints include the palms and can identify prints that might otherwise elude detection.

Sheehan told Reyes that he was personally investigating the murder of a woman on Ninety-seventh Street. Reyes said that he had not been there, though he had read about it in the newspapers. Sheehan reminded Reyes that the police would compare his major case prints with the fingerprints found in the apartment of the murder victim.

"What if your prints turn up?" asked Sheehan.

"They won't turn up," said Reyes.

"What if they do?" asked Sheehan.

But Reyes would not be intimidated by the possibility that his prints might be found in this victim's apartment.

Sheehan and Reyes went back and forth, but Reyes gave nothing up, and Sheehan stopped the interview. They broke for an hour.

At 11:30 P.M. Sheehan went back to work on Reyes, on the murder, with two other detectives present.

"I read there was a kid in the apartment," said Reyes. "Is that true?"

Yeah, said Sheehan, who then tried a new tack. Knowing that so many sex offenders are themselves victims of abuse, and sensing that Reyes may have been abused as a child, Sheehan asked him if anything had ever happened to him sexually when he was a child. At that point, Reyes asked to speak to Sheehan alone. The other two detectives left the room. Sheehan shifted into high gear.

"You don't have to be embarrassed," he said. "If something happened you can tell me."

Sheehan then told Reyes how when he was a kid he went down to Times Square to purchase a football helmet, went into a subway bathroom, and was propositioned by a guy. "I used the football helmet for the first time to crash it over the guy's head and I ran away. So, if something happened to you and it's embarrassing, you can tell me and I certainly won't laugh at it. I mean, things do happen."

Reyes then said that something had happened to him too, but he did not give any details. Did something bad happen to you sexually? asked Sheehan. And Reyes said yes.

"Well," asked Sheehan, "will you ever forget this guy? Because I won't ever forget the guy that approached me."

Reyes sat up straight. He became angry. "I'll never forget this guy, I'll never forget him," he proclaimed. And he slammed his hand on the table.

"Well," asked Sheehan, "do you think this kid at Ninety-seventh Street is ever going to forget the guy who raped and killed his mother?"

Reyes sat back in his chair. No, probably not, he said.

While Sheehan did not say it aloud, the point was clear. The "kid" would likely be able to implicate Reyes in his mother's murder. The identification could be in a line-up or in court. But the kid would not have forgotten Reyes's face, not in a lifetime.

Sheehan then showed Reyes a police drawing. The sketch in fact had nothing to do with the murder and was based on the description given by a victim of one of the rapes. But Sheehan said nothing of its source. He left the misimpression that it was based on a description by a child of the murder victim. The resemblance to Reyes was uncanny.

Reyes looked at the drawing. "That's me," he said.

Sheehan looked Reyes in the eyes. "You know," said Sheehan, "being a detective really isn't a big mystery. It's just interviewing several people, and that's how you get the answers to things. In this particular case, forget about the kid. Even without the kid, there's three people that have to be interviewed at Ninety-seventh Street."

"Who are they?" asked Reyes.

"Well," said Sheehan, "we'll go through it piece by piece, so you understand my job. There is the woman who is dead. But I can't interview her, because she's dead.

"The second person I'd like to interview is God. God was there. God was watching, and God knows what happened.

"The third person would be the killer. Only the person who was there can help me. I think it's you, and if you were there, I hope you tell me the truth. I don't know what happened. I wasn't there. I don't know if this was an accident. I don't know if it was a mistake. I don't know if the killer acted in self-defense."

"It wasn't self-defense," said Reyes, rubbing his head. "She defended her kids. She had the knife. I took it off her easily.

"It's a long story," Reyes said. "I hope I can trust you."

Sheehan assured Reyes that he could. And Reyes detailed his confession to murder.

Of course, putting his trust in Sheehan was not in Reyes's best interests, from a legal point of view. He went on, under Sheehan's protective wing, to make a videotaped confession early the next morning.

While the police now had enough to charge Reyes with murder, getting a homicide conviction would not be a walk in the park. The prosecution would have to prove Reyes's guilt beyond a reasonable doubt. In this case, a good criminal defense attorney had much fabric from which to spin reasonable doubt.

How could that be? How could there be room to question Reyes's role in the murder when Reyes himself had confessed?

The answer to those questions lies in the nature of proof in criminal cases. It is a universal truth among prosecutors and defense attorneys that criminal cases are built on three kinds of evidence. There is identification evidence, a witness coming into court and saying, That's him, that's the man. There is physical evidence, the victim's property or a weapon found in the defendant's pocket. Then there are confessions, admissions from the defendant's own mouth. Juries convict when all three kinds of evidence are present and when each kind corroborates the others. When there is only one kind of evidence, a jury may convict or they may not, depending on the weight and quality of the single leg of the triad of criminal proof.

There is considerable room for skepticism among jurors about any one kind of evidence standing alone. Identification witnesses may be mistaken. The victim's property may have been picked up innocently, or a weapon may have been planted on the suspect by a rogue police officer, the suspect "flaked," in street vernacular. A false confession may be the result of police coercion or the susceptibility to suggestion of a weak or frightened suspect, as confessions have been many times in the past. Corroboration of one form of evidence by other kinds is the key to obtaining criminal convictions, because when one piece of evidence corroborates another, the credibility of both pieces is enhanced.

After Matias Reyes confessed to murder, there certainly was a murder case against him, but it was based entirely on his confession.

There was no identification evidence. While the victims of the rapes had seen lineups and identified Reyes, the victim of the homicide, of course, could not. The police chose not to show her small children a lineup because it might have been too upsetting for them.

There was physical evidence tying Reyes to the rapes—the jewelry in his pocket from his last victim, and the tape of his 911 call following the earlier rape. But these items linked him solely to the rapes.

For the murder case, no identification witness pointed a finger at Reyes, and none of the victim's property or any weapon had been found in his pocket. In some respects, the murder case was still a good one. The cruel behavior reported by the rape victims could easily carry over to drag Reyes down on the murder charge. And the murder and rapes had a common modus operandi, the attack on the victims' eyes. But criminal juries often show a remarkable ability to make subtle distinctions, sometimes to a fault, as they pore over and dissect evidence. The murder case against Reyes, essentially built on his confession, might not have proved enough at trial to take the jury past reasonable doubt.

There were too many arguments the defense could make that could raise the prospect of reasonable doubt. Reyes had been in police custody since 3:00 in the afternoon. He did not confess to the murder until 1:30 in the morning. He had repeatedly denied the homicide to Sheehan through three hours of questioning about the murder and another rape. The confession, when it came, was prompted not by the presentation to Reyes of any evidence against him but by pressure.

That pressure was multifaceted. It was psychological. It was emotional. It was religious. A good attorney could turn Sheehan's skill in prompting the confession inside out, using it against the police and the prosecution. The circumstances and the disparate levels of sophistication between Sheehan and Reyes made psychological coercion inevitable, the argument would go. By 1:30 in the morning, the police could have had Reyes in such a state that he would have confessed to anything.

In support of this claim, the defense could point to the videotape of the confession, which the prosecution would surely offer into evidence at a trial. At the very beginning of the videotape, Reyes refused to answer questions. The questioning and the videotape were stopped and then, after a break, were resumed.

Why was the videotaping stopped, and what happened during the gap in time? According to Sheehan, Reyes told him off camera that he had stopped talking because he was afraid he would not remember the specifics of the crimes and the videotape resumed after Sheehan reassured Reyes not to worry about the details.

Here was a major opening for the defense. They could argue that Sheehan was lying, that the tape was stopped because Reyes had to be coerced into continuing. Or, more subtly and probably more effectively, the defense could have embraced Sheehan's testimony on this point, that Reyes could not remember details.

They would likely make the claim that Reyes could not remember the specifics because he was not there. What better proof was there of his lack of complicity in the crime than his inability to remember specifics? The only "specifics" Reyes knew about the murder were those he had gleaned from reading the newspapers and those fed to him by Sheehan over the three hours of factually detailed questioning. By the time Reyes finally gave in to police pressure and intimidation, he had gone through a small seminar on the details of the murder. What better education could there have been for a detailed confession? Sheehan ran his classroom well, but a coached confession, as expected, caused memory problems for the student. The police had put the words in his mouth.

The defense had even more to work with. Reyes, at age eighteen, had never before been arrested. To believe that after a lawful life he had suddenly committed the worst of all possible crimes was to accept the view that monsters can come out of nowhere. Rape, even ultraviolent rape, is one thing. Murder is a crime of special classification. (Or so a jury might believe.) The right jury or juror might be reluctant to take that leap from rape to murder based solely on a confession elicited in a precinct at 1:30 in the morning after hours of questioning and repeated denials.

This relentless focus on the doubts that a jury may have is as much an obsession of the criminal prosecutor as it is of the defense attorney. The successful prosecutor identifies possible doubts and finds ways to meet them head-on before the defense gets to raise them. The District Attorney's Office needed corroboration that Reyes had committed this murder.

Toward the goal of gaining that corroboration, semen recovered from the scenes of the murder and the rapes was sent to the FBI for DNA analysis. The FBI was also sent a sample of Reyes's blood, taken from him as part of the proceedings in the criminal case against him. The FBI was to compare the DNA from the crime scenes with the DNA in Reyes's known blood sample.

The results were heartening to the prosecution. The DNA contained in the semen from the murder and various rapes was consistent with that of Matias Reyes. According to the FBI report, the genetic characteristics of that DNA could be expected to occur randomly in one in every 49 million people in the Hispanic population in the United States.

But the battle did not end with these results. DNA evidence was still new at this time, and some courts in the United States were refusing to accept it. These courts, honestly concerned about an emerging controversy over the role of race in stating the significance of a DNA match, excluded not just evidence about the significance of a DNA match but all testimony about DNA. Sorry, they said. The jury will not get to hear these results. Nothing about DNA at all will get to the jury. The Supreme Judicial Court of Massachusetts was the most prominent of several courts that had taken this position at that time. If the New York courts followed suit, the DNA evidence against Reyes would never get to the jury, and the homicide case against him could be in jeopardy.

As we prosecutors in the District Attorney's Office prepared for the pretrial hearing, at which the judge would determine whether the DNA evidence would be admissible to the jury at trial, our doubts were allayed. Our witnesses were two of the nation's leading scientists. Our meetings with them were like graduate seminars in molecular biology for students who had been held back. These sessions were fascinating for us, probably painful for the scientists.

Dr. Thomas Caskey, after all, was the former president of the American Society of Human Genetics. The year before, Caskey had been hired by the United States government to use DNA technology to identify the remains of unknown members of the armed forces killed in Operation Desert Storm. Dr. Michael Conneally chaired the genetics task force of the Muscular Dystrophy Association and had been a leader in mapping human genes, including the Alzheimer's gene and the gene for cystic fibrosis.

Both Caskey and Conneally were entirely convinced of the reliability of the FBI's statement that Reyes's genetic characteristics could be expected to occur in one in every 49 million people in the Hispanic population. These scientific luminaries squarely endorsed the FBI's conclusions.

Our experts got set to testify, but before they were able to, the hearing had to be postponed because of an outbreak of violence in the courtroom. Reyes struck his attorney, John Ianuzzi, who then asked to be relieved from the case. He told the court that he would not and could not represent a client who had struck him. The prosecution, however, was ready to proceed, and the judge, refusing to reward Reyes for punching his attorney with a delay of his trial, would not let Ianuzzi out of the case. Ianuzzi went to the appellate court, which reversed the judge's decision. The DNA hearing was temporarily postponed while a new lawyer was appointed for Reyes.

Soon enough, though, these scientific experts testified in court at the pretrial hearing held to decide whether the DNA evidence would be admitted at trial. Their expertise, as well as the clarity and logic of their thought, were compelling.

The defense's last hope to keep the DNA evidence out at trial and maintain the prospect of an acquittal on the homicide charge was the testimony of their own scientific expert. We awaited his testimony confidently but with some concern. We, the prosecutors, had the burden of proof. It was up to us to show that DNA evidence was generally accepted as reliable by the scientific community. Anything less and the judge would exclude that evidence from the trial, and the jury would never learn of the DNA match.

The defense expert was Dr. William Shields, a geneticist at the New York State University at Syracuse. Shields testified to his disagreement with Drs. Caskey and Conneally. In his view, there were significant differences between ethnic groups within broad racial groups, so that statements assessing the significance of a DNA match for Hispanics were misleading. He offered data that he said supported this view.

On cross-examination, however, Dr. Shields made a number of admissions that dramatically undercut the usefulness of his testimony to the defense. Since he did not like the FBI method, I asked him on cross-examination if there was a method that he preferred, or that better took into account the reservations he had raised. He said yes, that there was such a method. I asked him if he had done a calculation of the numbers using that method in this case, and he said that he had done such a calculation. I asked him for the number, and he said that it was one in 692,585 rather than one in 49 million.

We had to show that this number hardly left Reyes in the clear. True, at almost a hundred times smaller than the FBI's figure, it did not seem to clang the prison doors shut on Reyes quite as conclusively. But, especially in a case where there was additional evidence, even Dr. Shields's number could support a verdict of guilty beyond a reasonable doubt. What we had to do was express that number in a way that made it seem as persuasive as the FBI number. Consider stopping random people on the street, we said. If one in 49 million people have a particular genetic profile, then 99.9999979 percent of those stopped would not have that profile. If we used Dr. Shields's number, then 99.9998556 percent of those stopped would not fit that profile. Not exactly an argument for the unreliability of DNA evidence, nor for acquittal. Shields admitted that my calculations were correct.

In fact, he went even further in admitting the weakness of Reyes's position. My final question on cross-examination built on a series of questions about how unusual it was that Reyes's DNA matched that from one murder and two rapes. That must be an extremely rare event, I asked Dr. Shields, and he agreed. So, in closing, I asked Shields whether his quarrel was with the population statistics generated by the FBI rather than with our conclusion drawn from these statistics that it was highly probable based on the DNA evidence that the defendant was the right guy. And he said yes. The defense expert had now as much as admitted that his client had committed all three crimes.

Three weeks later, the trial of Matias Reyes was set to begin. Judge Thomas Galligan had made it clear that he would admit the DNA evidence at trial. Given that, Matias Reyes had no defense to the evidence that put him at the murder scene. The corroboration of Reyes's confession to Detective Sheehan by DNA evidence was firmly in place.

On the morning that we were set to start picking a jury, October 7, 1991, the defense attorney said that Reyes wanted to plead guilty. Judge Galligan's plea offer was thirty-three years to life, the longest sentence we prosecutors had ever heard of on a plea bargain. A plea bargain would spare the victims the agony of reliving their encounters with Reyes and would eliminate the uncertainty that accompanies any criminal trial. Both the prosecution and the defense accepted the plea bargain, and Matias Reyes pled guilty.

Three weeks later, Reyes was sentenced. At sentencing, Judge Galligan made a record in court of his recommendation to the parole board that Reyes never be paroled, that he spend the rest of his life in jail. Reyes punched his lawyer and knocked him to the floor before he was led away to begin serving his sentence for rape and homicide.

At the time that Reyes was sentenced in 1991, the new genetic evidence that had played a crucial role in sending him to prison for life was just gaining wide acceptance. A new technology, it had first been used to solve a murder case in 1987. The story of the discovery of DNA analysis and that first use brings together science at its most wondrous and crime at its most heinous.

2 BREAKTHROUGH

THE BIBLE TELLS US THAT IT WAS THE FIRST MURDER in human history. Cain was a farmer, Abel a shepherd. Each offered a sacrifice to God. From Cain came produce, from Abel, sheep. The Lord preferred Abel's offering of meat to Cain's offering of produce, and Cain, in a jealous rage, killed his brother.

"Where is your brother Abel?" asked the Lord.

"I do not know," replied Cain. "Am I my brother's keeper?"

"What have you done?" asked the Lord. But then, in an instant, God knew what Cain had done.

"Hark," said the Lord, "your brother's blood cries out to Me from the ground!"

That cry, the cry of Abel's blood, told God that Cain had murdered his brother. The Lord immediately sentenced Cain to be a ceaseless wanderer upon the earth, and Cain soon left for the land of Nod, east of Eden.

Thousands of years would go by before blood would cry out again and positively identify a murderer.

In 1987, it would be man, not God, who would divine the identity of a murderer through blood. But the blood calling out the murderer's name would be not the victim's but the murderer's own. The means of identification would be DNA.

I ARRIVED IN THE MANHATTAN DISTRICT ATTORNEY'S Office in 1987, the year that DNA analysis was first used in a criminal case. As a brand-new assistant district attorney, I was still intrigued by every development in criminal law, and DNA captured my imagination.

After reading about DNA analysis, and thinking its potential extraordinary, I suggested to the chairman of a lawyers' committee to which I belonged that we study it. He asked me to chair the New York City Bar Association panel studying DNA evidence. I was soon immersed in DNA and in some of the most prominent court cases of our time, including the Central Park jogger case.

DNA and I must have been a good fit from the beginning, for I quickly became known as one of the few people in the country who could explain DNA evidence so that other people could understand it. This was not because I have a science background. In fact, my lack of such a background may have made me even more appreciative of how difficult the material can be for those untrained in science.

Another reason DNA and I were a good fit had to do with its great potential as a new tool for doing good. I came to the District Attorney's Office while I was still a young, idealistic lawyer. I firmly believed then, and I firmly believe now, that DNA analysis can promote a more just society, both by making punishment of the guilty more likely and by assuring exoneration of the innocent.

This is not to say that I came to the District Attorney's Office fresh out of law school. When I took that first job, prosecuting repeat felony offenders in the Major Offense/Career Criminal Bureau, I had already been an attorney for several years. But though I had clerked for a federal appeals judge and was then working for a major New York law firm, I had resisted taking the path of many young lawyers interested in public service, going to work at a public prosecutor's office, hoping that I would instead find a policy-related job in government.

But of course it's not that easy to find a paying job changing the world. Like many young idealists, I quickly settled into my corporate job, finding outlets for my concerns in community activities outside work. Yet as time went by, I found working in the world of major New York City law firms more and more dispiriting.

In the go-go 1980s, New York City law firms had a win-at-all-costs, us-against-them, wear-down-your-adversary, and exult-in-doing-it-twenty-four-hours-a-day atmosphere. To me, this was pure craziness. It had little to do with anything I wanted in life. I frequently felt wholly out of place. I might as well have been in a high school football locker room.

And, while the 1980s were a particularly strange time in New York City law firms, large law firms do not celebrate youth in the best of times. This point was dramatically brought home to me by one of the senior lawyers at the firm, who, when introduced to me as the new person on a case he was running, said, "Oh, so you're the new cannon fodder."

Believe it or not, he thought his candor charming. I found it more revelatory than charming and realized over time that it was a sign I would have to look elsewhere for satisfying work.

So I could not have been more pleased when I took a leave of absence from law firm life to work on a commission investigating corruption in New York City government. When that brief stint ended, I was more eager than ever to get into public service and newly energized by the prospect of becoming a prosecutor.

Besides, I had been recruited to come to the District Attorney's Office by the legendary Manhattan District Attorney Robert M. Morgenthau. He had seen me handle myself well at a symposium and invited me to talk to him about working in his office. So in 1987 I traded a solo office for a shared office, my view of the spires of St. Patrick's Cathedral for a view of the local jail, and my large salary for a substantially smaller one.

I was ecstatic. It was great. Besides an opportunity to do some good, there was a whole new level of excitement—cops and robbers, with an overlay of thought, intellect, and argument over subtle points of constitutional law. As prosecutors, it was our job to try to sort out the innocent from the guilty and to press for appropriate punishment for the guilty. There were certainly dismaying aspects to the job. Prosecution in large urban centers is a volume business, and most of the defendants have themselves been brutalized by society. Still, there is something profoundly idealistic and socially redeeming about the endeavor. Nowhere but in the criminal justice system do lawyers, both prosecutors and defense lawyers, routinely concern themselves with matters as basic and elemental as guilt, innocence, individual responsibility, and appropriate punishment.

Besides, some of the special responsibilities that came with being a prosecutor were emotionally and ethically rewarding. A corporate lawyer who agonized over the justice of his or her client's position before undertaking representation would raise eyebrows. On the other hand, despite those cynical stories so often heard—for example, the one in which the veteran prosecutor tells the new recruit, "Convicting the guilty is easy; it's convicting the innocent that takes talent"—to the vast majority of prosecutors I have worked with, the fact that a case was winnable was not enough justification to go forward. They also had to be convinced of the defendant's guilt.

While I loved my work as a prosecutor at the District Attorney's Office, the chance to become involved with DNA analysis offered something more, an opportunity to make a real difference in an entirely new area. I could be a prosecutor and help bring to the administration of justice something new, creative, and surely needed.

It was hard to imagine a system more in need of help than the criminal justice system. Throughout the 1980s and early 1990s, there was an explosion of violent crime in American society. As the fear of crime grew, it often focused on murder and rape, the most fearsome of all crimes. DNA analysis promised a perfect match for solving just these crimes, where blood or semen are most frequently left behind. DNA evidence could help put the worst of the worst behind bars and fully clear those falsely accused of the most serious crimes as no other evidentiary tool could.

This was also an alluring area to me because of its fundamental concern with actual guilt or innocence. The American judicial system, with its presumption of innocence and requirement of proof beyond a reasonable doubt, is rightly based on the premise that it is better that a guilty person go free than that an innocent person go to jail. Since all accused are innocent until proven guilty, protections built into that system to protect the innocent also, by necessity, protect those who have actually committed the crimes with which they have been charged.

Dialogue about the criminal justice process usually revolves around where to draw the line between society's right to protect itself and the right of criminal defendants to have their basic constitutional protections respected. This important debate frequently has little to do with actual guilt or innocence, for as it has been played out over the years it has become a way the law regulates police and prosecutorial behavior. Evidence obtained in violation of every citizen's Fourth Amendment right not to be subjected to unreasonable searches and seizures may be kept out of a trial not because it will result in an unfair verdict but in the hope that its exclusion will discourage future illegal searches by the police. In a similar way, a confession obtained in violation of an accused's Fifth Amendment protection against self-incrimination may be excluded not because it does not represent a true confession but to try to assure that the government is not encouraged to beat confessions out of suspects or in other ways to pressure them into providing evidence against themselves. In a sense, the law is willing to sacrifice justice in individual cases rather than undermine the constitutional safeguards that protect the individual from the power of the state.

By contrast, DNA evidence promised to go beyond balancing the rights of the accused and the rights of the state, and to aim straight at determination of the truth. Truth is sometimes an underrated commodity in the criminal justice system. In fact, there are judges who have prohibited lawyers from telling a jury that a trial is a search for the truth, insisting instead that a trial is a process, pursuant to the rules of evidence, to determine whether guilt has been proven beyond a reasonable doubt. For me, and for many others, the prospect of a focus on the truth in the criminal justice system was alluring, and I became an advocate for DNA analysis, pressing for its admissibility in speeches, in articles, and in the councils of government.

In 1995 I resigned from the District Attorney's Office to write this book. I believed it important to tell the story of DNA analysis, to help dispel some of the public bafflement surrounding this new technology, and to meet the strong desire of so many people to understand the controversy surrounding DNA testing. I have sought to explain the science of DNA and the legal issues involved in the simplest of terms, addressing them in the context of some of the most thrilling and dramatic court cases of our time. It is important that this story be told, because the controversy over DNA evidence has raised issues at the cutting edge of modern law and science and poses significant questions about the extent of our commitment to justice.

This is an account of high drama. It is a story of terrible

crimes solved through DNA, of the guilty receiving their just deserts, of innocent people rescued from crushing punishments for crimes they did not commit. It is a saga that has played itself out in obscure but extraordinary cases as well as in famous cases, like the Central Park jogger case, the World Trade Center bombing, and the O. J. Simpson trial. The story of this still young technology has already ranged all over this nation and the world—from the hunt for Austria's most notorious serial killer, to the murders of young teenage girls in a small English village, to cases from Los Angeles, Baltimore, and Virginia.

Despite its short history, the story of DNA analysis has unfolded in a series of striking developments. It started with the birth of DNA testing, rooted in the most important scientific developments of this era. This was followed by controversy over its reliability and the question of whether the criminal justice system would still embrace the new science wholeheartedly despite that controversy. Then came the rebirth and triumph of DNA, followed by further controversy, this time over the role of race in DNA analysis, and then the development of a new kind of scientific manhunt to catch criminals. Next came a second generation of extraordinary DNA tests and the assault on those tests in the O. J. Simpson trial. The story concludes with some reflections on the tremendous power of DNA, as illustrated in the cases of a doctor charged with rape and evil twins charged with murder.

For the beginnings of this fascinating and important story, our eyes turn backward to the frontier.

THE PRODUCERS OF STAR TREK GOT IT WRONG. Space is not the final frontier. Within each of the cells in the human body, there is a vastness comparable to that of outer space. The exploration of this inner frontier is already beginning to produce answers to some of humankind's most profound questions—about where we came from, how we are all alike, how each of us is an individual. Science is already beginning to yield answers to the most fundamental questions of human destiny: Who will live, and who will die? Who will be healthy, and who will be sick? Who will be content, and who will suffer from depression and derangement?

The answers to many of these questions lie in the mysterious patterns of DNA within each of our cells. Someday in the not too distant future, we will learn just how much of our destiny lies in our DNA and how much in our own hands. To the next generation, that knowledge will simply be a given, in much the same way that our children now accept with ennui that human beings have solved the myriad problems involved in getting humans to the moon and back.

Our inner space begins with the cell, the basic unit of life. Most of the cell is water. At the center of the cell is the nucleus. Packed within the nucleus are the chromosomes, containing the hereditary information transmitted from mother and father to child. The chromosomes, forty-six in number, consist primarily of proteins and nucleic acids, specifically DNA (deoxyribonucleic acid). The DNA is structured like a twisted ladder with rungs. But this is a ladder with 3 billion rungs.

The conjunction is mind-boggling. We begin with a unit too small to imagine, the human cell. At the center of that unit is a ladder with 3 billion rungs, a number too large to imagine.

Making up the twenty-three pairs of chromosomes are genes, nothing more than lengthy stretches of DNA. Each gene controls some aspect of our genetic identity by including coded instructions to cells regarding what role each cell must play in making each of us an individual.

Most of our human genes are identical from person to person. Less than 1 percent of any individual's DNA is different from that of other people. That is why we all have legs, arms, heads; our genes provide a code for protein synthesis, and we develop our familiar human structure. A bad gene, a stretch of DNA where the nucleic acids are not arranged as they should be, may cause us to develop a terrible genetic disease or to be predisposed to heart disease or cancer. Strangely, the key to making identifications in criminal cases lies primarily not in those stretches of DNA whose role in the grand plan has already been determined but in other stretches of DNA, which have no known function.

In 1980 Dr. Ray White, of the Howard Hughes Medical Institute at the University of Utah, developed a technique that revolutionized modern biology and made it much easier to find genes. It focused on cutting repetitive patterns of DNA and analyzing how often the patterns repeat. While these stretches of DNA have no known function, they frequently travel in tandem with genes and so could be used as markers to find specific genes. The lengths of these repetitive stretches of DNA were studied as a means to locate the genes that travel with them. The technique is known as RFLP analysis because a chemical known as a *restriction enzyme* is used to cut DNA into various *fragment lengths*, and the differences or *polymorphisms* in those fragment lengths are analyzed to locate genes in biological research or evaluate identity in criminal cases.

In diagnosing genetic disease, scientists analyze the length of repetitive DNA patterns as a means to find the genes that travel in tandem with those repetitive patterns. By contrast, these repetitive patterns are analyzed in criminal cases because it is the variation in their length, the variation in the number of times that these patterns repeat, that is at the heart of DNA analysis.

In court cases, witnesses for the prosecution frequently testify that no two individuals other than identical twins have the same DNA. This statement, absolutely true as a matter of scientific fact, can be highly misleading if it leads us to believe that the power of DNA analysis lies in its ability to identify and analyze all the characteristics of DNA unique to each individual. Science does not yet have that power.

Instead, the power of DNA analysis today lies in its ability to determine matches in the lengths of repetitive DNA patterns, which vary from individual to individual, the variations measured by RFLP analysis. These same variations may be found in all the DNA in the human body. The DNA in one cell is identical to that in every cell in a person's body where DNA is found. It may be in blood cells, semen cells, skin cells, or hair cells. Regardless, in every cell where it appears, the DNA found is identical to the DNA found in every other cell.

This means that the DNA in the semen cells a rapist may leave at a crime scene can be compared with the DNA in a blood sample taken from a suspect under court order. Assuming that the person whose blood is tested is the rapist, the DNA in the blood and the semen will be identical. There will be a DNA match, and the suspect will be implicated in the crime.

The results of this test are given dramatic, concrete, and lasting documentation. The analysis of the length of the DNA fragments at one genetic location is reflected on one piece of X-ray film; the DNA analysis process produces bands on the photographic film that reflect the length of the suspect's repetitive DNA fragments. There are two bands, one from the suspect's father, and one from the suspect's mother, and the lower each band is on the photographic film, the shorter the repetitive piece of DNA inherited from the parent who contributed it. These two bands are compared to the two bands from the scene of the crime. If the bands from the suspect and those from the crime scene are in alignment, there is a DNA match at that chromosome.

The presence or absence of a DNA match at one genetic location can be determined by examining the film. The power and significance of a match grows as more locations on the DNA ladder are analyzed and as matches are found on more pieces of X-ray film, with each individual piece of film reflecting a match at another chromosome. These visible matches over several pieces of film constitute what has been described as the "raw graphic power" of DNA evidence.

Why if no two people have the same DNA does DNA analysis get into numerical statements of the significance of a DNA match? DNA analysis does not measure the totality of the crime scene DNA against the totality of the defendant's, but only a piece of one against a piece of another. The more pieces from both match up, the more likely it is that the match indicates they came from the same person.

For instance, it may be that a DNA fragment in one sample that could be expected to occur in one person in 100 in the general population matches a fragment in the other sample. That is significant but hardly overwhelming. But if there is a DNA match at another location, reflected on a second piece of film, for a different repetitive pattern, the numbers suddenly grow exponentially. Assume that the second DNA profile also occurs in one out of every 100 people in the general population. The chances of the two DNA profiles matching randomly are one in 10,000, since one in 100 multiplied by one in 100 equals one in 10,000. If there is a match at a third location with the same one out of 100 figure in the general population, the numbers would go to one in 1 million; and if there is a fourth match of the same nature on yet another piece of film, it goes to one in 100 million. If a fifth similar match is added, the mathematical chances of the matches occurring at random goes to one in 10 billion.

Thus it is clear that the power of DNA as an identifying tool multiplies dramatically at each location where a DNA match is found on another piece of film. DNA numbers are then merely a means of stating the chances of there being matches on several pieces of film rather than a precise calculation of how often those matches actually all occur together. After all, there are only 5 billion people living on the face of the earth, but the chances of a particular set of DNA matches occurring together could be one in 10 billion.

This general type of DNA analysis, the most definitive, was first applied to criminal identification by Dr. Alec Jeffreys, working in his laboratory at Leicester University in England. In September 1984, Jeffreys discovered repetitive patterns of DNA present in all people that varied in length to an extraordinary degree. He realized that this variation could be used to establish identity and named his technique genetic fingerprinting. His scientific contribution was the discovery of particular locations on the DNA ladder where repetitive patterns show great variability in the number of times they repeat and the recognition that those variations could be used for purposes of identification. Jeffreys applied for a patent and entered into a contract with Imperial Chemical Industries to be his licensee for commercial use of the patent.

In 1985 Jeffreys published his discovery in the British science journal *Nature,* claiming that a genetic fingerprint is individually specific and that an individual's pattern does not belong to any other present or future person on earth. Jeffreys's approach provided results so definitive that it could have been fairly characterized as a fingerprint. Since it also had complex aspects that made his test somewhat difficult to interpret, his method was modified in favor of today's approach, not properly characterized as a fingerprint in most instances but still highly definitive. Both Jeffreys's technique and the variation used today are known as RFLP analysis. Its identifying power is dramatic.

THE POWER OF DNA TO CLEAR THE INNOCENT and convict the guilty was quickly put to the test in a case on which Dr. Jeffreys himself worked, the first time in human history that DNA was used to solve a homicide.

One year before Jeffreys made his discovery, a teenage girl was raped and murdered six miles from his laboratory. The murder took place in the small English village of Narborough.

On November 1, 1983, Lynda Mann was only fifteen years old. She went to school that day and briefly baby-sat for a neighbor's child after school. She then visited with her best friend, Karen Blackwell. At 7:30 P.M., Lynda left Karen's home to visit her friend Caroline. She never arrived at Caroline's.

Her parents were out for the evening. They arrived home at 1:30 in the morning. When they arrived at home, Lynda's older sister told them that Lynda was not yet home. They immediately called the police, and Lynda's father searched the neighborhood.

Her body was found at 7:20 the next morning, on a footpath adjoining the local psychiatric hospital. She was found by a hospital employee. The psychiatric hospital issued a statement seeking to reassure the public that there was no reason to suspect any connection between the death and the hospital.

An autopsy showed that Lynda Mann had died of strangulation. Her tongue was gouged by her teeth from the strangulation. There were seminal stains on her pubic hair, and the pathologist concluded that sexual intercourse had been attempted and premature ejaculation taken place. But penetration did occur after Lynda's death. Semen was recovered from her labia and vagina. According to the pathologist, the victim was five-feet-two-inches tall and weighed 112 pounds.

The investigation into Lynda Mann's death proved fruitless.

Then, almost three years later, it happened again. Another teenage girl was raped and murdered in the same small English village.

On July 31, 1986, at approximately 4:40 P.M., Dawn Ashworth was last seen alive by a local motorist as she was about to enter one of the village footpaths. Dawn was also fifteen years old. It was summer, and she was off from school, working at a local shop. The last day she was seen alive she was out visiting friends, and when she did not come home that night, a search began.

Two days went by before her body was found in a field off a village lane. She was surrounded by bushes and covered by tree branches, but the fingertips of one hand were visible. It was the police who found her.

Once again, an autopsy was performed, and there were similarities between the two murders. Like Lynda, Dawn was found to have died of strangulation. There were cuts and bruises on her face. The pattern of cuts and bruises on her mouth suggested that the killer had grabbed and held Dawn's mouth to muzzle her during the attack.

The killer had also raped her, penetrating both her vagina and her anus. The sexual attack was found to have occurred at or after death. Like Lynda, Dawn was found naked from the waist down. She was five-feet-five-inches tall.

Very quickly the police investigation led to the psychiatric hospital. The focus was a seventeen-year-old catering assistant, George Howard.

It was Howard's red motorcycle and red helmet that led the police to him. Several witnesses reported having seen a young man similarly outfitted near the scene of the murder on the day it happened. A young man with that gear had also been seen watching the search before Dawn's body was found.

After Dawn's body was found, Howard told a local officer that he had seen her in the area on the night she was murdered. Other witnesses soon reported that Howard had told them Dawn had already been dead even while the search was still continuing, when her fate could have been known only by the killer.

On August 8, 1986, the police came to Howard's home at 5:00 in the morning, and arrested him for the murder of Dawn Ashworth. They took him to the station house for questioning.

Under questioning, he acknowledged having seen Dawn but denied talking to her. But with further police questioning, his story changed. Howard said that he had walked with Dawn but did not kill her. The questioning continued that morning and into the afternoon.

The police sergeant conducting the questioning then offered the seventeen-year-old an excuse. He suggested that he did not think Howard had intended to kill her, that the killing was somehow accidental.

Howard agreed. He said he probably went mad and didn't know it. The sergeant then asked Howard if he had found Dawn attractive, and Howard answered that he had. The sergeant asked Howard to tell him exactly what had happened.

Howard then described his rape and murder of Dawn Ashworth. Later, however, he backed off his confession, saying he did not remember what happened. But that night, under further questioning, he again recounted the rape and murder. The next morning, the police showed Howard a typed version of his confession from the previous day. He acknowledged its accuracy.

It was apparent to the police that they had solved the murder of Dawn Ashworth. To them, it was also apparent that the seventeen-year-old who murdered Dawn Ashworth had committed the first murder too, that of Lynda Mann. But there was one wrinkle. The suspect would not confess to the earlier murder.

Articles in the local press had said that a scientist working in a nearby lab had discovered a kind of "genetic fingerprinting," so the police sent the semen recovered from the Lynda Mann rape and blood from the suspect to Dr. Alec Jeffreys.

The results were surprising. Dr. Jeffreys concluded that the DNA in the semen from the first rape was not that of the suspect. Howard had not committed the first rape. While this result was unexpected, what followed was startling.

The semen from the second rape, the rape to which Howard had confessed, was then sent to the laboratory by the police. The police expected that the results would further implicate the seventeen-year-old in the murder to which he had confessed. But these results were also negative.

The DNA from the Dawn Ashworth murder was identical to that from the Lynda Mann murder: The same man had committed both rapes. But Howard was not that man. Not only was he innocent of the first murder but he had falsely confessed to the rape and murder of Dawn Ashworth.

On November 21, 1986, Howard was released from custody. The police had thought they had an airtight case against him, but instead the DNA evidence cleared him of both murders.

The police then turned to DNA testing to try to catch the right man. In January 1987, they began a campaign of so-called voluntary blood testing for every male who lived or worked in the three local villages. The police started with men between seventeen and thirty-four years old, the age-group among whom they believed a rapist was most likely to be found. Each local man between seventeen and thirty-four received a notice asking him to voluntarily provide a blood sample to eliminate himself as a suspect. Most local men complied with the request. These are small villages, and the social pressure to comply was great.

Besides, it was clear to all that this testing program was

designed to protect the young women of the villages, the daughters and sisters of the men tested, from rape and violent death. Most of the young men saw the enterprise as entailing a minimal intrusion on their right to be let alone while promoting a much greater end, the detection of a murderer and the prevention of further violent crimes.

Some did resist the testing program. They maintained that they need not provide blood because they had alibis, but the police did not want to start drawing fine lines of distinction and insisted that these men too should give blood. One man viewed providing blood as too great an intrusion, but he was willing to provide a semen sample and did so after spending some time alone in a private room at the police station.

Overall, blood samples were taken from 4,582 men. But the police still had not found the killer. Then they received a major break.

On August 1, 1987, a baker named Ian Kelly was having lunch at a local pub with several other coworkers. The gossip during that lunch focused on a baker who was not at the table, named Colin Pitchfork. Kelly mentioned that he had taken the blood test for Pitchfork. He had agreed to pretend to be Pitchfork and give a blood sample during the first month of the testing program after Pitchfork told him a convoluted story about how he had already given blood for someone else. Pitchfork had been insistent, and Kelly had agreed to give blood in his place.

Another baker said that Pitchfork had offered him money to take the blood test for him but that he had declined. Pitchfork had told this man that he had a history of arrests for flashing and that he was scared to go anywhere near the police.

Six weeks later, after much hesitation, the manager of the bakery where Pitchfork worked, who had attended that lunch, called the police. She told them that Kelly had taken the blood test for Pitchfork and that before the two had made their deal Pitchfork had offered another man money to take the test in his place.

On September 19, 1987, the police arrested Colin Pitchfork at his home on suspicion of murder. The arresting officer asked Pitchfork why he had raped Dawn Ashworth.

Without missing a beat, Pitchfork told the officer that it was simply a matter of opportunity, that she was there and he was there.

At the station house, Pitchfork confessed in detail to the

rapes and murders of Lynda Mann and Dawn Ashworth. Shortly thereafter, a DNA test was done by Dr. Jeffreys.

Jeffreys compared the crime scene evidence from both murders and Pitchfork's blood. This time the DNA was an exact match. The genetic characteristics of Pitchfork's blood matched those from the semen of the man who raped Lynda Mann and Dawn Ashworth.

Rather than go to trial, Pitchfork pled guilty to both murders and rapes. He was sentenced to life imprisonment for each murder.

Ian Kelly, the man who gave blood for Pitchfork, was arrested the same day as Pitchfork and charged with obstruction of justice. He pled guilty and received an eighteen-month sentence, but the sentence was suspended.

It was an extraordinarily auspicious beginning for the new technology. In its first known application in a murder case, DNA testing fulfilled both its promises, clearing an innocent man and helping convict a guilty one. The power of DNA evidence to exonerate the innocent and implicate the guilty was combined in dramatic fashion.

With such a dramatic entrance, DNA analysis quickly caught the attention of the media and the world at large. Joseph Wambaugh, the premier writer of American true crime, described the Pitchfork case in vivid detail in his book The Blooding. DNA evidence was first used in an American courtroom to convict Tommy Lee Andrews of rape in Florida.

In 1987 DNA testing was completely new, but there was no doubt about its potential within the criminal justice system. Prosecutors and the press rushed to embrace the novel tool. Many even described it as foolproof, neglecting the home truth that any system run by humans must be subject to human error. Quickly, however, the first signs of trouble developed, and when that trouble came, it came far from England, in the Bronx.

3 THE TROUBLE WITH DNA

T HERE ARE FEW DECISIONS A PROSECUTOR MUST MAKE as difficult as the choice between offering a defendant a lesser sentence on a plea bargain and going to trial. After a trial, a convicted defendant will likely get an extremely lengthy sentence, something close to what he deserves. But if he is not convicted at trial, the defendant is a free man, free to go out and prey on society again. While the process of negotiating a plea of guilty is referred to as plea bargaining, it is in reality sentence bargaining, a negotiation over the sentence that a defendant will receive if he admits his guilt, forgoes a trial, and agrees to accept some form of punishment.

It stands to reason that a defendant who pleads guilty before a trial will receive a sentence significantly less than what would be imposed after conviction at trial. After all, why else would he agree to spare the state the obligation of proving him guilty beyond a reasonable doubt? The prosecutor must weigh the rewards and risks of going to trial and decide whether justice would be served by a bargained-down admission of guilt.

As the Bronx prosecutor, Risa Sugarman, contemplated offering Joseph Castro, a handyman in the building of two murder victims, a deal in exchange for his guilty plea, she thought most of all about the two innocents viciously murdered, who were entitled

33

to a full measure of justice. But she also had to consider the trouble with the DNA evidence, which pretrial hearings had indicated might be considerable.

Initially, Sugarman, the chief of homicide in the Bronx District Attorney's Office, believed that the DNA would clinch the case. But it later appeared that, despite the prosecutor's firm conviction that this was a very guilty man, Castro could conceivably win an acquittal at trial.

Every prosecutor's worst nightmare is an acquittal of a guilty man who has committed a heinous crime, a prospect that loomed particularly large in this case. The venue was the Bronx, and Bronx juries are notoriously friendly to defendants in criminal cases, much more so than those in Manhattan, where I worked as a prosecutor.

Besides, the likely defense here was obvious. There is an old axiom among experienced homicide detectives that the first step when a female body is found is to determine if the body had a husband. In this case, she did. David Rivera had returned home from work and found his wife and daughter murdered.

So the likely defense of Castro, the building handyman, was obvious: Who had better means, motive, and opportunity than the husband? After all, murders of wives by their husbands are common, and what marriage can stand close scrutiny without yielding up an old grudge or two capable of generating murderous rage? Even more surprising than the number of wives murdered by husbands is the number of children murdered by their parents, some 600 in the United States in a typical year. While we recoil from the prospect that a parent would murder his or her own offspring, far too many react to the stress of parenthood by lashing out at their children in uncontrolled rage. In such cases, confessions are hard to come by, because the parent knows that admitting guilt will engender more than the opprobrium of law enforcement figures. Friends, family, even fellow inmates will turn on the murderer with a passion.

Here, there was fertile ground for the defense. True, the tactic of blaming the victim, or the victim's loved one, who if innocent of the murder is certainly a victim himself, can be a risky tactic for a defense lawyer. There are few things more certain to incense a jury than a claim that a bereaved spouse is a murderer, and the potential that the tactic will backfire is great. It is a high-stakes gamble, and there are few lawyers sufficiently artful to walk that fine line between seeming to make an ugly charge against a grieving spouse and causing the jurors to start to suspect that the surviving spouse might indeed be the murderer.

In this case, one piece of evidence out of the couple's past seemed to demand a defense claim that the deaths of the mother and child could well have come at the hands of a volatile, violence-prone husband and father. By his own admission, Rivera had, a couple of years before, hit his wife and broken her jaw. This gave the defense lawyer that magic material that defense lawyers are always looking for—something more to work with than mere speculation. The husband's proven potential for violence would make him fair game and perhaps provide Joseph Castro, the handyman, a way to beat the murder rap. After all, the defense would not have to prove who killed the victim, only that there was reasonable doubt that the defendant had committed the crime.

At a trial the jury would have to decide. Was the husband's story, and his accusation of Joseph Castro, entirely true? Was the defense lawyer's argument that the husband murdered his family the foulest of lies? Was the husband a master actor responsible for the deaths of his wife and daughter? Or was there reasonable doubt about who had done what?

On the day that his common-law wife, Vilma Ponce, and his two-year-old daughter, Natasha, were murdered, David Rivera was twenty years old. Rivera and his family lived near Montefiore Hospital in the Bronx, one of New York City's largest and most prominent medical centers.

The neighborhood had been solidly Jewish, but most of the Jews had long since left, and it now had more Hispanic people than any other group. Still, the fundamental character of the area remained the same. It was a good neighborhood, a place where working people tried to give their children more than they had. Rivera and his wife lived in a nice, clean apartment in a well-kept building. The apartment was full of love and care; two-year-old Natasha's many dolls were lined up neatly on three rows of shelving.

Rivera worked as a caretaker at a Bronx housing project. Ponce's life was her family. She was twenty-two years old and six months' pregnant, looking forward to the birth of her and Rivera's second child.

Rivera's story was simple in its details but chilling as a reminder that any ordinary day in any ordinary life can easily turn into a life-destroying nightmare. On the morning of February 5, 1987, he left for work at 6:45, taking the number 10 bus to his job at the Marble Hill Houses. During the day, Rivera spoke to his wife on the telephone once, at 11:45 A.M. At 4:25 P.M., he left work, taking the bus home.

Once at his apartment building, Rivera took the elevator to the fifth floor and opened both locks, pushing his apartment door open. It was then he realized that something might be terribly wrong. Brown-haired Natasha was always at the front door to greet him when he came home, but that day there was only an eerie silence. Stranger yet, the chain was on the door.

The chain prevented Rivera from entering the apartment. He called out to his wife and daughter through the crack in the door. He called out each of their names—Vilma! Natasha!—more than five times. But there was no reply, or sound of movement.

Rivera went back downstairs. There, he pressed on the building intercom, ringing his apartment, hoping for a response. Then he went outside the building, looked to his apartment window, and whistled up toward the apartment.

On previous days when he had forgotten his keys, Rivera would whistle up from the street, and that would attract his wife's attention, and she would let him in the building. This day, Rivera had his keys, but the chain on the apartment door signaled that someone must be in the apartment. Why was there no answer to his whistle?

Rivera went to the grocery store around the corner. He dialed his home telephone number, hoping his wife was sleeping and the phone would rouse her. Again, no answer.

It was now approximately 5:15 P.M. Using the quarter with which he had just called home, Rivera called his mother. He thought that Vilma might have called her and that his mother might know what was going on. His mother told him she had not talked to his wife since 2:00 P.M., when Vilma had said that she did not know what they were having for dinner and the two women had talked about the television soaps. An ordinary conversation for an ordinary afternoon between a housewife and her mother-in-law.

Rivera told his mother that he was scared, that he thought something was wrong, and asked her to call the police. As soon as they hung up, his mother called the local police precinct and gave them her son's address. The officer who answered said the precinct would call 911 for her.

Rivera went back to his building, and once again he whistled up to his apartment. As he stood there, a man came out of the building.

Rivera and the man were face to face, less than ten feet away from each other. Rivera later remembered him as Hispanic, about thirty years old, 190 pounds, with medium-length hair and a mustache.

And he was covered with blood. He had blood on his wrist. He had blood on his face, covering his chin and his cheekbones. He had blood on his sneakers. The man also had an odd look in his eyes, which Rivera described as "chinky." There was nothing Asian about him; this was, according to Rivera, his way of saying that the man looked high.

As the man passed by, he looked straight at Rivera and smiled. Then he crossed the street and disappeared through a gate.

Seeing this frightful, almost Shakespearean apparition, Rivera ran back into his building. He took the elevator upstairs. No keys were needed this time to enter the apartment. And someone had taken the chain off the door from the inside.

Rivera pushed the door open slowly. He saw blood all over the apartment and ran headlong downstairs, hurtling toward the gate through which the blood-covered man had disappeared moments before. Just then the police arrived in a patrol car, summoned by the telephone call from Rivera's mother. Rivera ran toward them, and told the officers that he thought his family had been murdered.

The police went upstairs with Rivera. They entered the apartment, insisting that Rivera stay outside. Inside, there was a horrifying scene.

Vilma Ponce, five-feet-four-inches tall, 125 pounds, lay on the living room floor. She was naked except for her sneakers, socks, and a black shirt pushed up high on her chest. She had been stabbed fifty-eight times. Most of the stab wounds were to her chest. Although she was half naked, she had not been raped. But she was dead.

Her little girl, two years old, all of three feet tall and thirty-five pounds, lay on the cold bathroom floor. She was fully clothed, dressed like the little girl she was, in a T-shirt, shorts, and yellow thonglike shoes. She had been stabbed sixteen times, most often in the chest. She, too, was dead.

The officers went outside to talk to Rivera. They noted to themselves that he did not have any blood on him. The police told Rivera that his wife and daughter were dead, both stabbed to death. Rivera exploded in grief and anguish. In the words of one police officer, he went crazy. Most police officers place great store in their ability to judge the sincerity of a person's response to horrifying news that should be coming as a surprise. To these officers, Rivera's anguish appeared genuine.

Rivera left the building, to stay at his mother's home for the time being. The police secured the apartment and looked for fingerprints, but none other than the family's were found.

Two days later, Rivera went back to the apartment. He went back for one reason only; he had no clothes to wear other than the caretaker's uniform he had been wearing on the day of the murders. His clothes were in his apartment, and he needed them. His aunt and uncle drove him to the building.

Since the double murder, two detectives had been assigned to investigate the case. They met Rivera and accompanied him into the apartment while he gathered his clothes. Rivera left the building with his clothes; the detectives then pulled away in their car. Rivera's uncle started the car, and they were about to leave the scene when Rivera saw the man again, the same man he had seen on the afternoon of the tragedy. Today, of course, there was no blood on him. He was coming out of the same gate he had walked through on the day of the murders.

Every hair on Rivera's body stood on end. Rivera watched the man cross the street and then enter Rivera's own building. He looked different; he had shaved his head since their previous meeting. Still, he looked the same.

Rivera quickly left his uncle's car and ran after the man. Rivera approached him in the lobby and asked him his name. Joseph, said the man.

Rivera then made a strange and simple request: "Can you do me a favor and smile for me?"

The man smiled, and it was then that Rivera knew for certain that this was the man who two days earlier had been covered in the blood of Rivera's own family. He left the building and had his uncle drive him immediately to the local police precinct.

At the precinct, the police showed Rivera photographs of various people who had previously been arrested. Rivera identified a man named Joseph Castro from those pictures, and told the police that Castro was the man Rivera saw on the day of the murders, and the man who had smiled for him again, on request, that very day.

So the police investigated Rivera's story. They looked into Joseph Castro, to find out as much about him as they could. They discovered that Joseph Castro, age thirty-five, five-foot-eight-inches tall, and 160 pounds, helped out from time to time in local buildings, including Rivera's, doing odd jobs. The police found out that Castro lived across the street from Rivera. Castro's mother lived in the basement apartment; he lived next door, in the meter room.

The detectives also found at least the beginnings of a motive. Specifically, they learned that exactly one week before she was murdered, Vilma Ponce had been out on the street with her friend Barbara Troy and had pointed Castro out to Troy. That man, said Ponce, is always getting fresh with me, even though I'm pregnant.

This was more than a matter of simple annoyance. There was something about Castro that frightened Ponce, said her friend, and she would never have opened the door to him. Troy urged Ponce to tell her husband about this local man who was making unwelcome advances, but Ponce was afraid to tell Rivera, possibly fearful of provoking a violent confrontation between the two. This was, at the least, evidence of a significant link between one murder victim and Castro.

The detectives also discovered that Castro may have created his own opportunity to commit this crime. One troubling detail was the fact that he could not have expected his victim to open the door to him. But the police learned that the latch on the bottom lock to Ponce and Rivera's apartment had been put in facing in the wrong direction, rendering it useless. More interesting was that the new latch had been installed only two weeks before and that the person who installed it was Joseph Castro. Castro had been assisted by the building superintendent's nephew, Alex. At a trial, Alex could testify to Castro's role in installing the defective lock.

Beyond Castro's excessive interest in Vilma Ponce, and the

opportunity created by the installation of a defective lock, there was also the issue of timing. Certainly, this had been the most opportune time to surprise the young woman in her apartment. Her husband was at work, and she had just come home. Since she had just walked in the door, Ponce presumably had not yet had a chance to throw the second lock on her door, the lock that worked, the lock not installed by Castro.

The police put together this theory about timing from the fact that on the living room couch they found a brown bag containing six dollars' worth of chicken and chuck steak, obviously dinner for the family that night. The meat and chicken were still wrapped and unrefrigerated, telling proof that Ponce had not yet had a chance to put them in the refrigerator when she was attacked. There was also Ponce's 2:00 P.M. conversation with her mother-in-law, telling her that she did not yet know what they were having for dinner that night.

So, the scenario that the prosecution would describe at trial was apparent. Castro followed Ponce home as she returned with the food that would become her family's dinner and simply pushed open the door with the defective lock. He tried to force Ponce to have sex with him; that was why Ponce was naked but for her top, sneakers, and socks, why her shirt was pushed up on her chest. Ponce resisted, and Castro stabbed her to death. Castro had also stabbed and killed Ponce's two-year-old daughter. He may have stabbed Natasha to stop her screams, or because she tried to protect her mother. No one will ever know, but the bottom line was the same—Castro had murdered a two-year-old girl and her mother.

After a monthlong investigation, the prosecutor authorized Castro's arrest. The case looked like a relatively good one. It would be hard for the defense to explain away Castro's installation of the defective lock. Still, Rivera's admission that he had once broken his wife's jaw could throw a wrench into the prosecution's well-constructed case. Rivera's past violent act against his wife meant that the prosecution would likely have to defuse the claim that Rivera killed his wife and concocted a story about Castro to throw police off his own guilt. The dramatic story of a man's leaving the scene covered in blood, the coincidence of a second meeting the very next time Rivera was at the building, and the identification of Castro as that man, based entirely on

Rivera's testimony and nothing else, were almost too theatrical to be believed. The defense could even go so far as to suggest that Rivera manipulated the lock after Castro installed it, planning all along to blame his murder of his own wife on the most likely sap, a handyman known in the neighborhood to be making unwelcome advances to Rivera's wife.

To build their case, the police and the District Attorney's Office looked for additional evidence beyond Rivera's testimony. It was during this search for evidence that the police hoped would clinch the case that DNA came into the picture.

During the investigation, in the month between the crime and Castro's arrest, Castro was interviewed by a detective from the Bronx's Fifty-second precinct. The detective, while talking to him, noticed a stain on the band of Castro's watch that looked like dried blood. He took Castro's watch and watchband as evidence.

The blood on the watchband was subjected to DNA analysis to find out whether it had come from one of the two murder victims, from Castro, or from some other source. It was tested by the Lifecodes laboratory in Westchester, New York, the first private laboratory in the United States to do RFLP testing for criminal identification. The initial results suggested that this was the evidence that would win the case for the prosecution.

The results were compelling. Lifecodes concluded that the DNA pattern of the blood on the watchband matched Vilma Ponce's pattern at three different locations on the DNA ladder, at three different chromosomes. The laboratory stated that the frequency of this matching pattern was one in 100 million people in the Hispanic population. The focus of the case then shifted to a whole new terrain.

The Bronx criminal courthouse sits in the shadow of Yankee Stadium, and it sees more murder cases each year than there are home games at Yankee Stadium. Until now, this case had taken place on sad, awful, too familiar ground. The Bronx county courthouse is certainly a vale of tears, and it hears tales of homicide every day, the sad stories of the people's lives suddenly cut short for no rational reason.

At most homicide trials, be they in the Bronx or elsewhere, the evidence follows a familiar pattern. There is the testimony of eyewitnesses, police officers, a detective, the deceased's next of kin, and the doctor who performed the autopsy. The eyewitnesses, sometimes working people, sometimes drug dealers or prostitutes, tell the jury what they saw and identify the defendant as the person who committed the crime. The police officers testify to the defendant's arrest and to any evidence the defendant had on his person, such as a gun or a knife, that links him to the crime. The detective testifies to the defendant's confession, if there was one. The next of kin testifies to the identification of the body at the morgue, and provides some detail to humanize the deceased, so the jury will think of the fate of the victim as well as what awaits the defendant if they convict him. The doctor testifies to the cause of death.

This testimony is the simple, usual terrain of homicide. It is straightforward and often prosaic, yet at the same time highly dramatic, for it is by definition a story of life and death. It reminds everyone who hears it of the uncertain and unpredictable nature of our existence.

The Bronx criminal courts are used to bruising battles between prosecutors and defense attorneys. In this case, though, the figurative terrain of the dispute would be very different. The familiar field of controversy was replaced by an entirely new battleground, with totally unfamiliar forces wheeled up to fire on each other. It would still be a bruising battle, but now it would not be contradictory eyewitnesses challenging each other's testimony but some of the country's leading scientists. It would be a fight that would have reverberations well beyond the courtroom where it took place and briefly shake the newfound faith of many in the criminal justice system regarding the technology of DNA analysis.

All this took place even before the trial began. The judge had ordered that witnesses testify before him to help him decide whether this new DNA evidence had gained sufficient acceptance among scientists to be included in the evidence a jury would be allowed to hear at the trial.

At first, everything appeared to be just right with the DNA. The prosecution's first witness, Dr. Richard Roberts, worked closely at the time with Nobel Prize winner James Watson. Watson had become one of the world's best-known scientists when his unprecedented book, *The Double Helix,* provided the inside story of his discovery with Francis Crick and Maurice Wilkins of the helical structure of DNA in 1953. Watson was the director of the Cold Spring Harbor Laboratory, one of the world's most prominent biological laboratories, and Roberts was assistant director of the laboratory. This was a witness promethean by association. In years to come, Roberts too would win the Nobel Prize.

This impressive witness lent his full support to the new DNA technology. It was not possible, said Roberts, for DNA analysis to result in a false positive. It was hard to imagine a stronger general endorsement of DNA analysis than that provided by Roberts in court, an affirmative statement to the effect that this evidence could never contribute to a wrongful conviction.

Beyond endorsing DNA generally, Roberts also seemed to embrace the results in this case, to support the reliability of the results that implicated Joseph Castro. He testified that he had reviewed the X-ray films that embody the DNA results. Initially, he said, he was troubled by one of those films, which was not perfect. But a second and third set of experiments were carried out, and these gave a perfectly clean interpretation. Roberts was not specifically asked and did not specifically state that there was a DNA match here. Still, his testimony seemed to affirm the scientific reliability of the specific results generated by the DNA laboratory in this case.

Little did the prosecution realize that this would be the high point for their DNA evidence. From this point forward, there was nothing but trouble ahead.

The groundwork for that trouble had been laid the month before, on February 16, 1989, at a conference on the use of DNA in the criminal field held at Roberts's own laboratory at Cold Spring Harbor. The conference was sponsored by the Banbury Center at Cold Spring Harbor, which hosts multidisciplinary conferences and workshops on social issues relating to molecular biology. A scientist from Lifecodes, Dr. Michael Baird, spoke and showed films of casework done by his laboratory.

Attending the presentation was Dr. Eric Lander, then thirty-two. Lander was an MIT scientist, a former Rhodes scholar, and winner of a MacArthur "genius" fellowship, an award of $205,000 given without application or any strings to a person whose work deserves support. Lander was disturbed by aspects of the Lifecodes presentation. Most particularly, he was troubled by the possible inadequacy of the laboratory's controls.

Lander stood up at the meeting, and confronted the Lifecodes scientist about the adequacy of the controls used by the laboratory to guarantee the reliability of the lab's results.

During a break in the conference, Lander was approached by Peter Neufeld, then thirty-nine. Neufeld was one of Castro's two court-appointed lawyers for the DNA hearing. He had agreed to handle the DNA hearing with another attorney, his old friend, Barry Scheck, then forty.

Neufeld and Scheck, who had been brought into the Castro case specifically to handle the DNA hearing, were two of a very small group of lawyers who had knowledge about DNA evidence at this time. They were attending the "by-invitation-only" Banbury Conference as representatives of the defense bar who had previously worked on cases involving other forms of scientific evidence.

Neufeld showed Lander the evidence from the Castro case, the pieces of film that were the final result of the DNA analysis process, known as autoradiographs. Lander was unimpressed with the laboratory's results, and told Neufeld as much.

As far as Lander was concerned, that was the end of it. He would go back to his genetics laboratory, and the lawyers would return to their offices and their trials.

But Scheck and Neufeld believed that they had found their expert witness, their vehicle to undermine the DNA evidence. In Lander they saw a kindred spirit, a questioning scientist whose skepticism could translate to some measure of success for the defense side at the DNA hearing.

Certainly, Scheck, Neufeld, and Lander were almost peas in a pod. All three were New York born, well educated, highly intelligent, and extremely argumentative. All tended to speak in sweeping, categorical terms, and none lacked the arrogant certitude that he was right no matter how the rest of the world might feel. And a defense assault on DNA would certainly require that certitude, for the defense lawyers in particular were arrayed against a criminal justice establishment that repeatedly asserted that there could be no such event as a false DNA match. To challenge DNA was to stand out on a limb and challenge the tree. But that was what Scheck and Neufeld prepared to do.

Several days later, Neufeld called Lander and asked him to testify for the defense. Lander declined. He had other major commitments taking much of his time. Lander told Neufeld that he needed to become involved in a court case as much as he needed a hole in the head. Besides, Lander doubted that the problems with Lifecodes's work could be that egregious.

While Lander turned down Neufeld's request that he testify as an expert, he did agree to educate Scheck and Neufeld. The defense lawyers sent Lander daily copies of transcripts from the courtroom testimony, and the scientist reviewed that testimony, suggesting questions to the defense lawyers for their cross-examination of the witness from the Lifecodes DNA laboratory.

As Lander reviewed transcripts from the courtroom, he did not like the answers that the Lifecodes scientist was giving to the questions he had suggested. To Lander, they sounded like excuses for inadequate science. As his frustration mounted, Lander agreed to testify for the defense. He ultimately donated 350 hours of work to the case, including six days of testimony and a fifty-page expert witness report. It was Lander's testimony, his criticism of Lifecodes's procedures, delivered with the full force of his personality and intellect, that above all determined the outcome of the Castro DNA proceeding.

Aided by Lander's suggested questions, the defense won important concessions on its cross-examination of the prosecution's principal DNA witness, Dr. Michael Baird, of Lifecodes, whom Lander had confronted at the Cold Spring Harbor conference. On cross-examination by Barry Scheck, Baird admitted that Lifecodes's reports contained language implying that the laboratory used objective, mathematical standards in determining whether or not there was a DNA match. On the witness stand, he conceded that no such calculations were made and that DNA matches were declared simply based on visual observation.

To the feisty Scheck, the significance of Baird's admission was dramatic, and he threw both arms straight up in the air, pronouncing through his gesture that he had just scored a touchdown, as if the importance of the confession should have been apparent to all. "I mean, am I crazy?" he asked the judge. In the contentious atmosphere of the courtroom, the prosecutor asked Scheck if he "would like an answer to that question." The judge intervened to stop the hostilities.

The defense had scored a small but significant victory, an admission that the laboratory's printed materials were apparently misleading when they stated that the lab declares DNA matches objectively, and that in truth it made the determination subjectively.

This alone might not have been sufficient to block the admission of the DNA evidence, although it would certainly have been useful at trial in undercutting the lab's credibility with the jury. More would be needed to keep the DNA out of the trial altogether—and more would be supplied.

The bombshell came from Dr. Lander. Going beyond finding ambiguities and problems in the DNA evidence, he told the judge that the DNA evidence here "would indicate" that the blood on Castro's watchband did not come from the crime, that the analysis could show Castro "absolutely innocent."

His testimony was powerful and detailed, identifying a number of faults he had discovered with Lifecodes's procedures. Lander completed his testimony on April 26, 1989. Soon afterward, at the end of April, Lander and Roberts met at a professional conference at Cold Spring Harbor on various scientific issues unrelated to criminal justice. The two adversaries in the Castro case discussed the case, and Lander gave Roberts a copy of his fifty-page report. Roberts reviewed Lander's report, and decided that something had to be done. "I hadn't really seen the evidence in great detail before, and I quickly became rather concerned," Roberts later said.

Four days later, while in Boston on other business, Roberts visited Lander in nearby Cambridge. Roberts suggested that the experts on both sides meet and discuss the issues as scientists, with "none of this lawyerly talk." A meeting, without lawyers, was scheduled in New York for May 11.

The conclave led to an extraordinary two-page statement, issued jointly under the signatures of two prosecution witnesses and two defense witnesses. The scientists concluded that the DNA results in the Castro case were not sufficient to determine that the DNA did match or that it did not match. They agreed that the DNA results were inconclusive.

This was a dramatic departure from the prior testimony by the witnesses on both sides. Roberts, of course, had previously testified that the DNA results looked perfectly clean to him. And Lander had testified that the results would indicate that the blood did not come from the crime. But in their joint statement, the experts concluded that the DNA evidence neither implicated Joseph Castro nor cleared him. This statement was later endorsed by all the expert witnesses in the case except Lifecodes's Baird, who stuck to his view that the evidence implicated Castro.

The experts were troubled because at one location on a DNA print there were two faint, extra bands present in Vilma Ponce's DNA that were not present in the DNA from the watchband. Lifecodes had discounted these bands, viewing them as the likely result of bacterial contamination rather than genuine DNA bands, and had focused on the match between the more clearly visible DNA bands. Lander, on the other hand, believed the faint bands to be human DNA bands; that had been the basis of his conclusion that the DNA on Castro's watch did not match Ponce's. The experts agreed that the laboratory should have performed further tests regarding the source of those bands before declaring a DNA match. They decided that Lifecodes's failure to do so rendered the film inconclusive at that particular DNA location.

The experts also criticized Lifecodes's declaration of a DNA match because they believed that the laboratory had violated its own rules for declaring a match, that it did not use objective criteria. The criticism here went beyond a failure to perform the requisite mathematical calculations. According to the joint statement, those calculations, when actually performed, showed that the DNA patterns from the blood on the watchband and from Vilma Ponce's DNA, while similar, were sufficiently different that they fell outside Lifecodes's own mathematical standards for the confident declaration of a match.

The joint statement also concluded that Lifecodes's approach overstated the numerical significance of a DNA match. The laboratory had used very broad standards in determining the existence of a match. It had then used very narrow principles for calculating the numerical significance of a match. According to Lander, this was like catching DNA with a ten-foot-wide butterfly net and then showing the difficulty of that feat by demonstrating how hard it is to catch DNA with a six-inch-wide butterfly net.

After the experts issued their joint statement, the defense called Dr. Roberts back to the witness stand. Roberts now told the judge that he could not say whether the DNA in this case matched or not and that most scientists would share his view that the evidence against Castro was inconclusive.

Against this background, the judge ruled that the jury could not hear Lifecodes's conclusion that the blood on Joseph Castro's watchband was that of Vilma Ponce. This was the principal DNA evidence, and it would not go to the jury.

Justice Gerald Sheindlin, writing with an eye to the future, went out of his way to emphasize his finding that DNA testing is highly reliable and that his ruling rejecting the DNA evidence in this case was premised primarily on the laboratory's failure to conduct additional tests on the faint bands to determine whether they were human DNA or bacteria. Judge Sheindlin did not accept or reject the experts' conclusion that the laboratory violated its own standards for declaring a match, but he did find that the DNA numbers were exaggerated and wrote that he would have been forced to preclude or substantially reduce those numbers had he allowed evidence of the DNA match.

The judge did rule that the jury would be allowed to hear that DNA analysis showed the blood on the watch was not Castro's. Scheck and Neufeld had not challenged this DNA evidence at the hearing. This evidence could have had some value as proof against Castro at trial—after all, why was he walking around with someone else's blood on his watch?—but it would have had nowhere near the power of the excluded evidence, the barred conclusion that the blood on the watch was Vilma Ponce's.

Although the evidence of a DNA match had been excluded, the case could go forward, based primarily on Rivera's testimony and that of the young man who had been with Castro when he installed the lock that later proved defective. The prosecution and the defense had reached a momentous point. David Rivera would now confront Joseph Castro in court.

This confrontation was to take place immediately before the trial began, at yet another pretrial hearing. Castro was no longer represented by Scheck and Neufeld, his special DNA counsel, but by his original, court-appointed attorney. As Rivera took the witness stand, his rage at Castro was palpable. All present in the courtroom could feel it. The prosecutor asked Rivera a question about the building he lived in, and Rivera could not even bring himself to respond. There was a feeling in the air that Rivera might come out of the witness chair and physically attack Castro.

The judge told Rivera to look just at the DA, not at Castro. Rivera then recounted his story to the court. DNA or no DNA, it was evident that this was a man who had nothing to do with the murder of his wife and daughter, a man whose whole life has been wrenched by an evil act. It was also apparent that Rivera firmly believed that Castro was the man who murdered his family.

Credibility is key in the world of the courtroom. Credibility revolves about the consistency of a witness's story with those of other witnesses and about feasibility, whether or not the testimony affronts common sense. But judgments about credibility are also heavily influenced by intangibles, and Rivera was a man whom a jury would most likely believe.

The time had come for the prosecutor to decide whether to offer a plea bargain. In many respects, the case against Castro was still strong. Rivera would likely be an emotionally compelling witness at trial, but he was still vulnerable to cross-examination, and to the defense's speculation that he might have been the killer because he had broken his wife's jaw. And this was the Bronx, a tough county in which to get criminal convictions.

The prosecutor and the judge offered Castro a sentence of twenty years to life if he pled guilty to both murders without going to trial. The loss of the DNA evidence had cost the prosecution many years off Castro's sentence. Beating the DNA had saved Castro years in prison.

As he pled guilty, Castro admitted that he had stabbed each victim repeatedly and that he intended to kill both woman and child when he stabbed them. He also resolved a central question in the case. Castro confirmed that the blood on the watch came from the crime, essentially admitting that Lifecodes's conclusion was correct.

This provided some small measure of vindication for the DNA laboratory. But Castro's plea of guilty was virtually ignored in the publicity that followed the rejection of the DNA evidence in his case. To this day, much of the lingering popular perception that DNA evidence is somehow flawed has its origins in the press coverage of the Castro case.

Before this case, the press had been positively infatuated with DNA evidence. This reflected in part some of the overblown claims of the proponents of DNA, which included the claim that DNA analysis could never yield a mistake, a questionable claim about any system subject to the vagaries of human error. When the bubble of infatuation burst, the fallout was harsh. Where before there had been a vision of perfection, now there was the taint of "junk science."

This syndrome was most pronounced in the *New York Times*'s reporting on DNA testing in the aftermath of the Castro case. On January 29, 1990, the *Times* ran a front-page article titled "Some Scientists Doubt the Value of 'Genetic Fingerprint' Evidence," apparently inspired by the fallout from the Castro case, although it never specifically mentioned that case. The article, by *Times* reporter Gina Kolata, reported that "leading molecular biologists" say that DNA analysis is "too unreliable to be used in court."

The impact on the public's perception of this new evidentiary tool was enormous, for the article suggested that a technology that in previous press reports had been universally praised as foolproof was really invalid. But this press report was more than a little peculiar, for several of the "leading molecular biologists" quoted by Kolata were known to be avid supporters of DNA analysis in criminal cases.

Sure enough, four of the seven "leading molecular biologists" reported in the *Times* article to be supporters of the view that DNA is so unreliable that it should not be used in court joined together in a scorching letter to the editor of the *Times*. They characterized Kolata's article as a "misrepresentation" of the validity of DNA identification and stated that there is "excellent agreement among scientists that the validity of the DNA identification method is widely accepted." The biologists went on to write that the public deserves to have this powerful technology protecting its safety against violent criminals, and the wrongly accused deserve to have the technology prove their innocence. The letter pointed out that the Castro decision was based on technical aspects of the particular case and not the fundamental scientific validity of DNA technology.

Astonishingly, *the New York Times* did not print the scientists' letter. The public now moved to the view that the great promise invested in DNA was unraveling. This was a matter of substantial concern, because judges and jurors are also members of the public. It looked like the incorrect perception that DNA evidence was unreliable could be a burden to overcome in every case into which it might be introduced.

Fortunately, most judges continued to recognize the validity of DNA testing. They knew that the Castro case generally endorsed the reliability of DNA testing and excluded the results implicating Castro principally because Lifecodes had failed to conduct additional tests on faint DNA bands. As a consequence, the critical article did not do as much damage as had first been feared. After Castro, courts continued to accept DNA evidence as leading scientists continued to testify that this was an extremely reliable technology. And, for legal purposes, the Castro decision itself came to stand for that view, as well as for the possibility that a laboratory can perform DNA analysis and interpretation improperly in an individual case.

At the time of the Castro decision, there was already a very substantial body of law endorsing the reliability of DNA evidence. Defense critics argued that all those prior cases should be discounted because they did not follow a hearing as searching or extensive as that which took place in the Castro case. But in most of those cases capable defense lawyers had consulted with qualified scientific witnesses and been unable to find anything significant to challenge in the DNA evidence.

To some extent, the courts recognized that the Castro matter simply represented individual failings in one particular case. "There is a great danger of making too much of the Castro case," said Dr. Roberts at the time. "From the evidence I've seen of other cases, I don't think it is typical."

After all, it was unlikely that laboratories routinely violated their own match criteria, or that there were faint extra bands present in most cases. More likely, the Castro case represented a confluence of the reality that there were some ambiguities in the DNA evidence that the lab had not taken steps to resolve, conflicting statements by the lab regarding its own criteria, the retention of two very aggressive defense lawyers, and a remarkable expert witness they were able to persuade to join that case.

But there is no question that the Castro case heightened interest in some issues surrounding the reliability of DNA evidence that went beyond the guilt or innocence of Joseph Castro. Above all it demonstrated the need for developing appropriate standards and requiring adherence to those standards. The experts for the prosecution and defense in the Bronx case both complained about Lifecodes's failure to adhere to its own policy of using objective match criteria. They also agreed that Lifecodes

in 1989 was using statistical techniques that dramatically overstated the numerical significance of a DNA match.

Some of the concerns raised by the critics of DNA testing in
the first years of such testing were related to the private and commercial nature of the first DNA laboratories. The field of DNA
testing in the United States was originally developed and dominated by two private commercial laboratories, Lifecodes in New
York State and Cellmark in Maryland. At the beginning, only Lifecodes offered RFLP testing; Cellmark followed shortly thereafter.
Both offered their analysis to police departments and to district
attorneys' offices for a fee, leading inevitably to criticism that the
profit motive had driven private laboratories to rush DNA testing
to market before adequate standards to ensure reliability were
developed and put in place, and with overstated statistical claims
about the significance when a DNA match was found.

So in 1989 there was a great deal of ambivalence about DNA
testing. There had been the public relations debacle of the Castro
case, and the New York Times article suggesting to the public that
DNA testing was unreliable. More significant, there was an
unquestioned need for standards to guarantee the reliability of
DNA testing, particularly testing done by commercial laboratories run for profit, so that the results would not be subject to suspicion that they were monetarily motivated.

Above all, everybody involved with DNA knew that there
must be no more Castro cases, or the acceptance of DNA could
be irretrievably damaged. Where would the leadership come
from to advance the reputation of this fledgling but already powerful technology?

I FIRST MET FBI SPECIAL AGENT LARRY PRESLEY IN 1989, just before
the Castro decision came down. Presley, who would go on to a
stint as chief of the FBI's DNA analysis unit, was then a nine-year
veteran of the Federal Bureau of Investigation, assigned to the
Bureau's new DNA analysis unit.

Agent Presley is tall and fair haired, and has an all-American,
open manner. He is a graduate of Wheeling Jesuit College, and
he fulfills the expectations one would have of an FBI agent—
smart, serious, and reliable. Our first meeting was occasioned by
his visit to New York to participate in a program at the District
Attorney's Office. I was to do a mock prosecutor's examination of

a DNA expert for the new lawyers in the office, to show how to question an expert witness. A defense lawyer was then to cross-examine the expert.

Like all the FBI agents, Presley was new to testifying about DNA. As much as I wanted the experience of questioning a DNA expert, Presley, who would soon testify in hundreds of cases, wanted the experience of being questioned by a prosecutor and cross-examined by a defense attorney. Long before this meeting, the FBI had committed itself to getting DNA analysis established on a firm footing. Presley was part of that effort and had volunteered to play the expert in the New York exercise.

The FBI had moved slowly and cautiously into the field of DNA testing, starting its research in 1986 but not becoming involved in actual cases until later. While Lifecodes and Cellmark were handling cases, the FBI was still doing experiments. The Bureau was testing DNA samples and checking its own results, to make sure that it could do DNA analysis reliably. Soon, the FBI went beyond research to performing DNA analysis on actual criminal cases, accepting cases for analysis late in 1988 and reporting its first result in an actual case in March 1989.

The FBI made DNA testing available at no charge to law enforcement authorities. Agents traveled around the country to testify to the results of DNA tests performed by scientific personnel working in the FBI laboratory, putting the quality of the FBI lab and the credibility of the Bureau squarely behind DNA. Sometimes the agents testified for the prosecution and sometimes they testified for the defense.

But the FBI's efforts extended well beyond providing high-quality DNA testing and testimony in ongoing cases. At the time, eight scientists worked full-time at the Bureau on research and training. Their work was headed by Bruce Budowle, who quickly became a guru to DNA scientists all over the country.

At the time, the FBI was subject to heavy lobbying by the two private biotechnology companies active in the use of DNA for criminal identification, Lifecodes and Cellmark. Each used a system with different components, although each system used the RFLP method. Both companies understood that the FBI's use and endorsement of their technology could mean enormous profits. By adopting either corporation's technology, the FBI would enhance that company's prominence in the field of DNA testing. At the same time, that company would see an increase in income, from licensing fees and the sale of their products to the FBI and other crime laboratories.

There were two fundamental differences between the RFLP systems used by Lifecodes and Cellmark. First, each used a different chemical material to initially cut the DNA. When the FBI selected a third chemical material for use in its system, both Lifecodes and Cellmark switched to using that material. Second, Cellmark used the original system developed by Dr. Jeffreys, the inventor of DNA analysis. Lifecodes used a refinement on that technique, one that was less like a fingerprint but more easily interpretable. The Jeffreys "multi-locus probe" reflected many genetic areas on one piece of film; the Lifecodes "single-locus probe" reflected DNA analysis from each genetic location on a separate piece of X-ray film. The FBI adopted the Lifecodes approach for use in its RFLP system, and Cellmark soon switched to it too.

Neither company would buck the FBI. It was not that the FBI came into DNA testing as the principal leader in the field of serology, or blood analysis (as it was in other areas, like hair and fiber analysis)—that role had always fallen to Scotland Yard, and to the large urban crime labs in the United States. But the FBI laboratory was respected, its credibility unimpeached, and its endorsement crucial to the acceptance of DNA testing by courts, District Attorney's Offices, and local crime laboratories. And to place the new technology on a solid footing, Budowle sought the guidance of leading university scientists unaffiliated with the biotechnology companies—such as Ray White at the Howard Hughes Medical Institute at the University of Utah, Thomas Caskey at Baylor University, and Kenneth Kidd at Yale—listened carefully, and then performed numerous experiments.

Under Budowle's leadership, the FBI explored the boundaries of DNA technology. Bloodstains were exposed to sunlight, gasoline, motor oil, and detergent. More than 2,000 items were analyzed. In every case, the result before exposure was the same as afterward. Contamination could obliterate a DNA print, but it would not alter it. There would be a correct result, or no result, but environmental contamination would not produce a false result.

Budowle also sought to develop a means of stating the significance of a DNA match that would be both understandable by lay jury members and unimpeachable by scientist witnesses. In stating its results, the FBI specifically chose statistical methods that would, if anything, understate the significance of a match, a sharp contrast from Lifecodes's policy—so that defendants got a break from the FBI's statistical methods. There would be no pretense that six-inch butterfly nets had been used in stating the significance of a DNA match.

The FBI research and training efforts also included developing techniques for DNA analysis that would be easily interpretable. Before the Castro decision, the Bureau had already decided not to use the particular test that would generate the ambiguous results in that case. After developing its own testing techniques, the FBI trained scientists from all over the United States, and the world, in its techniques. As a result, the FBI techniques are those most widely used in local crime laboratories from coast to coast today.

Under Budowle, the FBI also sponsored an effort to develop standards that could be applied to all laboratories, providing objective rules for private as well as public laboratories. This effort drew on outside scientists, independent of the FBI, including Ray White, the Utah scientist who had developed RFLP analysis for genetic diagnostics.

This group of scientists first met in November 1988, and the FBI published their guidelines for DNA analysis in 1989. The guidelines were meant to set standards that would ensure the quality and reliability of DNA testing. They addressed all the concerns raised by the joint statement of the experts in the Castro case, requiring among other things that DNA matches be confirmed quantitatively, that standards be developed for determining when DNA analysis is inconclusive or unable to be read, and that scientifically valid statistics be used for stating the significance of a DNA match.

After 1989 the scientists met again and issued further reports, but the group of independent scientists working in association with the FBI were already well on their way to establishing a set of rules to govern DNA analysis, whether done in the FBI's laboratory, at Lifecodes, at Cellmark, or elsewhere.

As the decade drew to a close, much of the broad acceptance of DNA testing that the press reporting in the aftermath of the Castro decision had undermined was established once more.

DNA's return to a state of grace was confirmed when the Office of Technology Assessment of the United States Congress issued its long-awaited report on DNA testing in 1990. The report to the Congress noted that standards were still being developed and that more work needed to be done. Its most crucial finding, however, was devastating to the DNA debunkers.

Testing of DNA is reliable, concluded the report, and questions about the validity of DNA typing are "red herrings that do the courts and the public a disservice." Like the scientists who wrote the unpublished letter to the *New York Times,* the congressional Office of Technology Assessment recognized the fundamental reliability of DNA analysis and its important role in identifying the guilty and exonerating the innocent.

After one short year, DNA was back on track. DNA testing had been fundamentally reliable to begin with; by 1990, because of the exceptional efforts of the FBI, the standards and procedures necessary to protect its reliability using the RFLP method were mostly in place. The FBI effort was already well under way before the Castro decision, but the Bronx case raised the stakes, and gave much more impetus to the need for care and quality in DNA testing. It was one thing to want to do good, reliable work. It was another matter for a scientist to know that his or her work would be subject to the closest possible scrutiny by others who want to tear that work apart.

The scientific community met the challenge of setting standards to promote reliable DNA testing. Before, DNA testing had seemed simple, inevitable, infallible; now, in part because of the efforts of critics like Lander, Scheck, and Neufeld, it was apparent that DNA analysis was highly reliable but would require care in its use and interpretation. But the standards were apparently in place to govern that process, subject to the care and scrutiny of prosecutors, defense lawyers, and scientists. New approaches to protecting the integrity of DNA analysis would also be forthcoming; the influence of the Castro case would continue well into the future, for the joint statement of the prosecution and defense experts from that case urged that the National Academy of Sciences study DNA testing, and a report eventually published by that organization would figure dramatically in future cases and controversy over DNA analysis.

Still, in the wake of the trouble over DNA, the future of the new technology was far from assured. Would prosecutors and judges stand squarely behind the new technology, even when they did not like the results it generated? Defense lawyers could pick and choose between those cases in which they liked DNA results and those in which they did not, relying on favorable DNA results and attacking DNA tests that implicated their clients. Would prosecutors do the same, or fully support the reliability of DNA testing and find ways to work around DNA results and place them in the appropriate context when they did not like them but still believed a suspect to be guilty? This question was soon put to the test in one of the most notorious criminal cases of our time, the Central Park jogger case.

4 INSIDE THE CENTRAL PARK JOGGER TRIAL

IT WAS A HOT AUGUST DAY WHEN I RETURNED FROM COURT to my desk at the District Attorney's Office and found a telephone message from Elizabeth Lederer, the lead prosecutor on the Central Park Jogger case, asking that I call her. A handwritten note scrawled by the bureau secretary on the message said, "Very important."

Lederer, then thirty-eight, is a petite, shapely woman, with wide, captivating eyes. She is also extremely circumspect, as befits a prosecutor handling major cases, and I have rarely seen her in an unguarded moment. She is not a person given to great expressions of eagerness or anxiety. But this was to be an unusual day.

I called Lederer immediately, and she asked me to please come up to her office on the seventh floor of 80 Centre Street. I guessed that something was wrong the moment I walked in the door.

The DNA results had come in, and they were not good. "I feel," she said, "like I've been kicked in the stomach." This most composed woman was visibly shaken.

We had hoped and expected that the FBI would find the DNA

of our defendants when they performed DNA analysis on the evidence from the scene of the crime.

Instead, we learned over time in a series of discussions with the FBI that the single DNA band generated by semen found on a vaginal swab and on the jogger's sock did not match the DNA of any of the suspects. Nor did it match that of the jogger's boyfriend.

The FBI was over time somewhat equivocal about whether the single band should be characterized as a DNA profile. At first, they had called it an inconclusive result, because the initial test, on the vaginal swab, produced only one single weak DNA band at one chromosome. But after a second, later test on the jogger's sock produced the same single weak band at the same chromosome, the FBI moved to finally characterizing the single band on both the swab and the sock as a DNA profile.

There was no question that this result was going to hurt our case. There was also semen on the jogger's running tights; the DNA in that semen matched her boyfriend's DNA, but there was a legitimate reason for that DNA to be there. On the Sunday morning before the attack, the jogger had consensual sex with her boyfriend, put on the tights, and went running.

In fact, the DNA analysis of the stain on the tights and the other DNA results had more impact than any other factor on the prosecution's decision to call the jogger as a witness. She had to testify to explain how the stain on her tights got there, and to tell the jury that she had not had sex with anyone but her boyfriend. But the DNA in the semen from the vaginal swab and the jogger's socks did not match either her boyfriend or any of the identified suspects.

Did that mean we had the wrong guys in jail? Was there some simple explanation for this dilemma? Or was our case unraveling before our very eyes?

To answer that question, it is necessary to go back to the beginning, to Central Park and the scene of the crime.

CENTRAL PARK IS A PERFECTLY RECTANGULAR GREEN OASIS in a city of concrete streets. This vast area is bordered on the east by Fifth Avenue, on the west by Central Park West. Its south-to-north length runs from the glamorous area surrounding Manhattan's Plaza Hotel around Fifty-ninth Street all the way up into the southern edge of Harlem.

It is a credit to New York City that such a large chunk of the world's most valuable real estate has remained largely untouched by development and commerce since its design by the great Frederick Law Olmsted in the nineteenth century. The park continues to play a vital role in the recreation and relaxation of the people who live in New York City.

Contrary to popular perceptions, Central Park is a relatively safe place. It is an area where few crimes occur; the park has a crime rate lower than that of most New York City police precincts. In fact, the park is so safe that members of the New York Police Department mockingly refer to park duty as "squirrel patrol."

Violent crimes in Central Park do, however, often become national news stories. The why of this is a mystery. Maybe it is because these crimes strike at the heart of a city that is the media capital of the world. Maybe they conjure up the average citizen's worst fear, that he or she will become the victim of a random, senseless act of violence. After all, when Willie Sutton was asked why he robbed banks, he had an answer everyone understood—that's where the money is. And most people who suffer assault at or near home turn out to be victims of the rage of another family member, a friend, or at least an acquaintance. But when people enter the park for a stroll or a jog, or to fly a kite or walk the dog, what items of value can they be carrying on them worth the commission of a criminal act? And if not for money, then what is crime for? Park crime seems to be crime for crime's sake.

No crime of the late 1980s was more shocking, nor more an object of public fascination, than the assault on a female jogger who had presumed to go for a run in Central Park. Besides the fact that the crime took place in Central Park, there was the background of the victim, an Ivy League–educated investment banker, the new kind of young woman who did not fear competing with men for the top jobs and did not fear taking a nighttime jog through the park when that was the only time her busy schedule left her for the activity.

To the media, it was the "Central Park jogger case," named for the rape victim whose anonymity has been protected from the public to this day. In reality, the crime was more accurately the Central Park rampage, a series of attacks on many victims carried out over the course of about an hour by a pack of teenagers apparently gone mad. Indeed, the word one of the suspects used to describe the activity he had been engaged in—"wilding"— instantly entered the national vocabulary, standing for the mindless amorality that seemed to characterize so much urban teenage activity.

At about 9:00 P.M. on April 19, 1989, as Police Officer Raymond Alvarez drove through Central Park, he noticed a group of ten young men, aged fifteen to seventeen, playing and running around. The officer then saw another thirty teenagers join the first group. He shined his spotlight on the group, and the teenagers temporarily dispersed. But soon the two groups joined together again and headed south through the park. The night of terror was about to commence.

At the same time, a young woman was leaving her apartment building to go for a run in the park. She had worked at her investment banking firm, Salomon Brothers, until approximately 8:00 P.M. She had taken a taxi home from work, and changed into her running clothes. Next was her nightly run in Central Park.

As she left her apartment building, the young woman ran into a neighbor, James Lansing. It was just about 9:00 P.M., Lansing later remembered, as the young woman left her building at York Avenue and headed toward Central Park.

At that same time, Michael Vigna, a thirty-one-year-old investigator for the New York City Department of Health, was already riding his bicycle through Central Park. Vigna, a competitive cyclist, was on one of his nightly training rides. He was wearing cycling shorts, a cycling jersey, and cycling shoes as he rode his custom-made Italian racing bike along the main roadway that runs in a loop through Central Park. That roadway, closed to traffic on evenings and weekends, is extremely popular with cyclists and joggers.

As Vigna approached 102d Street in the park on the roadway, a gang of thirty-five youths spread across the road in front of him, forcing him to the extreme left. As Vigna passed by them on the left, one of the youths swung at his head. Vigna quickly jerked his head to the side, avoiding the punch. He could hear the force the fist would have delivered; even in missing it whooshed by his head. He did not get a good look at the face of any individual member of the group. It was 9:05 P.M.

As the gang continued heading downtown through the park,

they encountered a fifty-one-year-old unemployed man, Antonio Diaz, at 102d Street, who the gang members would later describe as "the bum." He had decided to walk home across the park, which separates the East Side and West Side of Manhattan, and was carrying a take-out dinner of chicken, rice, beans, and some beers.

The young men jumped Diaz. To Diaz, it seemed they had come out of nowhere. They knocked him to the ground, kicking him and hitting him on his head, eyes, and back. It was a severe beating, one that sent Diaz to the hospital. He could not see the faces of any of his attackers, nor did he know the time of the attack.

Just beneath 102d Street in the park, Gerald Malone, thirty-five, and his fiancée, Patricia Dean, both advertising executives, were riding a bicycle built for two. This was no romantic idyll but a practice session. Malone competed semiprofessionally on a regular basis, riding a tandem bicycle hand-built specifically for racing. He was riding in front; Dean sat on the backseat.

As they rode north toward 102d Street, Malone noticed a large group of teenagers on the right side of the roadway. There were thirty to forty of them, and they were all very close together, some 500 feet ahead. At this point, Malone and his fiancée were riding the bicycle at a speed between twenty-five and thirty miles per hour.

As Malone and Dean rode forward, the kids spread out in front of them, blocking the road ahead. Some crouched, bending at their knees while adopting what Malone characterized as a basketball stance, ready for action. Many pulled their hoods over their heads so that just their eyes were exposed, and got down very low to the ground. They stood several deep, all the way across the road, spread out evenly, making threatening noises, murmurs, grunts.

Suddenly, Malone felt his fiancée come up with a surge of power, and he responded the same way, pedaling furiously fast and hard. Malone steered the bicycle to the right, pretending that he was going to go that way.

But, within ten feet of the group, he veered to the left, and aimed straight at the first person in the very front, a young man much taller than the others. Malone aimed at that young man specifically because he seemed to be the leader of the group. Malone tried to hit him and hit him as hard as he could.

The tall young man jumped out of the way, and so did everybody else. But, as the two rode through the crowd, four young men grabbed at Patricia Dean, trying to wrench her off the bicycle. Three on her right pushed at her, while one on her left pulled upward on her thigh, trying to lift her off the bicycle.

The bicycle swerved and almost toppled. But the bicycle, and the cyclists, managed to stay upright, and Malone and Dean escaped, riding forward through the parted crowd. After they passed, some of the teenagers chased them but did not catch them.

During this brief, terrifying encounter, neither Malone nor Dean got a good look at the face of any one of the young men. It was 9:12 P.M.

Vigna, Diaz, Malone, and Dean all reported their encounters to the police. The word quickly went out on the police radio to the Central Park police, and to police from the neighboring precincts. A large group of teenagers was attacking people in Central Park. Police cars responded, searching for a large gang of young men, focusing on the main roadway through the park, since that was where the attacks were reported to have happened.

As the police cars began to enter the park, the teenagers, looking to hide, moved off the park's central roadway and headed to a road that runs through the park at 102d Street. This cross-drive is a shortcut from the park drive on the East Side to the park drive on the West Side. It is a less traveled road than the main loop running through the park.

It was there, on the cross-drive, that the teenagers came upon the Central Park jogger, and charged at her as she ran. There she was dragged off into the brush, sexually attacked, beaten into unconsciousness, and left for dead. This last phrase was not idly chosen. In later references to the event, at least some of the attackers spoke in ways that communicated that they assumed murder had been committed. Oddly, that fact did not cause them to end their night's activities.

On April 19, 1989, the jogger was twenty-eight years old, five-feet-five-inches tall, and weighed only 105 pounds. She had grown up in Pittsburgh, gone to college at Wellesley, business school at Yale. As an investment banker, she frequently worked from 7:30 in the morning until 8:00 at night, and ran in the evening.

After work, she ran in Central Park at 8:30 or 9:30 P.M., covering a full six or seven miles. She would run to the park from her apartment on Manhattan's Upper East Side, run north through the park, and cut across the park from the East Side to the West Side at 102d Street, on the cross-drive, because she thought this was safer than running farther uptown on the park drive.

Afterward, the jogger remembered absolutely nothing of the attack in Central Park that night. She did not even remember going running that day. Her last memory of April 19 was a telephone call she made at 5:00 P.M., canceling her dinner plans for that evening because she had to work late. Her next memory was of awakening, six weeks later, in a hospital room on Friday evening of Memorial Day weekend, 1989. The details of the attack on the jogger would be pieced together for the trial solely through the defendants' statements and the injuries the jogger suffered that night in the park.

After the young men left the jogger's beaten and apparently lifeless body they continued their predatory stalk. They walked farther downtown through the park, stopping in the woods that surround a reservoir at the center of the park.

The reservoir, a large, roughly circular body of water dotted with ducks, is one of the most picturesque places in New York City. It is surrounded by a track for walking and running. Walkers and runners on the track can see many of the most beautiful vistas of New York, including Frank Lloyd Wright's Guggenheim Museum, Fifth Avenue apartment buildings, and office towers that appear to be just beyond a foreground of shimmering water.

Just outside the perimeter of the walking and running track, in the woods just above that track, stood the young men. Poised at one of the most idyllic spots in New York City, they were ready to grab and hurt whoever came along.

On the path surrounding the reservoir, David Lewis, a thirty-one-year-old banker, was taking his daily run. As Lewis turned west at the top of the path around the reservoir, he heard a young man to his right, in the woods next to the path, say the word "ready."

Lewis looked to his right, just off the track into the woods, and saw two young men crouched in the stance of football running backs about to take off—knees bent, one arm forward, one arm down. Lewis asked the teenagers if they wanted to race, and they said, Yeah, we'll race, all right.

As Lewis then faced back toward the path and continued running, five young men stepped out of the trees onto the running path ahead of him. They stood in front of him, blocking his way.

Lewis ran at them full tilt and, just as he reached them, veered off to a small opening on the left. As Lewis ran by, one young man hit him on the arm. A group of teenagers pursued him, but Lewis escaped with a bruise on his upper arm, between his elbow and shoulder. He did not get a good look at the faces of any of the young men and was unable to identify any one individually.

Then David Good, a six-foot-four-inch, thirty-four-year-old engineer, ran by the same area on the reservoir path. As he did, a large group of teenagers threw sticks and stones at him from the woods surrounding the reservoir track. One yelled that he better run faster. A young man tried to block Good's way, but Good ran to the side and by him. The group chased him along the path, but they were not able to capture him. Good did not see the faces of any of the young men; the whole incident took less than a minute.

The young men did catch Robert Garner. Garner, thirty, was an analyst for British Airways. As Garner reached an old water pump station, the first of two old stone houses at the north end of the reservoir, a group of fifteen to twenty kids ran out from the trees on his right side. They were yelling and shouting; one shouted Merry Christmas.

The teenagers ran in front of Garner and behind him. Quickly, they surrounded him on the jogging track. In a group, they forced him off the track to a small embankment in the woods adjoining the running track, and knocked him to the ground.

"What do you want from me?" asked Garner.

"Money, of course," said one member of the group.

But the teenagers laughed, and it was clear that the group was not looking for Garner's money but to hurt him. They hit Garner's head with a stone; they struck him repeatedly. Garner was terrified and thought he was going to die. Then the teenagers, sighting another jogger, another victim, told Garner to get out of there. Garner did get out of there, running away. Like the night's other victims, Garner did not remember the faces of any of the young men.

As John Loughlin jogged toward the old stone house on the reservoir path, he thought that he saw a man in trouble, presumably Garner, on the ground, surrounded by a group of teenagers. Loughlin, an ex-Marine, a large man, six-feet-four-inches tall, 185 pounds, a teacher in the New York City public schools, was not the sort of person to ignore another person in trouble.

Loughlin slowed, and turned north on the track to face the scene taking place just off the running track. He was dressed in army-style camouflage jacket and pants.

One teenager from the group aggressively walked out of the woods toward Loughlin and onto the reservoir track itself, standing to Loughlin's right on the track as Loughlin faced north to the woods and the man in trouble.

"What are you, a vigilante?" asked the teenager.

Loughlin did not respond.

"Here is one of those vigilantes," the teenager shouted to his friends, three of whom were walking toward Loughlin.

"Vigilante," said the three teenagers, as they continued to walk toward Loughlin.

Loughlin did not remember what happened then. The next thing he knew, he was facedown on the ground, being hit on the back of his head with an object having the weight and hardness of a baseball bat. As Loughlin put up his right hand to his head to fend off a blow, he felt that the object was smooth.

As they beat him, Loughlin called out, "Fellows, why are you doing this to me? Stop." These kids were the same age as those students Loughlin taught in the New York City public schools. But the savage beating continued.

Loughlin was left bleeding and unconscious on the reservoir path. It was shortly before 10:00 P.M.

The rampage was over. The young men had taken less than one full hour to do all their damage and left the park.

During that hour, the police had received complaints in ever-increasing numbers. More and more police cars were dispatched to search the park for a large gang of teenagers. But, strangely, cruising through some of the same areas where all the crimes took place, they had not come across this large roving pack.

Two plainclothes police officers, Eric Reynolds and Robert Powers, took another approach. They decided to look outside the park, thinking that the teenagers might have left or be leaving the

park. They drove along Central Park West, the avenue that borders Central Park on the West Side just as Fifth Avenue borders
the park on the East Side.

At 102d Street and Central Park West, the officers saw a
group of ten to twenty teenagers walking northbound. Reynolds
and Powers identified themselves as police officers and ordered
the teens to stop, but they fled.

The police officers pursued them and managed to apprehend
and arrest five of the teenagers. Included was a young man named
Raymond Santana. And, as the police drove to the precinct, one of
the youths told the police that he knew who "had done the
murder." It was, said the youth, Antron McCray.

At that point, the police thought that the "murder" referred to
the savage assault on John Loughlin. The jogger, left in a secluded
wood, had not yet been found; she lay in thick brush, losing more
and more blood, on the verge of death but still clinging to life with
a tenacity that became one of the marvels of the case.

And the Central Park jogger would surely have died that night
but for a walk in the park by two men, Vinicio Moore and Carlos
Colon.

At about 1:30 in the morning, Moore and Colon made their
way across Central Park. Moore, thirty-eight years old, an unemployed construction worker, had been hanging out on the street
talking and drinking beer with his friend Colon, twenty-four
years old, an unemployed welder.

Initially, Moore and Colon were going to take the bus across
the park to get back to their respective homes. But it was a
moonlit, warm night, and Moore and Colon decided to walk.

Their night walk home followed a broken asphalt path
through the park that took them near the cross-drive where the
attack on the jogger had taken place. As they walked along, they
heard a groaning sound. The men looked toward the sound and
saw a form moving on the ground.

They knew immediately that the form was a body, and a body
in distress. They started running, afraid that whoever had hurt
that person might still be there and might hurt them.

As Moore and Colon came to the top of a hill, they saw a
police car. They approached the car, told Police Officer Joseph
Walsh that there was a body at the bottom of the hill in the

woods, and then returned to that spot with Walsh and his partner.

When Moore and Colon returned with the police, they found a ghastly scene. The young woman was naked but for her jogging bra, and severely beaten. One of her eyes was puffed out and almost closed. The side of her head was cracked and covered with blood. She was bound and gagged with her own shirt, her hands tied up in front of her face with her palms together. As if still fighting off her attackers, she was moving her hands up and down and kicking her feet out violently.

Walsh kept telling the woman that he was a police officer. Repeatedly, he asked, "Who did this to you?"

But there was no response. The woman seemed to be looking right through him, flailing with her arms and kicking with her legs.

Looking at the woman, the police were not able to determine her race or age. She was rushed by ambulance from the park to Metropolitan Hospital. The ambulance crew had placed her in mast trousers, designed to move blood from her lower organs to her vital organs, her heart and brain. She was classified by the police as "likely to die," a determination that turned out to be important because it allowed specially trained homicide detectives to enter the case.

The jogger was admitted into the emergency room at Metropolitan Hospital at 2:30 in the morning. Her identity was entirely unknown; her anonymity, today a matter of choice, was then simply a matter of fact. She was listed simply as Unknown Female, Patient Number 1127450.

At the hospital, the gritty young woman continued her "fight response," swinging her arms and kicking, even though she had lost three-quarters of the blood in her body, and her body temperature had dropped to eighty-four degrees. The level of blood loss was extremely life threatening; a person who has lost 80 percent of the body's blood—just 5 percent more than she had lost—invariably dies. She had a fractured skull, and the bones under one of her eyes were completely broken.

For that entire night, the jogger remained not only anonymous but also alone, except for the doctors and nurses trying to save her life and the police officers and detectives working on her case. Then, the next morning, at 10:00, she had a visitor.

Patrick Garrett, twenty-nine, was also an investment banker working at Salomon Brothers, the same firm as the jogger. He had joined the firm in 1986, as had the jogger, and they had become very close friends. They had never dated, and as friends only had shared an apartment for a year, some time ago. At work they sat next to each other on the fourteenth floor of One New York Plaza.

On the evening before the attack, Garrett had walked his friend to the door as she left work at 8:00 P.M. The young woman told Garrett that she was going to go home, and then go jogging, and would be back to her apartment by 10:00 P.M. The two arranged to meet at the woman's apartment at 10:00 P.M., after she returned from jogging, to look at her stereo.

On the night of the attack, as planned, Garrett rang his friend's doorbell at precisely 10:00 P.M., but there was no answer. He then went to the corner and called the young woman from a pay phone, but her answering machine picked up. Garrett left a message.

Garrett arrived at work the next morning at 8:00. His friend was not yet in, and that was unusual; she typically arrived at work at 7:30 A.M. Garrett asked the investment banker's secretary if she was supposed to be traveling that day and was told that she was not scheduled to travel. Garrett discussed her absence with his colleagues, and they called the police. Soon Garrett was asked to come to Metropolitan Hospital to see if the anonymous woman found in the park could be his friend.

At the hospital, a police officer showed Garrett pictures of the severely injured woman and asked if he could identify her from the pictures. He could not.

Garrett then went up to her room and looked at the anonymous jogger, but he still could not identify her, even after looking at her for ten minutes.

Only when a police officer showed him her ring could he tell the police that this was his friend.

The police now knew the identity of the female jogger. But neither she nor any of the other victims could answer Officer Walsh's first question to her—"Who did this to you?"

Since none of the victims of that night's rampage could initially identify any of the teenagers, the answer to that question would have to come from the young men who committed the assaults themselves. It was now up to the detectives to get the young men to talk, to make a case against themselves, where otherwise there would have been no case.

THE MANHATTAN NORTH HOMICIDE SQUAD is an elite group of detectives whose members are frequently brought in to help local precincts on homicide cases.

In theory, the primary responsibility for the case remains with the detective from the local precinct. That local precinct detective "catches" the case because he or she is next in the rotation among the detectives from the precinct.

The detectives from the homicide squad assist the precinct detective assigned to the case. Their assistance is necessary because the investigation of a major homicide case frequently requires several detectives. There will be many witnesses, and perhaps even many suspects, to be interviewed. The detectives from the homicide squad are the additional detectives necessary to interview witnesses and suspects. But they are also superb detectives and, because of the quality of their work, have a way of taking over cases they are brought in to help with.

These are some of the most experienced, toughest, and wiliest homicide detectives in the city, and they have an ability to get results where the precinct detectives might not. Their involvement in the jogger case was appropriate that night, although this was not yet a homicide case, because the jogger was listed by the police as likely to die.

In investigating the attack in the park, the place to start was the five youths apprehended the night before at One Hundredth Street and Central Park West. Above all, the detectives wanted to talk to those teenagers. But they had to wait, at least until morning. Since those involved were under sixteen, the detectives could not interview them without a parent present. So, all through the night, parents were notified and asked to come to the Central Park precinct, where their children were being held.

And, as the parents arrived, the interviews began.

Throughout the next day, April 20, scores of teenagers were interviewed. Young men would implicate other young men, and those young men too would be brought in for interviews.

That day, the precinct was filled with detectives, young men, and their parents. There were detectives from the Manhattan

North Homicide Squad, the Central Park precinct, the Twentieth Precinct, and the Twenty-fourth Precinct.

The interviews that the homicide detectives conducted were the heart of the jogger case. In retrospect, there would have been no case at all but for the admissions made to those detectives. None of the youths would have been arrested had they asserted their right to remain silent and simply refused to answer the detectives' questions.

It was certain that the techniques the detectives used to gain confessions from the teenagers would be subjected to the closest possible scrutiny by future jurors. This would be particularly true in a case with a racial dynamic like the jogger case. The detectives were predominantly white, middle-aged men, the victim white, the defendants young African Americans and Hispanics.

A Manhattan jury selected to hear this case would, because of the borough's racial demographics, be multiracial. That jury would become fully aware of the procedure used by the police in most American cities, New York included, to gain statements from suspects. Almost all of the preliminary questioning of those under suspicion by the police is conducted in interrogation rooms at the precinct, with no camera or recorder present. It is only after a suspect has committed himself firmly to a story that an assistant district attorney is called in and the suspect interviewed by the assistant district attorney on videotape. So a detective's account of how a suspect came to implicate himself is subjected to the closest possible scrutiny. The jurors will look particularly for any indication that a statement may have been coerced or fed to a vulnerable or impressionable defendant.

In this case, the detectives' accounts of the statements they took began with Detective Harry Hildebrandt. That day, April 20, Detective Hildebrandt of the Manhattan North Homicide Squad was assigned to interview Antron McCray at the Twentieth Precinct.

McCray, fifteen years old, had been named by one of the teenagers arrested on Central Park West as the person who "had done the murder," and he had been brought in for questioning, along with his parents, by detectives who had gone to his home.

Hildebrandt asked McCray to start from the beginning and tell him and the other detectives present for the interview what had happened last night in Central Park. McCray spoke for twenty minutes about assaults in the park but made no mention of a female jogger. He appeared nervous and fidgety.

The detective asked McCray's father if he could have a conversation with him outside the interrogation room, and the two stepped out. The detective told the father that it seemed his son was holding something back, and not telling them everything that had happened in the park. The father agreed and accepted the detective's suggestion that he go back into the room, talk with his son, and urge him to be truthful.

After a private conversation between father and son, the detectives returned to the room. The detectives then asked the teenager to tell them exactly who did what during the events in the park that night. McCray described the same activities, but this time he provided details, specifics about the blows inflicted. At one point, McCray's mother told him to tell everything that happened, telling her son that she and his father had brought him up better than this.

Still, McCray made no mention of a female jogger. When the detective asked him about her, he said he didn't know anything about a female jogger.

The detective again asked the father to step into the hall and told him that his son was still holding something back, and that it may be because his mother was present. The father agreed, said that he had raised his son to tell the truth, and suggested that his wife leave the room. The detective asked the father if he wanted to speak to his wife, and he said he would. The father spoke to the mother alone, and Mrs. McCray left the interrogation room.

The father turned to his son and said, I'm glad we had your mother leave the room. Now please tell them what happened. It was then that Antron McCray described how the jogger was attacked.

McCray spoke to the detectives about the attack for a half hour. The police took a written statement from him that afternoon.

Later, at approximately 1:00 in the morning, prosecutor Elizabeth Lederer took a videotaped statement in which McCray recounted the rampage in the park that night and the attack on the jogger.

The attacks that night, said McCray, began with the beating of a "bum." The group beat up the bum, poured his beer on him, and started to eat his food but did not finish because it was "nasty." They also saw a man and a woman on "a bike made for two people" and tried to catch them, but they got away. Then they proceeded downtown through the park.

They saw a "jogging lady" running on the path around the reservoir. They all charged her. The tall black kid hit her twice with a pipe. The gang ripped her clothes off; as they did, McCray held one hand while a Puerto Rican kid with a hood held the other.

According to McCray, a number of people had sex with the female jogger. The tall black kid got on top of her, then the Puerto Rican kid with the hood, then McCray himself.

On the video, McCray claimed that he did not penetrate the jogger but only rubbed against her, where earlier he had told the detectives that he had penetrated the jogger but had not ejaculated.

After McCray got off the jogger, a teenager named Clarence Thomas "went" next, and then Kevin Richardson. Then, "this guy" hit her over the head, and they all left. They left her there, by the reservoir, in the woods by the path. No one moved her body; they just left her there.

Then the group walked down to the reservoir and saw a jogger wearing a green army jacket. He said "something smart," and one kid pulled him down. They all kicked and punched him, and the tall kid hit him with a pipe. The group then left the park.

As they emerged on the West Side, the police pulled over and told them to stop, but McCray ran back into the park. He hid there, lying in the mud, avoiding the police. When he got home, McCray told his mother that he was dirty from playing tag.

McCray's statement was a compelling admission of his role in the attack on the jogger. In some respects, it was devastating, for it related both the facts of the attack on the jogger—which were unknown—and the known facts of the attempt to grab Malone and Dean on their tandem bike and the assault on John Loughlin.

But the statement also contained the seeds of potential disaster for the prosecution, because it got important facts wrong.

McCray said that the attack on the jogger had taken place at the reservoir, when it had actually occurred many blocks north of that in the park, at an entirely different place. And McCray said that they had left the jogger where they attacked her, when in fact she had been dragged deep into the woods, as evidenced by drag marks found by the police.

There was an area of potential doubt here, an area for the defense to exploit, for if McCray had actually been there, certainly he would not have gotten such important details wrong.

Or so the argument for the defense would go at trial.

WHEN DETECTIVE JOHN HARTIGEN OF THE Manhattan North Homicide Squad first interviewed Raymond Santana on the afternoon of April 20, Santana admitted a role in the other attacks the night before. But he denied any knowledge of a female jogger.

Later that afternoon, Detective Hartigen confronted Santana's father about the teenager's statement as the son sat in the room. Hartigen told the teenager's father that the detectives believed his son was withholding additional information. At that point, the son asked his father if he could talk with Detective Hartigen alone. The father agreed and Raymond Santana's father stepped into the next room.

When Raymond Santana spoke to the detective alone, he told the detective that he had participated in knocking down, striking, and beating the female jogger.

The detective immediately stopped Santana and said that he couldn't tell him these things without his parents being present. The detective stepped out, looking for Santana's father. But the father had left the building. The interview would have to wait.

Later, at 2:30 in the morning on April 21, at the precinct, Raymond Santana told his story to prosecutor Elizabeth Lederer, in a videotaped interview in the presence of his father. Santana told Lederer that a group of thirty-three kids had gone into the park to beat up people and take bikes and money. They had scattered when they saw a police car, but then they had regrouped. When they got to the reservoir, they had tried to grab two joggers, but both had gotten away.

A third jogger came by, said Santana, and he was jogging too slowly. They thought he might be a cop. Jermaine, a member of the group with a gold tooth, picked up the male jogger and threw him to the ground. Everyone, including Santana, began beating the male jogger and kicking him, and one member of the group hit him on the head and back with a lead pipe. Jermaine was particularly savage in his beating, said Santana. It was like he was trying to murder the man. Santana did not take the man's headset because it was simply a radio, and everyone wants one that plays cassettes.

The group then proceeded from the reservoir to the roadway, continued Santana. There, they attacked the female jogger. Kevin Richardson took the lead, grabbing her by her wrist and tripping her with his leg. One youth pulled off her clothes. As Richardson entered her, the jogger screamed for help, but Steve Lopez held her mouth, telling her, "Shut up, bitch." But the jogger kept screaming. So Lopez took a brick and hit her twice in the head with the brick, all while Richardson had sex with her and Santana grabbed her breasts. At that point, after she was hit twice with a brick, she stopped screaming.

"She was like shocked," said Santana.

Santana did not see whether anyone else raped the jogger after Richardson because he left. "My conscience told me to leave," he said.

Once again, the police had a devastating confession. But once again, there was a problem, for the defendant's statement included a major inaccuracy, grist for the defense argument that these statements were not firsthand accounts by people who had actually been there but recycled stories fed to the defendants by the police. According to Santana, the attack on the female jogger followed the attacks on the male joggers at the reservoir. This was inconsistent with the statements of the other defendants, who said that the attack on the male jogger at the reservoir had been the last attack.

THE SHREWDEST OF THE MANHATTAN NORTH HOMICIDE DETECTIVES was Thomas McKenna. McKenna was assigned to interview the most arrogant of the three young men who would soon stand trial, Yusef Salaam.

From the outset, Salaam thought that he could outwit this middle-aged homicide detective. The police had come to pick up Salaam on April 20. Another young man from the group had implicated him in the attack on the jogger.

Salaam was fifteen, but he told the officer who picked him up that he was a year older. He showed the detective identification that represented his age as sixteen. Salaam had previously used the fake identification to impress teenage girls, or, as he put it, "older women."

At the precinct, Detective McKenna told Salaam that he wanted to talk to him about an assault that had taken place the night before in Central Park. But Salaam stopped him. "Before you go any further, I wasn't in Central Park," he said.

"I know you were in Central Park," McKenna replied. But Salaam denied having been in the park.

"Look," said McKenna, "I don't care if you tell me anything, I don't care what you say to me, we have fingerprints on the jogger's pants or her running shorts, they're satin, they're a very smooth surface. We have been able to get fingerprints off them.

"I'm just going to compare your prints," continued the detective, "to the prints that we have on the pants, and if they match up, you don't have to tell me anything because you're going down for rape."

Salaam looked at McKenna.

"I was there," said Salaam, "but I didn't rape her."

Salaam told the detective about how he and a group of friends were going into the park to "have some fun." They joined up with a group of fifteen others, from the Taft Houses. After entering the park, they attacked "the bum." Then they tried to block a man and a woman on a tandem bike. The man, who was in front, sped up, coming right at Salaam, Salaam stepped out of the way, and the bikers got through the crowd.

Next, a female jogger came down the path. Kevin Richardson ran out and stopped her. But she struggled, so Salaam ran out and hit her with a pipe. She went down, but she was still struggling, so he hit her again.

They took her off the road toward the trees and removed her shirt and pants. Salaam felt her breasts, and various members of the group—Kevin, Corey, and two other guys whom he didn't know—all had sex with her.

Then, he said, he just left. He went down to the trees, where he met up with the guy with the gold tooth. They were standing by the tree line when a jogger with a green army jacket came by. The guy with the gold tooth stepped out and punched the jogger in the head. The jogger crouched down, and Salaam came out and gave him three hits to the head with his fist.

As the questioning continued, a detective came to the door of the room. Salaam's mother was downstairs, and she was insisting that Salaam was only fifteen. Shortly thereafter, Salaam's mother said that she was getting a lawyer for her son. At that point, no further questioning was allowed by law.

There would be no written statement, nor any videotape, from Yusef Salaam.

But Salaam would say one more incriminating thing. On April 21, 1989, at approximately 6:30 P.M., he wanted to go to the bathroom and was escorted there by Detective Joseph Neenan. As Salaam was washing his face at the sink, he asked Neenan, "How much time am I looking at for what happened?" It was not a question one would expect from a person who was innocent.

Still, none of Salaam's statements were in writing or on videotape. The proof that he made statements admitting his participation in the attack on the jogger would depend solely on the testimony of police detectives. Surely, the case against Salaam was the weakest of the three that would soon go to trial.

AT ITS HEART, THE PROSECUTION'S CASE AGAINST these three defendants was based on the statements that they had made to the detectives, and the substantial similarity among their accounts of what happened in Central Park and those of the victims. They had given details of a night of terror that in most respects matched the stories provided by the people they had injured or sought to injure.

The defendants' statements were the greatest strength of the prosecution case. In fact, for the most part, the defendants' statements *were* the prosecution case. John Loughlin had eventually identified one suspect, not prosecuted at the trial of these three defendants, in a lineup, but no other victim was able to identify any of his or her attackers, and the jogger herself could remember nothing of the night. There was little more to implicate the three teenagers than their own incriminating statements.

If the heart of the case was the defendants' own statements to the detectives, its Achilles' heel was the DNA evidence. Here was a gang rape, and the only DNA found that could have linked the defendants to the crime belonged to someone else.

This inconsistency appeared to give the defense their greatest opportunity. The defense could argue that the defendants' statements were rehearsed, force-fed to them by the police. The defense could point to the DNA evidence and argue that it showed that the police and the prosecutors had the wrong

guys, and that the jury should not credit the defendants' supposed confessions to the police, because they were contradicted
by the DNA evidence. The prosecution team had to find a way to
meet that argument at trial.

So when the DNA results came in, Lederer and I began to discuss how we could address this problem. We dismissed out of
hand the possibility of attacking the reliability of DNA testing. We
saw such testing as a development that our office should, and
would, embrace as part of a consistent posture. We knew that a
district attorney's office cannot argue for the reliability of DNA
testing in some instances and denigrate it in others. As a public
institution with public responsibilities, we had to be consistent in
advocating the position we viewed to be correct, and could not
pick and choose when to support DNA and when to oppose DNA.

We also started from the premise that we did have the right
guys. Besides the statements by these defendants, which the jury
would hear, there were statements by other suspects, not on trial
in this first case, implicating these defendants, even though they
would never make it to the jury because they were hearsay.

So we had to figure out what had gone wrong here, why the
DNA results had turned out the way they did, and how to keep
the DNA results from destroying our case. Toward that end, I
was asked to work with Linda Fairstein, Lederer's mentor, chief
of the District Attorney's Sex Crimes Bureau, and a pioneer in
the prosecution of sex crimes.

To the amusement of both, Elizabeth Lederer and Linda
Fairstein are frequently confused. Both are physically striking
women who have prosecuted high-profile sex crimes, and they
have in common a precise manner of speech that suggests to
their peers and to juries that the words they speak are carefully,
deliberately chosen and entirely correct.

Fairstein and I sought expert advice and spent a fair amount
of time simply talking to each other to figure out how to address
the DNA problem. As we did, it quickly became clear to us that
the explanation for the results lay not in the complex world of
DNA technology but in the simple facts of the crime.

Lederer should focus on developing facts from the case consistent with guilt but explaining the absence of the semen of these
defendants. She should look for facts indicating that these defendants may not have ejaculated. She should search for evidence

suggesting that other young men, never identified, raped the jogger. And she should look for indications that the hospital's collection of semen was less than ideal and may have missed some DNA that may actually have been present.

And that is precisely what Lederer did.

It is often said that facts are cold, hard things, but nothing could be further from the truth in criminal law. In criminal cases, as facts are extracted, developed, and argued, they become the plot twists of a real-life thriller. The skill and artistry with which facts are developed and argued often determines success or failure, and the prosecutor or defense attorney will prevail who has developed and argued the facts in a manner that has the ring of truth. So Lederer set about developing facts to explain why we got the apparently wrong DNA, even though these suspects were actually guilty.

The law did not require that the defendants' semen be found inside the jogger. The legal definition of rape requires penetration but not ejaculation. And even if one young man did not penetrate the jogger, he would still be guilty of rape as an accomplice if he helped others to rape her.

Besides, there was a good explanation for the presence of a DNA print from a person other than the identified suspects. Both McCray and Salaam said that two guys they did not know had gotten on top of the jogger. McCray specifically mentioned a black guy and a Puerto Rican guy with a black hood. The DNA print could belong to one of these two men, who was never identified and from whom no DNA sample was taken.

In explaining the absence of DNA from any identified suspect, Lederer also brought out details involving the collection of evidence. The doctor and the nurse who took the vaginal swab testified that this examination was different from those done in most rape cases. The injuries to the Central Park jogger were so severe that they could not take the time to do a rape kit procedure until several hours after she was brought in. She had been assaulted at about 9:30 P.M., and brought to the hospital at 2:30 A.M., but the sample was not taken until 6:15 in the morning. During the time that elapsed, the doctors were working to save her life.

When a sample finally was taken, the conditions for taking a vaginal swab were poor. At the time, the jogger was waiting to have a CAT scan. None of the equipment usually used for a pelvic examination was available in that room. The jogger was not placed in stirrups. She was unconscious, still flailing her arms and legs, and unable to cooperate. Lighting conditions required the use of a flashlight to aid the doctor in taking a sample.

Had the tests been done sooner, had the tests been done under better conditions, perhaps more evidence would have been gathered, and a better-quality sample might have been taken. Then, perhaps, the DNA profiles of other assailants might also have been found. But there was nothing peculiar about the absence of the defendants' DNA here.

In short, Lederer sought to convince the jury that the DNA evidence was consistent with the other evidence, and that it was consistent with guilt. In this scenario, far from representing a problem, these results were exactly what one would expect in the circumstances. It was a reasonable, credible argument, but whether it would be sufficient to convince the jury remained to be seen.

MOST EXPERIENCED TRIAL LAWYERS AGREE THAT a defendant's choice to testify or not to testify is the most important decision that a defendant and a defense lawyer will make. The ultimate decision is the defendant's, and the choice to testify can be a very risky one.

Juries are generally extremely scrupulous in following the law that a defendant need not prove anything in a criminal case, and in evaluating the proof offered by the prosecution in determining whether guilt has been proven beyond a reasonable doubt. Generally, juries will pick apart that proof meticulously before they decide to convict a criminal defendant.

But when a defendant testifies, the burden tends to shift. This is not a shift recognized or accepted by the law; in fact, judges are most specific in their instructions regarding the burden of proof, and juries are told that the burden does not change as a legal matter because a defendant testifies. But, as a practical matter, the jury reverts to a much more visceral standard when a defendant testifies, to some extent balancing the believability of the prosecution witnesses and that of the defendant. A defendant who testifies and is not credible may sink himself, regardless of weaknesses in the prosecution's case.

That was the risk Yusef Salaam took when he decided to testify at trial in the jogger case.

Salaam, tall and slender, took the witness stand, and, on direct examination by his own attorney, denied that he told Detective McKenna he had participated in an attack on a female jogger, or in any other attacks. Salaam claimed that he never admitted any involvement in that night's events to McKenna. But he also offered his version of what happened in the park that night, and it was there that he ran into trouble.

According to Salaam, he had entered the park with a group of fifty young men, with no specific purpose in mind. But, Salaam said, he quickly got separated from the group. As he walked through the park, he saw a bum, thought he was dead, and started running because he didn't want to be blamed for killing someone he didn't kill. Then he came upon a group that looked like they were beating somebody up. Again, said Salaam, he started running.

Then, something very strange happened during Salaam's questioning by his own attorney. Salaam made the startling admission on his direct examination that he had in fact had a pipe as he entered the park that night. According to Salaam, he didn't do anything with the pipe. It just fell out of his pocket, somewhere in the park. Besides, it wasn't even his pipe. It was his friend Kharey's pipe. Kharey told him to hold it for him, and Salaam forgot that he had it.

As the prosecutor began her cross-examination, she headed straight for the implausibilities and admissions within Salaam's story, and sought to highlight them for the jury.

You were walking with a group, asked Lederer, and suddenly everybody was gone? We were walking up a hill, said Salaam. I got real tired, lagged behind them, and suddenly everybody was gone. I don't know where they went.

Then, said Lederer, you came upon a person who you thought was dead. Yes, said Salaam.

Did you go over to see if he was bleeding? asked Lederer. No, said Salaam.

You just decided to run away from him? asked Lederer. If I touched him, said Salaam, my fingerprints would have been on him.

You just ran away from him? asked Lederer. Yes, I did, answered Salaam.

You didn't call for help for him? No, said Salaam.

Then, asked Lederer, you ran further into the park? I ran south, answered Salaam. You stayed in the park? Yes.

You weren't going home at that time? I was trying to catch a train, answered Salaam.

You were running south in Central Park trying to get to a train, is that your testimony? Yes, answered Salaam.

You had a pipe in your pocket? asked Lederer. Yes, said Salaam.

Do you always carry a pipe in your pocket? asked Lederer. No, said Salaam, I don't have a pipe of my own.

You weren't going into the park for a picnic? asked Lederer. No, I wasn't. It was nighttime. I don't have a picnic in the nighttime, said Salaam smugly.

Good point, said Lederer.

Did you have any jogging clothes on when you went into the park that night? asked Lederer. No, I didn't, said Salaam.

You didn't take a bicycle to go biking in the park that night, did you? I didn't have a bicycle, said Salaam.

You didn't take any sports equipment; you weren't going to play any sporting games, were you? No, said Salaam.

And you went in with a pipe and you thought it would be fun, isn't that right? Yes, said Salaam.

BEFORE HE TESTIFIED, THE CASE AGAINST YUSEF SALAAM had been the weakest against any of the three defendants, since Salaam had been the one defendant who had not made a signed or videotaped statement. Now, the case against Salaam was the strongest, by virtue of his testimony and Lederer's cross-examination. And while the judge would tell the jury that the evidence against each defendant must be evaluated separately, Salaam's testimony, both his attorney's on direct examination and on Lederer's cross-examination, was in many respects the defining moment of the trial. It certainly sealed Salaam's fate, but its significance went well beyond his individual future.

His extraordinary testimony was also extremely influential in condemning the other defendants. So far as the jury could credit Salaam's admissions to the police, which were neither written nor on videotape, surely the jury could credit the admissions of the other defendants to the police and prosecutor, which were on videotape. Just as the weakest case was now the strongest, so the cases against the other defendants grew stronger, as the credibility of the statements to the police was fortified by Salaam's testimony.

It was true that the other two defendants, Antron McCray and Raymond Santana, had made errors in their videotaped statements. McCray had placed the attack on the jogger at the wrong location, and Santana had described the sequence of attacks in an order contrary to that offered by the other defendants. All along, it was apparent that the prosecution would argue that errors of that sort were hardly surprising when made by teenagers recollecting and describing a night of violence, frenzy, and rape. Indeed, if the detectives were feeding information to the defendants, they would have fed consistent information. And now the willingness of the jurors to credit the prosecution's explanation for the defendants' mistakes and to credit the prosecution's videotapes surely grew after the Salaam testimony.

In criminal cases, there are always aspects that do not exactly fit. A jury's willingness to convict follows from the prosecution's offering a credible, coherent story and reasonable, rational explanations for aspects of the case that might be troubling to the jury. Certainly Salaam's testimony created an atmosphere in which members of the jury were more willing to credit and accept an explanation for DNA results that might otherwise have troubled them.

At its core, the prosecution had built a case based on the defendants' statements and the corroboration of those statements by the people attacked in the park that night. That is why it was so crucial that the events in the park that night were presented to the jury as the Central Park rampage, rather than only the Central Park jogger case. Those victims, unlike the female jogger, could remember what happened in the park and described a rampage that mirrored the atrocities described by the defendants themselves. The truth of the teenagers' detailed statements were corroborated by the people whom they hurt and tried to hurt, as well as by the injuries suffered by the female jogger.

In her summation for the prosecution, Elizabeth Lederer focused on the evidence that she had built to lead the jury to the inescapable conclusion that these defendants had participated in the rampage and rape in Central Park. Finally, though, she spoke about the issue of individual responsibility.

"Antron McCray, Yusef Salaam, and Raymond Santana had their fun in Central Park on April 19, 1989. Today they have no one to blame for the predicament that they are in but themselves. They showed no sympathy and no mercy . . . in the park on that night.

"They have had a fair trial, ladies and gentlemen, and what they deserve from you now is a fair and just verdict, based on the evidence in this case. And the only fair and just and true verdict in this case, based on this evidence, is a verdict of guilty as to each of the defendants on each of the counts."

The Central Park jogger case went to the jury on August 9, 1990. The jury, consisting of four African Americans, four Hispanics, three Caucasians, and one Asian American, did not reach a verdict in this difficult case for ten days.

On August 18, 1990, the jurors returned their verdict. They convicted Antron McCray, Raymond Santana, and Yusef Salaam of rape, assault, and riot. On September 11, all three were sentenced to state prison, despite their status as juvenile offenders— and despite the absence of their DNA.

The prosecutors in the Central Park jogger case had stood squarely behind DNA analysis and explained the absence of DNA evidence against the defendants in reasonable and logical terms. There was no assault on DNA testing, no argument that such testing itself was somehow flawed.

Over the years, this would become the norm among the best and most ethical prosecutors. They would follow the DNA evidence wherever it led. Soon the new science would lead to striking developments in a case in Baltimore County, where a young prosecutor would have the courage to follow the DNA evidence to a surprising conclusion.

5 THE TRIUMPH OF DNA

JUST OUTSIDE the city of Baltimore lies a neighborhood known as Parkville, the first suburb beyond the city limits to the northeast. Parkville is no Scarsdale or Winnetka. It is home to and bedroom for blue-collar people, Baltimore's lower middle class.

Parkville is substantially safer than Baltimore; homicide drops sharply as you leave the city limits. The scourges of Parkville are different from those of the inner city. At lunchtime at a typical restaurant, there are more people to be found drinking at the bar than eating at the tables.

The road from Baltimore through Parkville is named Harford Road, and the first stretch of that road beyond the city limits travels through Parkville's business district, a series of one- and two-story office buildings and restaurants scattered among private homes and apartment buildings. Three miles farther out, the business district ends. There, the last restaurant on the right side of Harford Road is named the House of Kabob. Five hundred feet farther, on the right, is the local VFW post. Between the restaurant and the VFW post, on the other side of the road, a hundred feet from the restaurant, is 8002 Harford Road, a two-story, red-brick apartment building.

The front of the building is attractive; ivy covers it, and the window frames are bright with white paint. The front entranceway of 8002 Harford Road leads to a hall. There is one apartment on the first floor and another on the second floor.

In the back of the building, there are separate entrances to the first- and second-floor apartments, with a wood stairway leading to a second-floor landing. Access to the second-floor apartment is through a screen door and a wood-and-glass-paneled door. A wood canopy covers the landing on the second floor, and an enormous television antenna tops off that covering.

In August 1990, two women, Carol Sanders, then age twenty-eight, and Alice Walters, then twenty-five, shared the second-story apartment, though by midmonth Alice Walters would move out. Sanders, a high-school graduate employed as an accounts representative for a Baltimore paper company, was separated from her husband. Her seven-year-old daughter lived with the two women.

It is never easy to understand the peculiar dynamic that generates mutual obsession between a particular man and a particular woman, and that was certainly true of the relationship between Carol Sanders and John Davis. From the outside, there was nothing particularly remarkable about Sanders or Davis, and one might wonder what drew them together with such intensity. Carol Sanders was a brown-haired woman, five feet four inches tall, of average physical appearance, with what might be called a pink-collar job. Her sometime boyfriend, a bricklayer, was a dime-a-dozen Baltimore guy, a hard-drinking, twenty-eight-year-old self-described "asshole." Physically, Davis was almost Mr. Average: five-feet-ten-inches tall, with a medium build, brown hair, blue eyes, and a tattoo on his arm. His most distinctive feature was likely his shaggy brown hair, parted in the middle, which gave him the look briefly made popular in the early 1970s by the actor David Cassidy in his role as the teen heartthrob Keith on the television program *The Partridge Family*. The haircut, now seen rarely in most of America, remains popular among young working-class Baltimore men. Along with it, Davis also had a mustache.

Davis's walk on the wild side, however, was not limited to his hairstyle and mustache; it extended to some minor criminal charges. Over the years he had been arrested for assault, possession of marijuana, and breaking and entering.

The relationship between Sanders and Davis had been a stormy one virtually from the beginning. They had met four years earlier, after Sanders was separated from her husband. They dated and then decided to rent an apartment together, where they lived with Sanders's daughter.

This experiment in shared living was short-lived. There were arguments, including shoving, pushing, and pinching by Davis that left bruises on Sanders's face. Sanders moved back with her parents, but soon she and Davis were back together again in the apartment. There were more arguments. Soon, Davis stopped coming home some nights. Both Sanders and Davis moved back with their parents.

But apparently Sanders and Davis could not stay away from each other. They started dating again, and continued for a full year, but once again there were arguments. The relationship continued along this rocky course.

In 1987 Davis approached Sanders in a parking lot, beat on the windows of her car while she was inside, screamed that he would get her, and ripped off the car's side mirrors. Sanders escaped, driving to a nearby Kmart, and got out of the car. From out of nowhere, Davis appeared, grabbed her, and threw her to the ground. He was charged with assault and also with making harassing phone calls to Sanders, but both cases were marked inactive and never reopened.

Soon afterward, Sanders ran into Davis at a local bar named Straps. The two made a date, but Davis stood her up. They must have connected soon afterward, however, for they moved back in together for four months. That stay ended when Sanders told Davis to leave because she suspected that he was using drugs.

On August 15, 1988, Sanders came home to find her home broken into. Her bed was slashed, the phone cords cut, plants thrown around, her jean skirt shoved down the toilet. On her mirror, there was a message: "Fuck you, babe." Sanders's daughter lived with her through all these fights, breakups, and reconciliations.

Two months later, in another incident, Davis threw a couch, a lamp, and a lit cigarette at Sanders. He was charged with assault and battery, but he did not show up for his court date.

Over the next two years, Sanders was the victim of an extraordinary campaign of anonymous harassment. Her car tires were slashed. Her daughter's bird was stolen, as were her pots and pans. Her car was stolen and torched with gasoline. She moved and changed her telephone number to escape from the harassment.

Though Sanders could not prove who was making her life a living hell, she felt sure it was Davis—a view he disputes to this day, denying that he had anything to do with these various acts. Yet in June 1990, when they ran into each other in the neighborhood, the two started talking, one thing led to another, and they had consensual sex. To put it succinctly, Sanders's feelings toward this man were intense and conflicted.

Maryland, while not quite a southern state, is a border state. In Baltimore, August nights are hot and humid. Thursday night, August 16, 1990, was particularly hot, even by Baltimore standards.

Earlier that evening, Carol Sanders and her seven-year-old daughter had been out for a crab dinner with a friend. Because of the excitement of the evening and the heat of the night, the young child was not falling asleep. It did not help the situation that the fan in her bedroom was not working. So her mother made a bed for her on the living room floor and lay on the couch waiting for her to fall asleep. The television was on in the living room, but all the other lights in the apartment were off.

As Carol Sanders waited for her daughter to drop off, she herself fell asleep on the couch. The mother and daughter were alone in the apartment, since Sanders's roommate had moved out of the apartment during the past week.

Before she allowed herself to sleep that night, Sanders had checked the locks on both the front and back doors. But the back door, made of wood and glass, had a broken windowpane. That broken windowpane was the one closest to the inside lock.

At 4:00 in the morning, Sanders was awakened by something being pulled over her face, and someone jumping on top of her. A pillowcase had been pulled over her head. At first, Sanders thought that it was her daughter. "What do you want?" she asked, thinking that she was speaking to her little girl.

But she then realized that the person on top of her was not her daughter. The pillowcase was wrapped around her head and held from behind. The intruder partially lifted up the pillowcase to just above her mouth. Her eyes were still covered, but the pillowcase was raised enough for the man to kiss Sanders on the lips.

She recognized the kiss. It was John Davis's.

"Johnny, what are you doing?" she asked. But there was no response.

The man then began to punch her in the face. She did not scream, because she was afraid to wake her daughter. Repeatedly, the man hit her in the face, as she cried and tried to protect herself, holding her arms up, burying her face in the sofa to avoid the blows. She told the man she would do whatever he wanted if he would just not hurt her daughter. But he continued to hit her, this time a series of punches to the stomach. It didn't hurt anymore; by now, she was numb.

Then the punching and hitting abruptly stopped. The man grabbed at her jeans, unbuttoned the top button, and unzipped them. With one hand, he rolled down her jeans and panties at the same time, while holding the pillowcase over her head with his other hand.

Sanders tried to talk to the man through the pillowcase. "Why are you doing this?" she asked, but the man did not answer. She tried to pull the pillowcase off her head, but her attacker was too powerful. Then the man pulled his pants down. At that point, Sanders tried to fight and flailed at him. But her fight only brought more punches from the man, more punches to her face and stomach. The man then tried to position himself on top of her. Again, she tried to fight him off. This time, he punched her repeatedly through the pillowcase with a closed fist.

It was now clear that resistance was not going to work. Sanders's nose was broken, her lip split. Her will to resist crushed, and believing that any further struggle might endanger her life and that of her daughter, she pretended to be unconscious, lying on her back on the couch.

Her assailant spread her legs and entered her. As he had intercourse with her, she began to cough, choking inside the pillowcase on the blood streaming from her broken nose and her cut lip. And as she coughed, she spat blood that permeated the pillowcase.

At that point, the rapist panicked and withdrew from inside her. He pulled up his pants and ran out the back door.

As the screen door slammed behind him, Sanders's daughter awoke. She had slept through the entire attack, only awakened by the slamming of the door. When the seven-year-old awoke, she saw her half-naked, bleeding mother and began to scream hysterically. Sanders calmed her daughter, put on her pants, and called 911 for help. But her daughter began to cry hysterically again when she heard her mother talking to the police.

After speaking with the police, Sanders hung up the phone, calmed her daughter again, and went with her to the apartment of their downstairs neighbor and landlady. There they waited for the police to arrive.

The police promptly took Sanders to a local hospital, the Greater Baltimore Medical Center. There doctors treated her broken nose, split lip, and bruising to her face. They noted what they characterized as substantial blunt force trauma. They also took vaginal swabs from the rape for use as evidence.

From that morning forward, Carol Sanders was interviewed time and again by various investigators and prosecutors. From the beginning and through it all, she was adamant that her rapist had been John Davis.

It was, of course, hard to argue with a woman's identification of her ex-boyfriend as the man who had raped her. It really shouldn't take much more than a glimpse for a woman to identify a man with whom she used to live.

Still, there were several reasons why the police and prosecutors had to be careful in relying entirely on Carol Sanders's identification of John Davis. After all, she had been sleeping and awoke from her sleep to find a pillowcase on her head. She had not had even a moment to realize what was going on before she was in the middle of a violent assault, her nose broken, her lip split and bleeding. Her reaction was a panic-driven struggle to avoid rape and then save her own life, the terrifying thought racing through her mind that she and her daughter might be facing death or serious physical injury that very evening. During most of the attack, by her own account, her head had been covered by a pillowcase. And even in that brief moment when she was able to uncover her eyes, the room was dark except for the flicker of the television set. These circumstances were not conducive to making a calm, reasonable determination of who her attacker was.

There was also a troubling inconsistency in the details of the victim's story as recorded in the police reports. The woman told one police investigator that she had briefly pulled the pillowcase up over her head during the struggle on the couch and seen her attacker's face at that time. She had also seen that Davis was wearing jeans but not a shirt. She saw a shirt hanging from his back pocket.

But a second police report stated that Sanders could not see the rapist, although she had seen him from behind when he fled out the back door. That report made no mention of the victim's pulling the pillowcase over her head and seeing his face. In fact, it seemed inconsistent with Sanders's claim that she had seen Davis's face during the attack.

Her story left prosecutors a little skittish, wondering to what extent Carol Sanders truly got a good look at her assailant. Certainly Sanders had reason to believe it might be her ex-boyfriend. She knew in her heart that it had been Davis who had previously trashed her home, slashed her tires, and stolen her daughter's bird but that he had gotten away with all those acts because she could not prove his involvement. It is likely that more than once some police officer had said to her, "But no one saw Davis do it." Now Davis might just as easily get away with this rape if she didn't give the police everything they needed to arrest him, indict him, and convict him. This is not said to justify such thoughts, if indeed Sanders was thinking them. Not only are such attempts by victims to help the police amass enough evidence to go to trial wrong but they also have a way of wrecking the case at trial.

Carol Sanders must have believed Davis's past behavior was entirely relevant to the issue of whether he had committed this particular crime. One of the more difficult legal principles for laypeople to accept is the protections against a jury's learning about a defendant's prior "bad acts" or criminal convictions. Why are the courts so concerned, people often ask, that a jury not be prejudiced against a defendant based on evidence of his previous misconduct? Yet in most jurisdictions courts will bar testimony about prior behavior unless there are extremely strong similarities between its mode of operation and the crime for which the defendant is being tried. One of the other exceptions is when a defendant takes the stand in his or her own defense. Then courts allow prosecutors to inquire into the defendant's past under the general rule that wide latitude is given to cross-examiners in their attempts to attack the credibility of the witness, and thus of the testimony he or she has given.

It was to be expected that Carol Sanders would not know the niceties of trial practice and would believe that Davis's past behavior could be used to convict him of this new crime. She had saved the police reports, and the repair bills, from those incidents, and she got together and delivered to the prosecutors in a neat package the documentation of the costs of her earlier victimization ranging from the $500 bill for her daughter's pet cockatoo to a $71 bill for two new tires. Now, especially after the rape, she told the police, she wanted Davis to get what he deserved. She would like him to go to jail, she said, to die. She never wanted to lay eyes on him again, and she was afraid of what he might attempt next, that if Davis was found not guilty she would never be able to raise her little girl.

No one else would do this to her, she told investigators. Davis, she said, was obsessed with her, and she knew that he was the person responsible for the rape.

So when the prosecutors pressed her for details, when they asked her, again and again, she would simply insist it was Davis. "I could tell," she would say. "I knew it was him."

"She said it sounded like him; it felt like him. She said it was him," said Scott Shellenberger, a Baltimore County prosecutor.

This was Sanders's position right from the start. In the early morning hours of August 17, the victim told the police who responded to her 911 call that it was John Davis who had attacked her, and she gave them Davis's address at his mother's home. The address, only one street light away from Sanders's own address, was transmitted by police radio to the Communications Division of the police department, which dispatched officers to arrest him.

The officers roused Davis from his sleep, arrested him, and brought him down to the precinct. There he was questioned by the detective assigned to handle the case, Terry Woodhouse.

That night, and over the months to come, Davis adamantly denied having anything to do with the rape of Carol Sanders. He claimed that he had been sleeping at his mother's house at the time of the attack.

Davis was in big trouble. His defense was not the kind of claim a jury would likely credit at a trial. He would be relying for his defense on an alibi, a claim that he was somewhere else at the time of the crime. But his alibi would not be supported by a disinterested witness. Instead, he had his own self-interested testi-

mony that he was home sleeping at the time of the crime, supported only by testimony to the same effect by the one woman in
the world who would be expected to lie to save him from jail, his
mother. And even if his mother said Davis was home all night,
how could she be sure? How would she have known if he quietly
had ducked out around 4:00 in the morning, a time when she
would most likely have been in deep sleep?

It looked like things were only going to get worse for Davis. On
the morning of his arrest, Davis agreed to give a blood sample to be
used in investigating the crime. Indeed, he remained amenable to
everything the police suggested, even agreeing to allow them to
search his home.

These sound like the responses of an innocent man who
believes that if the police are allowed unfettered access to all the
information they want, they will come to believe him innocent of
the crime. They could also, however, have been the responses of
a guilty man who was both not terribly intelligent and easily
cowed by police pressure. Or maybe those of a man who thought
that since he had covered his victim's eyes there could be no eyewitness identification of him and that without such an identification he would be home free.

When Detective Woodhouse came back to take Davis's blood
for a DNA test, Davis had a new lead for him. While he was in jail
at the local precinct in Parkville, said Davis, the police had
brought in an acquaintance of his named Gregory Ritter. Ritter,
said Davis, had been the on-and-off boyfriend of Sanders's roommate, Alice Walters.

Ritter and Davis recognized each other, and each asked the
other what he was in there for. When Davis told Ritter that he
had been arrested for raping Carol Sanders, Ritter got this funny
look on his face. And, said Davis, to look at this guy, he could
pass for my brother.

When Davis told Detective Woodhouse that he should investigate Ritter, the detective wrote down Ritter's name. Woodhouse also mentioned to the prosecutor, Shellenberger, Davis's
claim that they should investigate his look-alike. "I remember
saying, Yeah, right," said Shellenberger later, recounting his sar-
castic reaction. The focus remained on Davis.

Still, Shellenberger, an extremely energetic and conscientious
prosecutor, was eager to know that he had the right guy in jail.

The FBI's DNA test takes six to eight weeks to run, and at the time a backlog of cases in the FBI lab was further slowing the process. Shellenberger wanted the DNA results. Davis was still insisting that he was innocent, and his lawyer had offered to arrange payment to a private genetics laboratory to perform the DNA test if that would move the results out faster. But the prosecutors made several calls to the FBI, which agreed to give the Baltimore County case a high priority.

On December 19, 1990, an FBI agent called the prosecutor's office and informed them of a startling result. The DNA recovered from the semen was not that of John Davis.

The prosecutor's office asked to have that conclusion put in writing. The FBI sent a teletype to the prosecution that same day advising them that Davis could not be the source of the DNA in this case.

Stunned by this result, the prosecutors immediately arranged for Davis's release from jail. Still, they did not immediately dismiss the case against him. Before doing so, Shellenberger wanted to talk to the FBI in detail, and also to talk to the victim in person. While assessing what this new, genetic evidence meant, Shellenberger said he wanted to "take baby steps." After talking to the victim, and to the FBI, Shellenberger decided that only one conclusion was possible. Davis was innocent.

On January 9, 1991, the prosecutors went to court and dismissed the case against John Davis. In doing so, they based their decision on the DNA evidence. "If you're going to rely on it, you're going to rely on it," said Shellenberger, who believes, like almost all prosecutors, that DNA testing cannot be a one-way street, held out by prosecutors as conclusive evidence only when they like the results it yields. It seemed at this moment that the case was over, one more unsolved rape to go with all the others.

The police did, though, have one small lead, however far-fetched. When Detective Woodhouse had taken Davis's blood, Davis had told the detective about Gregory Ritter, the man in jail who looked like Davis and who had dated the victim's roommate. Though the detective could not have been surprised to hear a man facing hard time point the finger at someone else, he wrote down Gregory Ritter's name, and still had it in his file.

The prosecutor and the detective decided to look into Ritter.

It was the longest of long shots. "We said, What the heck?" according to Shellenberger.

Detective Woodhouse went to visit Sanders and asked her about Ritter, an unemployed Baltimore bricklayer. Yes, said Sanders, she knew Gregory Ritter. He had dated her roommate, Alice Walters, but she had broken off the relationship four months earlier, in April. In fact, said Sanders, Ritter blamed her for the breakup. Sanders had told her roommate to get rid of Ritter, that he was no good. There was certainly no love lost between these two.

Sanders also told the detective that one week before the rape, on Friday night, August 10, at 11:30 P.M., Ritter had come by the building to see his former girlfriend. Sanders had been in Washington, D.C., visiting friends, but she had heard about the visit from her roommate.

Ritter knocked on the front door to the apartment building, and Walters came downstairs and answered the door. Ritter told her that he had been drinking and that he wanted to come upstairs. He wanted, he said, to start up their relationship again. But his former girlfriend would not let him in the apartment and insisted that they talk in the hallway.

An argument started. The owner of the building, who lived in the first-floor apartment, came out into the hallway, and told Ritter and Walters that this was her home and she did not want all this commotion in the hallway. But her demand for peace and quiet had little effect on Ritter. He pushed Walters against the wall, slapped her face, spat at her, and called her a stream of obscenities.

This was too much for the landlady. She intervened to help Walters. The two of them pushed and pulled at Ritter, forcing him out the front door of the apartment building and locking the door behind him.

A few minutes later, Ritter tried to push his way back in. He actually cracked the building door but did not succeed in getting into the building. At that point, Walters called 911, but Ritter left before the police arrived. The police officers interviewed Walters and the landlady, and took a report.

Sanders had a copy of the report from that prior incident. In Baltimore County, the police generally give the victim of a crime a copy of the complaint report, and they had left one at the apartment after Ritter's late-night visit. Sanders gave it to the detective investigating the rape.

The detective found Sanders's story very interesting, noting the similarities between the two incidents.

Exactly one week before the rape, Ritter, having had too much to drink, had tried to enter Carol Sanders's apartment, seeking sex with his old girlfriend. When the girlfriend refused, he had tried to break into the apartment building.

Then, one week later, a rapist with alcohol on his breath had raped Carol Sanders.

Given these common threads, several motives suggested themselves to support the possibility that Ritter was the rapist. Ritter, drunk and angry at his old girlfriend, could have mistaken Sanders for his old girlfriend. He could have intentionally raped Carol Sanders in retribution for her role in prompting the breakup of his relationship with Walters. Or Ritter could not have much cared which of the two women he was raping. After all, he was angry at both.

Of course, the investigators had now entered a realm of wild speculation. They needed evidence that had to do with the night of the rape, and they needed to know more about Ritter.

They started with the arrest that had brought Ritter to the Parkville police precinct, where he had encountered John Davis. Ordinarily, Davis would have been moved from the precinct holding facility to a local jail two days after a crime. But at that time the Baltimore County jails were particularly crowded, so it was not unusual for a prisoner to be held in a cell at a police precinct up to a week before being transferred to the jail where he would stay pending trial.

Two days after the rape, shortly after late Saturday night passed into early Sunday, August 19, 1990, Ritter had been arrested at 12:35 A.M. Intoxicated, he had driven his pickup truck off the road and straight into another car. The passenger in the car he hit suffered a neck injury and was taken to the hospital.

When the police arrived at the scene, Ritter was swaying, wobbling, staggering; in his encounter with the police, he was both cocky and cursing. He refused a Breathalyzer test but told the police that he had drunk four beers. Ritter was arrested for driving while intoxicated and also charged with driving with a revoked license. That arrest had been only the latest in a series of encounters between Ritter and the law. He had previously been convicted of theft, possession of drugs, destruction of property, and battery.

In some respects, Ritter's record was similar to Davis's. He was a troublemaker but had no history of serious violent crime. If he had raped Carol Sanders, it would have been, by far, his most serious crime. His record suggested that it was possible but by no means certain that he was the man who had committed the rape.

Since Ritter had a criminal record, his photograph was on file with the police. Detective Woodhouse pulled this photo, and he also pulled the physical descriptions of both Ritter and Davis from their arrest reports.

It was startling. There was a similarity in the appearance of the two men that began with both men having the same look, but that went much further.

Both men had the same, distinctive Baltimore bad-boy hairstyle, with brown hair, and a mustache.

Each had thick eyebrows.

Each had a small, upturned knob at the bottom of his nose.

Ritter was five-foot-ten; so was Davis. Each had the same medium build. Ritter was twenty-six; Davis, twenty-eight.

In a darkened room, one man could easily have been confused for the other.

In one way, Ritter fit the description Sanders had given of her attacker better than Davis. Ritter's police photo also showed a substantial amount of hair on his chest sticking out from the top of his shirt. When Carol Sanders had described her assailant to the police, she said that she had felt hair on his chest. That description had initially troubled Detective Woodhouse, because when Davis was providing a blood sample, Woodhouse had seen him shirtless, and Davis's chest was hairless. But in no state in the country can a conviction for rape be based on the fact that both the assailant and the accused have hairy chests. The police knew that they needed more, much more, to develop a case against Ritter, and they turned to the possibility of a DNA match. At this point, the prosecutors and the police believed that they already had enough evidence to get a warrant to take Ritter's blood.

The law views taking blood for DNA testing as a form of search, requiring a court order equivalent to a warrant. So, to get an order to take blood, the police and prosecutors have to do what any prosecutor seeking a search warrant does. They have to put together their evidence in formal papers and spell out for a judge why they believe there is probable cause that the suspect committed the crime.

Seizing a suspect's blood does not violate a suspect's privilege against self-incrimination because that privilege applies only to oral testimony. Blood is evidence, not testimony; it can be seized pursuant to a search warrant, just as a gun or a knife can be seized from a suspect's apartment through a search warrant.

"Probable cause" to get a search warrant requires much less proof than that required at trial to convict a defendant in a criminal case. It simply requires proof that it is more likely than not that the suspect committed the crime.

Here, the search warrant application was thin at best. The police were hard-pressed to argue that it was more likely than not that Ritter had committed the rape, but they made the argument, laying out every detail they had supporting the view that Ritter had likely raped Carol Sanders.

The application for a search warrant was made on January 25, 1991. The supporting paperwork submitted with the request that the judge sign a search warrant was a sworn statement signed by Detective Woodhouse, reciting numerous facts that he had learned from his investigation of the case, but relying primarily on the resemblance between Davis and Ritter, Ritter's angry visit to the apartment one week before the rape, Ritter's prior arrest record, and his hairy chest.

Judge Gordon Boone, Jr., of the Baltimore County District Court signed the search warrant on January 25, authorizing the police to seize a vial of Ritter's blood for DNA testing.

Detective Woodhouse did not have to look far to find Ritter. Since the rape, Ritter had been sentenced to prison for a violation of probation on one of his prior criminal convictions. On January 25, the detective went to visit him at nearby Patuxent Prison, and Ritter was brought to the prison infirmary, where a nurse took a vial of his blood and gave it to the detective.

Three weeks later, on February 14, the detective personally brought Ritter's blood sample to the FBI's headquarters in Washington, D.C., for DNA testing. The DNA from the rape had been transported to the FBI when the initial tests were done on Davis's DNA, and the FBI still held that evidence.

On May 21, the FBI called Detective Woodhouse. The DNA testing was complete, and the DNA profile found matched that of Gregory Ritter at the three genetic locations the FBI was able to analyze. These particular genetic characteristics could be expected to occur randomly in one in every 500,000 whites, one in every 300,000 Hispanics, and one in every 2 million blacks. That same day, the detective obtained a warrant for Ritter's arrest, and the next day he arrested Ritter at Patuxent Prison for the rape of Carol Sanders.

When Detective Woodhouse arrested Ritter, he read him his Miranda rights and then asked Ritter about the rape. Ritter's response was peculiar indeed. For ten days, beginning three days before the rape, Ritter said he had been drinking and smoking PCP. Ritter claimed that he did not remember his actions during the ten-day period. He maintained that he did not even know he had been arrested until he woke up at the police station. Asked about the rape, Ritter commented that he didn't recall anything about the rape, but it was possible that he did it.

The prosecution was now in an odd position. The DNA results implicated Ritter, as did other facts. But the victim still maintained that Davis was the man who raped her. DNA or no DNA, she insisted it had been Davis.

Looking forward, prosecutor Shellenberger imagined the trial of Ritter. The FBI would come in and say the DNA could not be Davis's DNA, but was fully consistent with Ritter's. The victim, on the other hand, would testify that it was Davis who raped her, and that Ritter was an innocent man. Shellenberger would be in the unenviable position of having to argue that the prosecution's key witness, the victim in the case, was telling the truth about the fact that she was raped but was mistaken about the identity of the man who raped her.

To prepare for trial, Shellenberger had blowups made of photographs of Davis and Ritter. He would use them to show the jury how close the resemblance was between the two men. Beyond that, Shellenberger subpoenaed Davis to testify at trial. Davis would deny the rape on the witness stand, and the jury would see firsthand the close resemblance between the two men. Asked now, Shellenberger expresses the belief that Ritter would have been convicted at trial. But he still preferred not to roll the dice on a jury trial in this unusual situation.

Shellenberger asked Carol Sanders if she would approve a plea offer to Ritter in which he would plead guilty to the lesser charge of second-degree rape and receive a sentence of up to forty years, instead of the life sentence that he would likely receive after his conviction at trial for first-degree rape. Under Maryland law, Ritter could be found guilty of first-degree rape if the jury determined that any of three aggravating factors was present: breaking and entering, serious bodily injury, or suffocation. But it was also possible that a jury could acquit outright or be unable to reach a unanimous verdict given Carol Sanders's prior identification of Davis and her continuing belief that Davis was responsible.

The victim told the prosecutor that a lesser plea by Ritter was probably OK, but that she wanted to think about it some more. Shellenberger told Sanders that he needed to know by February 3. But she did not get back to him.

So the prosecutor decided to go ahead with the plea bargain, and Ritter pled guilty to rape in the second degree on February 4, 1992.

On April 27, 1992, Ritter was sentenced to forty years' imprisonment. Davis had no comment. "He's decided he doesn't want to be interviewed. He just wants to get on with his life," said Detective Woodhouse, who spoke to Davis on the day of sentencing.

Prosecutor Shellenberger spoke that day about DNA: "In this one instance, it has freed an innocent man and sent away a guilty man. Five years ago, Davis might have been sent to prison."

In some respects, Shellenberger understated the matter when he said that Davis "might" have been sent to prison before DNA testing. For it is hard to imagine a jury acquitting a defendant in a brutal rape when his former girlfriend claims that she saw him and recognized him, no matter how brief the glimpse or how troubling the inconsistencies. Certainly the inconsistencies were not dramatic enough to stop the prosecutors from indicting Davis in the first place, and keeping him in jail for months until DNA exonerated him. Nor would they likely have been sufficient to save him from a conviction and from spending most, if not all, of his adult life in jail.

The last word, though, was reserved for the rape victim, who finally seemed reconciled to the fact that it was Ritter, not Davis, who had raped her. "It's been very upsetting, very traumatizing. But I got what I wanted today," said Carol Sanders on the day of Ritter's sentencing.

Following the debacle in the Joseph Castro case, DNA evidence was strongly back on track, doing what it was supposed to do. The questions about its validity had diminished dramatically as the FBI had entered the field, both doing DNA work itself and gathering scientists to set standards for DNA analysis.

But even as DNA analysis regained strength, a new storm was gathering. A vitriolic controversy over DNA and race was about to sweep the nation and once more throw the future of DNA testing into doubt.

6 VITRIOL

T HE CONTROVERSY OVER DNA HOLDS a great paradox. It is the very fact that DNA evidence is so powerful—so much so, in fact, that it is often seen as impervious to challenge—that causes concern about its use. After all, no legal scribe ever envisioned a judicial system where the responsibility to act as the finder of fact would be taken from the defendant's own peers and handed over to bench technicians.

Of course, it is true that, over the long history of Anglo-American jurisprudence, courts have opened their doors to numerous new forms of scientific evidence. Many of these innovations have provoked controversy but few as much as DNA evidence, for never before have we seen a new form of scientific findings so persuasive that it often stands above all other evidence, or lack of evidence, and by itself spells the difference between conviction and acquittal. The challenge the courts face is in allowing DNA evidence the opportunity to inform jury decisions with appropriate credibility, neither too much nor too little.

The power of a DNA match is typically stated in the millions, a denomination hard to imagine or understand. While the numbers are extraordinary, in most cases scientists are not saying that the match is unique. This conjunction of awesome numbers representing an event that could yet conceivably be a coincidence has made courts uncomfortable; some courts sufficiently troubled by the issues surrounding the meaning of a DNA match have excluded DNA evidence entirely.

The original battles over DNA evidence were clashes over the adequacy of standards and controls used by laboratories performing DNA analysis. But by the fall of 1991, those battles were for the most part over. Rarely did defense lawyers question whether there was actually a DNA match when a DNA laboratory declared such a match. Instead, the controversy shifted to the gargantuan numbers used by DNA laboratories to convey that the match was likely more than mere coincidence. Underlying this controversy was the role of race and ethnicity in stating the power of a DNA match.

Strangely, this debate became more intense as it left the courtroom and, in late 1991, moved to America's most prestigious scientific institutions and publications. Issues relating to race, ethnicity, and DNA had been litigated fiercely in courtrooms for several years. But scientists fighting for principle displayed an intensity, even a savagery, unmatched by the most aggressive lawyers. The momentum generated by these academic disputes carried over to the legal controversy over DNA. At times it threatened the very admissibility of DNA evidence in court and raised the prospect that DNA laboratories would declare DNA matches but that jurors would never learn of their findings. What would the impact be on the system of justice if this most persuasive evidence was kept from juries?

The focus on race was also fueled and driven by defense lawyers, and this was hardly surprising. It is no secret that a legacy of racism, social injustice, and economic deprivation has resulted in African Americans being disproportionately involved in the criminal justice system. In a country that is approximately 12 percent African American, 45 percent of those arrested for murder, rape, robbery, and aggravated assault are from this one racial group. Overwhelmingly, jurors put aside their racial backgrounds and do the right thing in individual criminal cases, following the evidence wherever it leads, be that conviction or acquittal. But these facts cannot help but play themselves out in jury deliberations in any criminal trial in which race is an issue. So in a system that requires a unanimous verdict, a racial theme that may have emotional resonance with jurors will be seized upon by defense attorneys.

It was not supposed to be this way. At its origins, part of the promise of DNA evidence included moving all emotional issues, including racial ones, off center stage. DNA would provide "objective" scientific proof of identity or innocence. There is no racial issue in determining whether a suspect's DNA matches the DNA from a crime scene because the match is to an individual's DNA.

But there are differences in the frequency with which known patterns of DNA repeat from race to race. This has led to an attempt to state the frequency of a DNA match occurring within a specific race.

The FBI generally states the significance of a DNA match in reference to broad racial groups, such as whites, blacks, and Hispanics. In the Matias Reyes case, for example, the Bureau stated that the particular DNA profile at issue could be expected to be found in one in every 49 million people in the Hispanic population. There is no suggestion by the critics of DNA evidence or by defense lawyers that stating results of DNA analysis in racial terms reflects racial prejudice or insensitivity. Indeed, in the Reyes case, if the chances of a match had been calculated for the population at large, not just for Hispanics, it might have been one in 100 million or even higher, seeming to provide even stronger evidence against Reyes.

Some critics argue that the FBI's racial breakdowns are "terribly misleading" and "unjustifiable" because they do not go far enough in taking race and ethnicity into account. These critics maintain that people tend to marry within their own ethnic groups. As a result, say the critics, America is composed of separate ethnic populations that are genetically very different from each other. These ethnic groups are said to have genetic differences one from another larger than those among broad racial groups. The critics argue that breakdowns based on large racial groups cannot be used reliably in court, whether those breakdowns are for whites, Hispanics, or African Americans.

These critics thus go to the other extreme and reject the broad racial classifications used by the FBI not because they balkanize Americans but because the balkanization is not far-reaching enough. The classification "whites," for example, is said to be misleading because whites, after all, consist, among others, of Italians, Irish, and Poles.

Hispanics are said by the critics to be a "biological hodge-podge." The designation "Hispanic" includes people of Mexican, Puerto Rican, Guatemalan, Cuban, Spanish, and other ancestries. But many Guatemalans coming to this country are pure Indian, and many Mexicans have large and variable components of Indian ancestry. Puerto Ricans and Cubans, however, have little or no Indian ancestry but much African ancestry.

"Blacks" is also said to be an inadequate category, because blacks from around the country are said to vary genetically. The critics claim that blacks from South Carolina have 3.7 percent "white" ancestry, while blacks from Detroit have 26 percent white ancestry. These variations among ethnic and geographic groups are said to render deficient the broad racial categories used by the FBI.

These claims are rejected wholesale by the scientists supportive of the FBI approach. Broad racial populations are meaningful and more than adequate for DNA analysis, say these scientists. In their view, the United States' population has been characterized by extensive mobility and the mixing of ethnic groups within broad racial groups since World War II. Even a small amount of mixing will quickly homogenize populations for genetic purposes, and mixing in the years following World War II has been considerable. In the view of these scientists, supportive of interracial but not intraracial distinctions, each American race is closer to its own genetic "melting pot" than to being rigidly subdivided into the discrete ethnic groups that came to this country.

For several years before 1991, the debate over the role of race played out in courtrooms across the country. Expert witnesses for the prosecution and the defense did battle at pretrial hearings on the admissibility of DNA evidence. Overwhelmingly, the courts ruled for the prosecution and allowed DNA evidence and the FBI numbers into court, as happened in the Matias Reyes case.

The courts admitted DNA evidence in most cases despite the arguments of critics. The scientists hired by prosecutors were in many instances world renowned. Their credibility in supporting the FBI approach weighed heavily with the courts. They testified that, genetically speaking, the ethnic variation within broad racial groups is slight or nonexistent. They also testified that the FBI had built assumptions into its approach that significantly understated the power of a DNA match, whether ethnic populations vary genetically or not.

The experts supporting the FBI approach also told judges

through their testimony that any variation within broad ethnic groups could as easily benefit as harm a defendant. Make no mistake about the fact that these experts vigorously maintained that there is no substantial variation; however, if the numbers were somehow skewed, they could as easily be skewed in favor of a defendant as against him or her. While a defense expert could claim that an estimate of one in 50 million is potentially skewed so that the actual number could be one in 500,000, the number could just as easlly vary upward by the same magnitude to one in 5 billion. There was no basis to claim that the numbers were biased against defendants.

At pretrial hearings, the scientific experts also labored mightily to make it clear that the FBI numbers are estimates of the meaning of a DNA match. There are no precise numbers in this realm. The estimate is designed to give a jury an idea of how rare it would be to have two such samples match solely through coincidence. "I'm a statistician," said scientist Bruce Weir. "I get paid to estimate variability."

The testimony of the scientists in favor of admissibility was strongly aided by the argument of prosecutors that this is an issue jurors can handle. Any quarrels between experts over the effects of ethnicity can be considered by a jury. Scientific disagreement about aspects of statistical probability is not a reason to bar DNA evidence in its entirety.

Instead, disagreements about the significance of ethnic populations can be addressed through expert witnesses, cross-examination, and arguments by lawyers for both sides on summation, and they can have their applicability to the case at hand decided by juries. A sufficiently weighty defense argument will raise doubt about the prosecution's claim of positive identification; if weighty enough, the argument may raise reasonable doubt about guilt. Speaking in legal terms, this is appropriately a matter of "weight," not "admissibility."

These compelling scientific and legal arguments generally led judges to admit DNA evidence into court. The judges had to determine whether they could reconcile the criticisms of DNA evidence with the rule that new scientific evidence can only go to the jury if there is "general acceptance" that it is reliable.

This rule requiring "general acceptance" in the scientific community before novel scientific evidence can be admitted in court is known as the *"Frye* standard." It is named for a 1923 District of Columbia court decision refusing to allow a jury to learn the results of a crude predecessor of the modern lie detector test. Under the *Frye* standard, the courts required special judicial screening of new scientific evidence before it can be heard by a jury. In 1991 this rule still applied in most state courts, and a modified though somewhat more relaxed form of the rule applied in most federal courts.

A compelling logic underlay the rule. While judicial screening is not required for most evidence submitted in court, scientific evidence is different. Scientific evidence can be extraordinarily powerful evidence, so much so that laypeople, who often lack the ability to evaluate scientific matters, can be intimidated into accepting it rather than persuaded to do so. Judicial screening thus protects the process, as judges filter out evidence that is not legitimately "scientific."

Prior scrutiny by judges is also required before scientific evidence goes to a jury because expert witnesses are allowed to testify to their opinions in courtrooms. All other witnesses may testify only to facts based on firsthand knowledge and observation. Before scientific experts can provide their opinions, the courts must ensure that these opinions are based on sufficiently solid scientific grounds.

The "general acceptance" required in this instance meant different things to different judges. Some understood it to mean that any dispute about expressing numerical findings barred DNA's introduction as evidence. To these judges, controversy by definition demonstrated a lack of general acceptance. To most judges, "general acceptance" was understood to require much less. In this view, scientists could argue about DNA just as competing teams of doctors, engineers, and other experts argue about other evidence in court, so long as there was general acceptance in the scientific community that the science underlying the evidence is reliable.

In late 1991, the issue of race and ethnicity lingered. Disputes about the accuracy of using broad racial categories had blocked the acceptance of DNA evidence in some trials. The Massachusetts Supreme Judicial Court had barred DNA evidence in its entirety. A handful of courts troubled by DNA numbers had allowed experts to tell jurors about the meaning of a DNA match in words rather than numbers, by stating that the prospects of a specific DNA match occurring at random are "remote" or "very remote." These restrictions, however, were very much the exception rather than the rule, since the evidence of the "general acceptance" of the FBI approach was fairly strong. For the most part, DNA evidence and the FBI numbers were admitted in court, despite the controversy over race and its role. That is exactly what happened in late 1991 in the Matias Reyes case, as issues of race and ethnicity were raised but rejected at the pretrial admissibility hearing.

Then, all hell broke loose.

Science, the nation's leading scientific magazine, accepted for publication an article severely critical of the FBI approach. The article was written by Drs. Richard Lewontin and Daniel Hartl, scientists at Harvard and Washington universities.

Lewontin and Hartl had recently testified for the defense in a major case in Ohio. In his decision in that case, the judge had chosen to rely not on their testimony but on the testimony of the prosecution experts, most notably Dr. Thomas Caskey of Baylor University, the former president of the American Society of Human Genetics. Lewontin and Hartl then brought their losing courtroom criticism to the pages of *Science* magazine. The impending publication of their article threatened the admissibility of DNA analysis in a way that their courtroom testimony never could. This threat arose because of the particular importance in the legal system of scientific articles that have undergone "peer review."

Leading scientific journals will accept an article for publication only after having sent it out to be reviewed by several scientists not associated with the authors of the piece. The scientists determine that the scientific methodology described in the article, not necessarily its conclusions, is sound enough to merit publication. While the review process cannot be used to imply that publication has endorsed the conclusions of an article, publication by a journal such as *Science* does provide an ironclad imprimatur of legitimacy to its point of view. Publication by a prestigious journal enhances the credibility of the argument made in an article. Such publication can have substantial consequences when courts are trying to determine whose views enjoy general acceptance within the scientific community.

In reviewing testimony in a *Frye* hearing, a court can choose to discount the views of an expert witness who testifies for the defense. This is all the more true when the testimony is disputed by leading scientists and by the entire criminal justice establishment. But an article by a Harvard scientist in the nation's leading scientific journal would be much harder to discount.

The stakes were extremely high. The article would provide potentially deadly ammunition to the critics of DNA evidence, jeopardizing its very admissibility in court. Defense lawyers would cite Lewontin and Hartl's article to support their claim that the FBI methods for stating the significance of a DNA match are not generally accepted by the scientific community. The FBI numbers, they would say, must be excluded.

The critics would argue that all evidence of a DNA match must be excluded as a consequence of the exclusion of the DNA numbers. They would argue that evidence of a DNA match is "meaningless" without a number stating its significance. So, if the number stating the significance of the match has been excluded, the fact of a match too must be excluded from evidence. Even before the acceptance of the Lewontin and Hartl article for publication, this argument for the exclusion of DNA evidence had already won judicial acceptance in some cases. Now it was immeasurably strengthened.

The Lewontin and Hartl article was also significant in another important respect. It urged that methods be used that would produce numbers more modest and more favorable to defendants than those generated by the FBI approach. But, in the eyes of the proponents of DNA evidence, these numbers would dramatically understate the power of the technology and the power and meaning of a DNA match.

In cases where there is a great deal of other evidence against a defendant, modesty in stating the significance of a DNA match may not matter for all practical purposes. That the defendant's DNA could be expected to match DNA found at the crime scene in one out of every 100,000 people may be more than enough to lock things up when it is also shown that the defendant was at the scene at about the time of the crime, had threatened to commit the crime, and was found in possession of some item taken from the crime scene. But in those criminal cases where there is little evidence against a defendant other than a DNA match, the size of the numbers stating the match's significance may be the difference between conviction and exoneration. The difference between larger and smaller numbers will also be particularly important in criminal cases based on a match made from a DNA data bank of convicted offenders. A number that is not large enough to reflect the true chance of the match being a coincidence could free a murderer or a rapist; a number that is too large could unfairly implicate a person in a crime he or she did not commit.

The importance of the *Science* article was underscored by the intense controversy that surrounded its publication. Months before its publication, prosecutors and prosecution experts all around the country had read the Lewontin and Hartl submission. The leak reportedly came from the office of Dr. Hartl, at Washington University in St. Louis. An aide of Hartl's had sent the prepublication manuscript to a defense expert witness in an Oregon multiple homicide case. That witness had introduced the manuscript in court as an exhibit, rendering it a public document. From court, the prepublication draft was circulated among prosecutors and experts interested in DNA evidence. Among those receiving a copy was James R. Wooley, a federal prosecutor in Ohio. Wooley's reaction to the paper generated a storm of controversy in both the popular and scientific press.

Wooley was surprised and concerned by the paper. He had previously cross-examined Lewontin and Hartl in a lenghty federal court hearing in Ohio. That hearing, in a murder trial, had been the forum for an extensive legal challenge to DNA population statistics mounted by DNA defense lawyers Barry Scheck and Peter Neufeld. The federal judge had chosen to rely on Dr. Caskey's positive view of DNA evidence over the more negative opinions of Drs. Lewontin and Hartl.

After the hearing, Wooley had an off-the-record conversation with Hartl. According to Wooley, Hartl made derogatory statements about the defense efforts in the case. Hartl said that he had been badly misled by the individuals who had asked him to get involved in DNA litigation and that he regretted his involvement in the entire matter. Wooley recounted that the scientist told him that he considered the defendants "barnacles on the walls of society" that should be "scraped off."

These comments caused Wooley to believe that Hartl had

reconsidered his earlier pro-defense positions. So when Wooley received a draft of the paper, he was perplexed. In early October 1991, Wooley called Hartl and asked him about the "discrepancy." Hartl told Wooley that he had never intended to lead Wooley to believe that he had altered his substantive views. The two discussed the paper at great length. Wooley expressed his concerns about the paper's substance and his view that it could have a substantial impact on current cases. "I told him that I thought the paper would be misconstrued, that it will confuse and mislead— and that with the credentials of Drs. Hartl and Lewontin, it would have an impact on cases disproportionate to its significance."

Hartl's account of the call differed sharply from Wooley's. He stated that Wooley warned him of the "political consequences" of publishing and asked him to reconsider because of the possibly disastrous consequences for future DNA cases. In short, Hartl claimed that Wooley asked him not to publish his article because it would hurt the admissibility of DNA evidence in court.

The telephone call from the prosecutor generated an extraordinary response from Richard Lewontin, Hartl's coauthor. He fired off a letter to Wooley accusing him of a "very serious breach of ethics": "You have attempted, in the interest of what you regard as public policy to suppress scientific evidence and to attempt to have scholars withhold their true views in support of that policy."

The differences between prosecutor and scientist went well beyond the specific content of the telephone call. Lewontin saw governmental coercion: "When someone who is an official in the Department of Justice Criminal Division Strike Force telephones a private citizen to request an action that citizen would not ordinarily take, then a form of intimidation has been used. It is always alarming when agencies of the State—be it the FBI, the IRS or the Criminal Division Strike Force—are used as intimidating devices against citizens who oppose a stated policy of the government."

By contrast, Wooley saw himself not primarily as an agent of the federal government but as a spirited advocate in the debate over DNA evidence. In the world of scientific and legal controversy about DNA testing, scientists have routinely offered opinions on the shape the law should take, and lawyers have addressed scientific issues with confidence. Scientists and lawyers have frequently

interacted as part of the ongoing dialogue. They attend conferences together, talk on the telephone, and speak each other's rar-
efied languages.

Wooley had lectured and written extensively on DNA and
engaged in numerous conversations with scientists. It was no
secret in the community of those involved that he was a vigorous
advocate of DNA evidence. Wooley saw his call to Hartl as
another conversation among vigorous advocates engaged in an
important debate. In his view, Lewontin's fears were exaggerated. To Wooley, the power of a federal prosecutor in Ohio to
intimidate or affect a team of tenured scientists from Massachusetts and Missouri was limited or nonexistent. The scientists saw
the matter differently. But this much was clear. The aggressive
advocacy surrounding the publication of the *Science* article was
fierce.

The prospect that the impending publication of the *Science*
article would threaten the admissibility of DNA evidence in court
concerned scientists as well as prosecutors. Dr. Caskey and Dr.
Kenneth Kidd had reviewed the prepublication manuscript, and
both were extremely troubled by it.

Their concern was based heavily on their understanding of
the governing law. "I felt publishing the article would create a
very serious problem in the legal system, and that was their
intent," said Kidd, a professor in the Department of Genetics at
Yale University's School of Medicine. He believed that defense
attorneys who wanted to block the admission of DNA evidence in
court would play on the fact that the article had survived the
review by scientists necessary to gain publication in a top scientific journal.

Kidd's concern about the authors' intent was supported by
the article's conclusion, which asserted that estimates of DNA
probabilities are "generally unreliable." These words echoed the
governing legal standard for admissibility of scientific evidence
and asserted that it was not met.

At the International Congress of Human Genetics in Washington, D.C., Kidd and Caskey cornered one of *Science*'s editors.
They urged that the Lewontin and Hartl article not be published
without a rebuttal. "I thought there were major scientific points
on which they were wrong or on which there are very legitimate
alternative viewpoints, and for the article to appear without some

form of rebuttal is inappropriate," said Kidd. The editor at the conference passed on Kidd's and Caskey's concerns to Daniel Koshland, the top editor at *Science*.

Koshland agreed to commission a rebuttal from Dr. Kidd and Dr. Ranajit Chakraborty of the University of Texas. "Pure politics," said Lewontin. "I think it is quite extraordinary that an editor would go out and hire two guys to write a rebuttal" after an article had been peer reviewed and accepted. The *Science* editor portrayed his action as the essence of fairness. Said Koshland, "I did it to give a more balanced view of the subject. I was trying to be fair."

The editor also took a second look at the Lewontin and Hartl article and said he was "disturbed that the data did not support the paper's conclusions." He called Lewontin to "ask him for revisions." Lewontin hit the roof and replied that any attempt to hold up the paper or withdraw it "would be met with the biggest stink he had ever heard."

On December 20, 1991, *Science* published the original article and a rebuttal. Surprisingly, the "rebuttal" appeared in the magazine's pages before the original article. The article by Kidd and Chakraborty vigorously supported the use of broad racial groups. The article by Lewontin and Hartl attacked the use of numbers based on such classifications on the ground that they are misleading because they do not consider the crucial role of ethnicity.

A major news story, titled "Fight Erupts over DNA Fingerprinting," was published in *Science* accompanying the articles. This story described the controversy surrounding publication of the paired articles in great detail. There was a substantial danger that courts reviewing the articles and the news story in *Science* would take the controversy as evidence of a lack of the requisite general acceptance within the scientific community and refuse to allow DNA analysis into court.

At this point, all those concerned with DNA testing and its future in court looked to Washington, D.C., and to the National Academy of Sciences. In January 1990, the National Academy had initiated a study of DNA testing. By late 1991, when the *Science* articles were published, there had for months been rumors that the academy report was imminent. Most hoped, indeed expected, that the report would bring order out of chaos and resolve the battle over DNA evidence.

This hope was premised on the prestige of the National Academy of Sciences. Since 1863, the academy had been a private society of distinguished scholars with a mandate from Congress to advise the federal government on scientific and technical matters. Its principal operating agency is the National Research Council. The academy had convened a high-powered committee, including scientists, a law professor, and a federal judge, to produce this eagerly awaited report. But the report would not come for several months. When the first press account of its conclusions appeared in April of 1992, it was a bombshell.

On April 14, 1992, the *New York Times* reported in a page-one story that a "long-awaited Federal report on a powerful new genetic technique for identifying criminal suspects says it should not be allowed in court in the future unless a more scientific basis is established." The article, by science reporter Gina Kolata, the same reporter who had written the earlier controversial story on DNA testing, reported that the National Academy of Sciences "says courts should cease to admit DNA evidence until laboratory standards have been tightened and the technique has been established on a stronger scientific basis." The story did not mention race and ethnicity, the issue that had dominated the DNA debate, until its twenty-sixth paragraph. The focus of the story was a report that the National Academy had found laboratory standards inadequate and called for a DNA moratorium.

On the morning the *Times* story appeared, the chair of the academy's DNA committee hastily called a news conference. The report had not been scheduled for publication until the next day, but the press conference was urgent.

"Forgive me if I seem to be a little bit out of breath," began Dr. Victor McKusick of Johns Hopkins University. "I was very upset when I saw the article this morning. It seriously misrepresents our findings." The report of a recommended moratorium is "not so. On the contrary, we confirm the general reliability of using DNA typing in forensic science." Specifically, he said, "[we] recommend that courts accept the reliability of the technology and recognize that current laboratory techniques are fundamentally sound." The National Academy of Sciences also issued a statement that day saying that the major conclusion of the *Times* article was "incorrect," and that the academy had concluded that DNA typing provides "strong evidence" of identity.

The next day's *Times* carried a page-one article and headline, also written by Kolata, admitting and explaining its mistake. "Chief Says Panel Backs Courts' Use of a Genetic Test—Times Account in Error," read the headline. The article stated that the *Times* "erred in our article and headline in saying that the panel called directly for a moratorium on the use of DNA typing." This article had it substantially right, but by introducing the word "directly," it seemed to be offering the excuse that the report could reasonably be read as calling for a moratorium. It could not. While the report had called for implementation in the long run of its own program to promote the quality of testing, it supported DNA testing in the meantime pursuant to the standards issued by the independent scientists working in association with the FBI.

How could the *Times,* the nation's leading newspaper, have made such a major mistake? The *Times* explained the error in its own front-page news story. "We based our interpretation of the report on the views of legal experts," said Nicholas Wade, its science editor. The newspaper reported that it was told by several law professors that the panel's call for laboratories to meet high standards was "tantamount to saying that DNA evidence should not be admissible at this time." The *Times* quoted one prominent lawyer critical of DNA testing as saying: "There's no question it says that."

On its face, the report was a strong endorsement of DNA technology, the special "spin" in the original *Times* article notwithstanding. Besides endorsing DNA analysis, the report tried to offer a way out of the woods of the debate over race and ethnicity. The National Academy took no position on which side was right: Instead, it assumed for the sake of discussion that there may be significant differences between ethnic groups within racial groups. It then proposed an approach for making estimates of the significance of a DNA match that are independent of the race or ethnic group of the suspect. The statement of the significance of a DNA match would make no reference to race.

The proposed approach had some important aspects in common with the FBI approach. A DNA match consists of finding a match on each of several chromosomes, usually two, three, or four chromosomes. Both the FBI approach and the National

Academy approach assigned a significance to each match at an individual chromosome. The overall significance of a DNA match was determined by the multiplication of those values at each of several matching chromosomes.

But the National Academy report proposed that a limit, a "ceiling," be imposed on those values before they are multiplied. Under the FBI approach, the frequency assigned to a match at a chromosome is that in the suspect's broad racial group. The academy required study of the frequency of such matches in many ethnic populations. But it would not then assign a frequency to a match at a location on a chromosome reflecting the suspect's particular ethnic background. Instead, it assigned for a match at an individual chromosome the frequency for that ethnic group in which the match would appear most commonly, giving the suspect the benefit of the most common frequency among any of the ethnic groups. So, if a suspect were Italian, the value assigned at a chromosome where a DNA match was found would be that for the group where a match would appear most frequently, be it Italian, Ecuadoran, or Alabama blacks. There would also be an additional limit imposed on the value that could be assigned for a match on any given chromosome, regardless of the actual numbers.

The academy described its approach as "the ceiling principle," since it imposed a ceiling on the significance of a DNA match, requiring that the lowest possible number for all ethnic groups be used for each separate chromosome where a match was found.

This approach, if implemented, would have dramatically reduced the stated significance of a DNA match. A match that previously may have been deemed a one in 50 million in a broad racial population might be stated as a one in 500,000 match in the general population; what may have been considered a one in 1 million match might now be one in 10,000.

In most cases, such as the Matias Reyes case, where there was evidence besides DNA, this approach would likely make little difference. But in cases where there was little other evidence, particularly cases built on matches from DNA data banks, the impact could be huge. Some such prosecutions would be effectively precluded by the National Academy's ceiling principle.

At first, it looked like the limits built into the National Academy's proposal were the price that law enforcement and prosecutors would have to pay to get DNA into court. Some few cases would be sacrificed, but overall DNA evidence would be admitted at trial. Several court cases decided soon after the report was issued required compliance with this new manner of calculating DNA numbers, and it was widely assumed that the courts would require compliance with the academy's proposal, and admit DNA evidence only on this limited basis.

This likely response was heralded by the California courts. Before the National Academy report was issued, California law had allowed the FBI numbers to go to the jury. After the report and the *Science* articles were published, California took a different tack. A decision from California's First District Court of Appeal said that there must be some "common ground" for admitting DNA evidence and that the National Academy report appeared to point the way to that common ground in future cases. It rejected the FBI numbers, stating that they should not have been allowed in court. In finding a lack of "general acceptance" of the FBI approach, the California court focused on the "bitter" and "raging" disagreement reflected by the *Science* articles.

Most assumed, like the California appellate court, that the National Academy report would be the gold standard that the courts would look to in admitting DNA evidence, the "common ground" that would solve this dilemma of "general acceptance." After all, who would argue with the National Academy of Sciences?

This view, however, was short-lived, for many scientists were extremely eager to argue with this particular report of the National Academy of Sciences. A broad coalition of scientists attacked the report through 1992 and 1993. The scorching assault proceeded in numerous conferences, speeches, and scientific publications. It was for the most part an attack not only critical of the National Academy of Sciences approach but supportive of the FBI and its methods for stating the significance of a DNA match.

A British geneticist, Dr. Newton Morton, likened the National Academy of Sciences to the scientific establishment of Galileo's time. He attacked the academy's way of stating the significance of a DNA match as "incompetent" and "illogical." "If I were asked if there is any scientific justification to the ceiling principle, I'd have to say no," said Neil Risch of Yale University. The scientists decried the report's "principle" as a political compromise masquerading as science. They claimed that it was neither "scientific" nor a "principle" and would lead to marked understatement of the significance of a DNA match in the name of science while it had no basis in science.

This controversy was unsettling to the courts. The California appellate judge who had written the earlier decision that looked to the National Academy report as potentially providing the "common ground" that would allow the routine acceptance of DNA evidence in court was extremely disturbed. In a new decision, in a new case, Judge Ming Chin of the First District California Court of Appeal noted that, though it was only eight months later, the prospect of "common ground" was vanishing. Chin admonished the critics of the National Academy report to censor themselves or potentially lose the admissibility of DNA evidence in court entirely. The "persistence of disputes threatens the admissibility" of DNA testing, he wrote. "This is no time for a purist insistence that DNA evidence should be admitted on one's own terms or not at all."

This call for self-censorship was jarring, seeking as it did the sacrifice of abstract "scientific truth" to the perceived "public interest" in getting DNA evidence into court. But there was no question that the judge's view appeared at the time to have some basis in cautious good common sense. After all, the admissibility of DNA evidence did require general acceptance. The controversy over the National Academy report seemed to threaten the most likely path to general acceptance, leaving only more chaos and uncertainty. Judge Ming Chin was concerned that further controversy over the issue could lead to the exclusion of DNA evidence entirely.

But the fierce controversy over the report did not lead to the rejection of DNA evidence in court. Instead, the scientific critics of the report enjoyed an extraordinary victory. Their criticisms led the National Academy of Sciences to agree to reexamine the issue of race and ethnicity. This decision dramatically diminished the impact of the National Academy's report on this issue. The admissibility of DNA evidence by the courts has for the most part not been limited in the manner proposed by the academy. It is hardly surprising that a roundly criticized report currently subject to reexamination by the entity that issued it is much less powerful, and that absolute compliance with its approach is not required by the courts.

In this atmosphere, the FBI approach continued, for the most part, to prevail in court. It was the genetic equivalent of the only guy left standing after a barroom brawl. It was the best available estimate of the actual meaning of a DNA match.

To the extent that courts are troubled by the *Science* articles and the dispute over race and ethnicity, the National Academy method is also available to the jury as an alternative view. The National Academy's ceiling principle can be offered to a jury by a defense expert or brought out by the prosecutor or defense attorney on examination of the government's DNA witness. A jury may choose to rely on the National Academy's approach or the FBI's. Oddly, it is conceivable that in certain cases a prosecutor might agree to use the more modest numbers simply to deprive the defense of a contentious issue and thereby avoid having the jury speculate about whether the whole area of DNA analysis is really settled science.

The trend toward allowing the FBI numbers to be presented to a jury got more support from a decision of the United States Supreme Court on June 28, 1993. In *Daubert,* a products liability case, the Court determined that the "general acceptance" standard for admissibility of scientific evidence no longer applies in federal court. It decided that the *Frye* standard had been supplanted by the Federal Rules of Evidence, characterizing the "general acceptance" rule as an "austere standard" and stating its preference for a more "flexible" standard. The trial judge would still act as a "gatekeeper" who would ensure that scientific evidence is "not only relevant but reliable." Evidentiary reliability would be based upon "scientific validity," and scientific conclusions would have to be based on "good grounds based on what is known." According to this more relaxed standard, a judge must ensure that scientific evidence "rests on a reliable foundation" before admitting it. General acceptance within the scientific community would remain one aspect of admissibility because it is a factor that bears on reliability (along with empirical testing, peer review and publication, and error rates) but would not be an absolute prerequisite for the admissibility of scientific evidence in federal court.

The high Court's decision has eased the introduction of DNA evidence in federal courts. There may be some room for continued disagreement in court over whether there is "general acceptance" of the FBI methods. But there is unquestionably a "reliable" scientific basis for the FBI approach. So the FBI numbers should be admitted in federal court with little controversy.

The Court's decision will also likely foster the admissibility of DNA evidence in state courts. Most DNA cases are state court prosecutions for rape and other violent crimes, and the Supreme Court decision binds only federal courts. It does not control state courts. Still, a decision of the United States Supreme Court is bound to influence state courts in setting and interpreting their own standards.

In the wake of *Daubert*, some state courts may choose to abandon the Frye "general acceptance" standard in favor of a "reliability" standard for the introduction of scientific evidence. More likely, the Supreme Court decision will influence state courts to take a more relaxed view of the meaning of "general acceptance." Many states already allow general acceptance to be found even where vigorous controversy over some aspect of the science remains, a view conducive to the admissibility of DNA evidence. The Supreme Court endorsement of a more relaxed approach to the introduction of scientific evidence should foster this trend.

At long last, the debate over race and ethnicity as a possible block to the admissibility of DNA evidence appeared to be at an end. The momentum in that direction snowballed in October 1994, when a major advocate and a leading critic of DNA evidence jointly published an article declaring that the controversy "has been resolved." An article in *Nature* by the FBI's Bruce Budowle and Dr. Eric Lander of the Whitehead Institute for Biomedical Research urged that courts allow experts to testify both to the FBI approach and to the "ultra-conservative" National Academy approach. "Now," they wrote, "it is time to move on." So the FBI's head DNA scientist and the leading defense scientist declared the DNA wars over race and ethnicity at an end.

Over time, the courts have more and more routinely admitted DNA evidence. But the proclaimed resolution of the dispute went to the issue of admissibility of DNA evidence only. It reflected a judgment that matters relating to race and ethnicity are not so substantial as to block the admissibility of DNA evidence in court.

Still, the weight that a jury may choose to give a DNA match is another matter. Defense lawyers and scientists remain free to question and criticize DNA evidence in court. Race and ethnicity remain an issue for trial. In some cases, where DNA evidence is less than overwhelming and other evidence is slight, the issue may be crucial. It may provide a means for the defense to minimize the significance of a DNA match and secure a hung jury or acquittal.

Meanwhile, another important and related issue quickly gained the spotlight. Many advocates of the FBI's approach to stating the significance of a DNA match had fought for that approach and for the use of large numbers in order to preserve a position they would need in the coming battle over gaining convictions in cases built against suspects identified through DNA data banking. The prospect of catching felony offenders by collecting their DNA and keeping it on file to check against future offenses now moved to center stage. It was to be the next area of passion and action in the debate over DNA.

7 MANHUNT

J EAN ANN BRODERICK had moved to Minneapolis to go to college, and she had stayed on to work there after school. She was twenty-three years old, and had come to Minneapolis from her hometown of Omaha, Nebraska.

She and her friends were an idealistic group, young people who had taken jobs with public-spirited, civic organizations. Four of them, three women and one man, had rented the first floor of a large house close to downtown Minneapolis.

There were four bedrooms on the first floor, and the young people, who knew each other variously from college and postcollege life, rented all four. The house that they rented was located in a neighborhood known as Lowry Hill.

Lowry Hill was full of large, old, Victorian homes. It had once been a wealthy neighborhood and had gone full cycle from decline in the 1960s to rebirth in the 1980s and '90s. It was a good neighborhood on the edge of some bad neighborhoods.

On Saturday night, November 17, 1991, Jean Ann Broderick and one of her female roommates, her best friend, went out for the evening. Their third female roommate was away for the weekend, and their male roommate did not come along. The two women drove into downtown Minneapolis. Because each had had a couple of drinks over the course of the evening, they decided they would walk home that night rather than drive, and retrieve their car later.

It was a cool, bracing fall night, a nice night for a walk, and they were responsible people, who would walk rather than drive after a couple of drinks. As they walked home that night, the two young women passed by a halfway house for sex offenders three blocks from where they lived. Soon they reached home.

The two talked for a while before retiring to their individual bedrooms. Then they both went to sleep.

The next morning, their male roommate left early, leaving the house at about 8:00 A.M. As he left, he noticed that the back door was unlocked. But, since the roommates had left the back door unlocked on prior occasions, this did not alarm him.

Broderick's best friend slept in that morning. She did not find Broderick's body until 2:00 in the afternoon.

The man who killed Jean Ann Broderick first went into the bedroom of the roommate who was out of town for the weekend. He took a pair of tights, and cut them into several pieces. He then slipped into Broderick's bedroom. He stuffed one piece of the tights into her mouth, silencing her so her roommates could not hear her cries. He tied her hands behind her back and then raped Jean Ann Broderick. Finally, he strangled her to death with another piece of her absent roommate's tights.

When her best friend found Broderick, she was facedown on her bed, with her hands tied behind her back and a dried semen stain on her buttocks.

The police immediately focused on the halfway house. But an investigation of the men who lived there quickly led nowhere. There were no suspects and no leads.

Fifty percent of rapes in the United States are unsolved crimes, and Minnesota had been one of the first states in the country to pass a law requiring that convicted sex offenders provide samples of their blood for DNA analysis. With a data bank in place, investigators can then compare the DNA profile from an unsolved sex crime to see if they already have the same profile on file.

When the Minnesota authorities checked their data bank, they found a DNA profile that matched that of Martin Perez, a thirty-seven-year-old illegal immigrant from Mexico, who was just then in jail in Minnesota on a new burglary charge but had not been at the time of the murder. Perez's prior criminal history included convictions for rape, sexual assault, and burglary in Minnesota, Texas, and Georgia.

In March 1991, he had been deported to Mexico. The authorities did not know if Perez was even in the United States when Jean Ann Broderick was murdered on November 17, 1991. Perhaps he had been in Mexico and had returned to the United

States only just before his most recent burglary. But, as it turned out, Perez not only had been back in the United States between his deportation and the murder, but had even been in and out of jail during that time.

On August 28, 1991, Perez had been arrested in the burglary of the apartment of a St. Paul woman. As a repeat offender, he should have received years in jail for the burglary and should not have been free to murder Jean Ann Broderick. But Perez successfully conned the Minnesota authorities, giving them the phony name Andrew Cruz Cortez. He presented to the police as his own a genuine birth certificate for Andrew Cruz Cortez, deceased since 1989. Perez went through the criminal justice system under that false name and, as a presumed first-time offender, was released from jail after only two months.

Three months later, at the time of the murder of Jean Ann Broderick, Perez was not in custody and was presumably in the area of the Twin Cities.

As the Minneapolis police investigated the murder, they discovered that this had not been the first time a man had made unlawful entry in the middle of the night to the house where Broderick was murdered. Broderick and her friends had only recently moved into the Lowry Hill house, and that summer other people had lived in those same first-floor bedrooms. Police reports on file with the Minneapolis authorities showed that during that summer a man in one of those bedrooms had surprised and confronted a burglar, who then fled from the house without being apprehended. The man who had confronted the burglar had left Minneapolis soon afterward and was now a student at the Columbia School of Journalism in New York City.

The Minneapolis police enlisted the assistance of the New York City Police Department. Because they had a match between the DNA of the semen found at the scene and Perez's DNA as carried in their DNA data bank, the Minneapolis police sent Perez's photograph, along with pictures of several other men of similar appearance, to the New York City police. Detectives from the New York City Police Department then visited the student and showed him the pictures. The journalism student picked out Perez's photograph, recognizing him as the burglar he had surprised that summer in that same house.

At trial, the student again identified Perez as the man he had confronted, in what was later Jean Ann Broderick's home, only a few months before her murder. It was powerful evidence.

The judge also allowed prosecutors to introduce evidence of Perez's 1984 conviction for attempted rape of a woman ten blocks from Broderick's home. Perez had almost choked that woman into unconsciousness as he tried to rape her. The crime, which took place outdoors, was stopped only because the woman's neighbors intervened.

But, most of all, it was the DNA evidence that made the case against Perez. A large amount of semen was recovered, so scientists were able to match genetic characteristics at six separate genetic locations. An expert witness testified that, with matches at that many locations, he could state with a reasonable degree of scientific certainty that this semen came from Perez.

On April 22, 1993, after one hour and twenty minutes of deliberation, a Minneapolis jury convicted Perez of first-degree murder and rape. He was sentenced to life imprisonment without parole.

Broderick's murder would never have been solved without a DNA data bank. "Without a DNA pool, there is no way we would have been able to identify the suspect," said prosecutor Steve Redding. "And we certainly would not have been able to get the conviction."

It was the first case in American history in which the new tool of DNA data banking was used to solve a rape or murder. Significantly, a data bank had been used to identify a suspect. Then additional evidence was developed against that suspect and presented to the jury. This pointed the way to the most likely use of DNA data banking—not trying to prove cases against suspects solely on the basis of DNA evidence, but taking a data bank match as a starting point and then adding supporting evidence to bring about the conviction. Used in such a way it is a tool of great promise.

All the same, the progress toward wider use of DNA data banking was slow at best. By early 1993, only twenty-one states had passed laws requiring convicted sex offenders to provide blood for DNA data banks. Despite the FBI's plan to establish an interstate data bank, and the high mobility of serial killers and rapists, many states had not yet taken the samples that would be necessary to build a useful national database.

But soon the costs of inaction became clear.

THERE IS IN MANHATTAN A SMALL TOWN in the middle of a great city, a place of tree-lined walkways and red-brick buildings with a park and a fountain at its center. Twenty thousand people live in Stuyvesant Town, a development built in 1947 by the Metropolitan Life Insurance Company.

Stuyvesant Town covers eighteen blocks in lower Manhattan, and it is a place where the middle class thrives in a borough of extremes. Teachers and librarians, cops and prosecutors; these are the people of Stuyvesant Town. There are 8,000 applications on the waiting list for this urban village.

But during five months in late 1993 and early 1994, the residents of Stuyvesant Town lived in a state of terror. A serial rapist was on the loose. Each of his victims was an attractive, fair-skinned, petite, and very slender woman. The ages of the victims ranged from twenty-one to thirty-two.

Nothing could have been done to stop the first rape. But the second and third rapes could have been prevented.

The first took place on November 18, 1993, at approximately 7:15 P.M. A young woman was returning home to her apartment building after grocery shopping, carrying several bags as she walked across Fourteenth Street. While she opened the door to the outside of her apartment building, a man approached behind her jingling a set of keys. The jingling keys made the woman believe the man lived in the building, and, as she walked into the lobby, the man followed her in.

As they rode up together in the building's elevator, her grocery bags at her feet, the man grabbed at the woman's crotch. She dropped her mail and slapped his hand away, asking him what he thought he was doing. It was then that the man grabbed the young woman, put his hand over her mouth, and held a knife to her throat. He repeatedly called her a bitch and told her that he would kill her if she screamed. The man pushed the elevator button for the top floor and forced the young woman to an area inside the apartment building that led out onto the roof.

On the roof landing, the man forced the woman to take her clothes off and ordered her to get on her knees and perform oral sex on him. He could not maintain an erection and told the woman it was her fault, that she wasn't acting as if she enjoyed what she was doing. The man then forced her to get down on her hands and knees, with her face pressed against the step that led to the roof. He penetrated her vaginally from the rear.

Then he left. The young woman was treated at Beth Israel Hospital, where vaginal swabs were taken and saved as evidence.

On January 16, 1994, at approximately 5:45 P.M., a second young woman went to visit her parents, who lived two blocks south of Stuyvesant Town. The woman had been shopping, and she carried bags as she walked across Fourteenth Street toward her parents' building.

As she came to the front door of her parents' building, the young woman had difficulty unlocking the door because of the intense cold. Just as she managed to get it open, a man came up behind her. He placed his hand over her mouth, held a box cutter to her throat, and forced her behind the stairwell on the first floor. There he forced the young woman to her knees and ordered her to perform oral sex on him, indicating as well that she should take his scrotum in her mouth. He kissed the young woman's breasts and repeatedly called her a bitch. Then he ordered her to turn around and bend over, and he penetrated her vaginally from behind. After that he left.

A neighbor carrying out the trash found the young woman sobbing under the stairs, so traumatized that she could not speak. She had to use gestures to describe what had happened to her and was too hysterical to call the police; the neighbor made the call on her behalf. At St. Vincent's Hospital, vaginal swabs were taken.

Two weeks later, on February 1, 1994, at approximately 2:00 on a bright, sunny afternoon, a third young woman walked home across Fourteenth Street, carrying books. A man approached her on the street and told her that she had a nice walk. The young woman kept walking, and the man walked in front of her until she turned into her apartment house.

As the young woman opened the front door to her building, the man suddenly came up behind her. He put his hand over her mouth, held a box cutter to her throat, and ordered the woman to take him to her apartment, telling her that if she didn't live alone he would kill her.

At her front door, the woman trembled so much that she was unable to get the key in the lock. The man punched her on the side of the head, and she opened the door. The man then made the woman take her clothes off.

He forced the young woman to perform oral sex and, again, to take his scrotum in her mouth. He ordered her to hold his buttocks while she did so. He told her to lie down on her stomach on her bed but then told her to roll over on her back, and he vaginally penetrated her. The man fondled the young woman's breasts and repeatedly kissed her on the mouth. Then he told her to get on her hands and knees, and again he penetrated her vaginally, this time from the rear. Again and again, the man called the woman a bitch. He bragged about how much she was enjoying these sexual acts. He could tell how much she was enjoying it, he said.

All in all, the man held the young woman captive in her apartment for forty-five minutes. Before leaving, he removed the cord to her phone from the wall and told her to take care. He then left the apartment. His victim was treated at Beth Israel Hospital, and again vaginal swabs were taken.

As the people of Stuyvesant Town grew more and more nervous, the police were making no progress. They circulated posters with police sketches based on the victims' descriptions of the rapist. He was described as a Hispanic man in his late twenties or early thirties, five feet seven inches tall, with a lean and muscular body, balding, with a mustache and possibly a beard. The posters were circulated in Stuyvesant Town and the surrounding area, but to little apparent effect.

The investigation was now a waiting game. Female police officers, decoys dressed in casual clothes, walked from streets into building lobbies. The streets were watched by officers with binoculars stationed in unmarked police cars and the windows of office buildings. The police looked for any men scouting women, and they looked for the man in the sketch. It was a nervous time in this usually peaceful downtown community.

Then, on March 30, 1994, the police received assistance from an unexpected source. Michelle L. Monagas, then twenty-eight, had worked as a secretary during the day and gone to college at night. She had then gone on to law school, graduating from Cardozo Law School in 1992. In 1994 she was an assistant district attorney in the Bronx District Attorney's Office.

Her half brother, Anthony Monagas, then thirty-four, had lived his life on the other side of the law. In 1983 Anthony Monagas had been charged with and pled guilty to two rapes and one attempted rape in Florida's Dade County.

In Florida, Monagas had been sentenced to a term of twenty-two years to life in prison. But he had been released by the Florida authorities after serving ten years of his sentence. His release came in July 1993, five months before the Stuyvesant Town rapes started. In that time, Monagas had made his way to New York City. He was working as a handyman and going to school at night to learn the upholstery trade. He had a girlfriend on East Fourteenth Street.

The Bronx prosecutor, Michelle Monagas, did not know that her half brother's South Florida rapes had striking similarities to those in Stuyvesant Town. In both Florida rapes, Monagas had forced the women to have oral sex with him and then ordered them to lie on their stomachs so that he could penetrate them vaginally from the rear. And in one of the rapes, Monagas had ordered the woman to "put a lot of feeling into it, act like you like it."

But the Bronx prosecutor did know that her brother had suddenly left New York City in suspicious circumstances. In mid-March, she had a telephone conversation with her sister Lorraine, who lived in South Florida. Her sister told Michelle Monagas that their brother Anthony had seen a sketch that looked like him, panicked, and fled New York. He was now staying with Lorraine in Leisure City, Florida.

Upon hearing this news, the prosecutor discussed the situation with her boyfriend, a New York City police officer stationed at the East 169th Street station house in the Bronx. She then looked through wanted posters at the Central Booking Office in the Bronx.

There, among the posters, she saw what looked like a drawing of her brother, wanted for the Stuyvesant Town rapes. The decision to turn her brother in was extremely upsetting to the Bronx prosecutor. "She was terribly upset about how it was going to affect her, about how it was going to affect her family," said a colleague.

On March 30, 1994, Michelle Monagas met with a police lieutenant, two sergeants, and a detective. She described all the circumstances to them, including where she knew her brother to be.

That same day, the police showed the victim of the latest rape a group of photographs that included one of Anthony Monagas. The victim identified Monagas as the man who raped her. The next day, New York City police detectives flew to Florida to arrest the prosecutor's half brother at her sister's home.

Monagas was brought back to New York. On the trip he told the detective who arrested him that women get raped because of the way they dress, that it does something to a man—although his victims had in fact all been wearing winter coats when they were accosted. Monagas also boasted that he heard the newspapers had given him a name, the Stuyvesant Town Rapist, and asked the detective if Mayor Giuliani had made any great statement about him.

Upon his return to New York, Monagas was placed in a lineup, and identified by the victim of the third rape. The victim of the first rape could not make any identification in the lineup, and the victim of the second rape said that Monagas looked like her attacker, only older.

So at first Monagas was charged with only the third rape. The District Attorney's Office sought a court order to take his blood so that DNA testing could be conducted. Monagas's attorneys fought that effort, arguing that there was no probable cause linking him to the two rapes in which he had not been identified. But the District Attorney's Office prevailed in court, and Monagas was ordered to give a blood sample for DNA analysis.

The FBI found that Monagas's DNA profile matched those on the vaginal swabs from the victims of all three Stuyvesant Town rapes. In each, the DNA profile was one that could be expected to occur randomly in one in every 50 million people in the Hispanic population.

Monagas was charged with two more rapes. Faced with overwhelming DNA evidence, he pled guilty to all three rapes and was sentenced to a prison term of twenty to forty years, with the judge recommending that he serve his maximum sentence.

IT IS NOT HARD TO SEE THAT ANTHONY MONAGAS could have been promptly identified and stopped in his tracks after the first rape if there were a functioning national DNA data bank in place. An entire community could have been spared months of terror. And, more important, two women could have been spared the horror of rape.

In 1992, New York's Governor Mario M. Cuomo had proposed legislation to establish a data bank consisting of the DNA of criminals convicted of rape and other violent crimes in that state. Under the plan, New York would have participated in a national program, run by the FBI, providing for the interstate investigation of unsolved crimes. Since Anthony Monagas had been convicted of rape in Florida, he would have been identified after the first Stuyvesant Town rape if New York and Florida were participants in such a federal program.

For three years, the state legislature blocked Cuomo's bill, mostly because of disagreements over which agency of state government would administer the DNA legislation. But after the Monagas case, there was a whole new drumbeat. The issue had been made simple for the legislators. DNA data banking could stop serial rapists before they raped again, and to delay any further was to allow women to be raped in situations where they need not have had to endure such an outrage.

Cuomo's commissioner of criminal justice, Richard Girgenti, did not mince any words. "I believe that some of the Stuyvesant Town rapes could have been prevented," he said. "That's the price tag for not passing this legislation. There were victims who did not have to suffer. There was a community terrorized that did not have to be. It did not have to happen this way." Others also criticized the legislature. "To sit and wait while people are being harmed is very problematic," said one Manhattan prosecutor.

After the Monagas case, the failure to pass a DNA data-banking law meant the responsibility for future rapes would be shared by the state legislators. The lawmakers would perhaps never experience the fear and trembling of a rape victim, or of a community plagued by a serial rapist. But, if they did not act, they might face the prospect that the public would hold them responsible, not for every new rape that occurred, but for having failed to take steps that could have prevented at least some of them. This was not a responsibility that most politicians wanted to assume.

Besides, in 1994 New York's top court ruled that DNA evidence was reliable and should be accepted in court. Lawmakers resistant to DNA data banking could no longer hide behind the argument that they were awaiting the view of the state's appellate courts on the reliability of DNA.

So, after failing to pass a data banking law in 1992 and in 1993, the New York State legislature finally passed a DNA data banking law in 1994.

BY THE BEGINNING OF 1996, FORTY-ONE STATES had passed laws requiring that sex offenders and other designated convicts provide blood samples so that their DNA profiles can be kept on file to investigate future sex crimes. And a second generation of DNA technology gathering new strength and power offered the promise within the next several years of developing DNA data banks with far less cost and labor, bringing much closer to fruition the idea of a functioning and fully funded national data bank that would investigate all unsolved crimes.

8 SUDDEN INSIGHT: THE WORLD TRADE CENTER BOMBING AND BEYOND

T IME AND AGAIN, prosecutors and detectives were stymied by the most notable limitation of the power of the new DNA technology. In many crimes, some DNA was found, but the amount of evidence recovered—blood, semen, hair, or saliva—was not large enough to run a successful DNA test. In some cases, the evidence was simply too small to begin with. In others, the DNA broke into pieces too small to test successfully, degraded by bacteria that grow in heat or moisture. The bacteria had not altered the DNA profile it ate, but had made it indeterminable.

This barrier to learning the truth was squarely addressed by a breakthrough to a second generation of DNA technology, whose origins lay in a Friday night ride in California.

*   *   *

As Kary Mullis drove to his country home, his thoughts alternated between a problem that was troubling him at work and the new ponds he was digging on his country property. Suddenly, Mullis had an epiphany. He pulled over to the side of the road and tried to tell his dozing passenger, Jennifer, that he had discovered something fantastic. But Jennifer continued to doze, refusing to be disturbed.

That night, at his Mendocino country home, Mullis could not sleep, imagining a brilliant future for himself. And he was proven to be correct in his joyous optimism. His flash of insight would win him the 1993 Nobel Prize for Chemistry.

The problem he had solved involved one of the most frustrating barriers to using DNA, the fact that frequently there was too little DNA to work with. His insight had the classic attributes of creative solutions—simplicity and elegance. Mullis's idea: Find the particular part of the DNA you want to work with and copy it, again and again, until you have literally copied it a million times, and then run your tests on the copies.

The process Mullis used to accomplish this feat came to be called PCR, and it bears these initials because a substance called a *polymerase* causes the *chain reaction* that reproduces the DNA.

When Mullis had his idea, the tools to implement such molecular copying had been available for about fifteen years but had gone unrecognized. His brilliance lay in seeing an application of old findings to new problems. This is the way great science has always been done.

Mullis reports that the lack of great complexity in his solution to a problem so many people were wrestling with has led other scientists, some admiring, some jealous, to put one question to him again and again: "Why didn't I think of this before you did?"

"Nobody really knows why; surely I don't," wrote Mullis in an article recounting his discovery. "I just ran into it one night."

When Mullis invented PCR, he had no thoughts of crime or criminals. The problem he was focused on during his car ride related to the genetics of sickle cell anemia.

Mullis eventually left the genetics company for which he worked when he discovered PCR, an entity named Cetus Corporation. There was considerable bitterness between Mullis and Cetus over the issue of credit for the invention of PCR. Cetus owned legal rights to the technique, although the patent was listed under Mullis's name.

Over time, the PCR technique was applied in a number of fields. Most dramatic is its use in medicine, where the applications are many and varied.

Genetic diseases are detected in fetuses by the analysis of small amounts of tissue multiplied through PCR. Doctors following the course of leukemia in a patient use the new technique; they extract cells from the patient, copy the relevant DNA through PCR, analyze the nature and extent of the genetic mutations caused by the disease, and prescribe a course of treatment. The technique is also used for matching the tissue of organ donors and recipients. Bodily tissue is extracted, copied through PCR, and then matched, so that transplanted organs will be less likely to be rejected.

Esoteric uses for PCR, uses less crucial to human well-being, have developed outside the medical field. In one notable study, scientists extracted tissue from a 40,000-year-old woolly mammoth, frozen in ice until 1978. They then used PCR to copy the woolly mammoth's DNA, which had degraded—broken down into small pieces—and compared it with the DNA of the modern elephant. Not surprisingly, the two have very similar DNA.

None of these applications of PCR specifically related to the identification of individuals. The transition of this new technique to the realm of criminal identification was led by Dr. Henry Erlich, a leading scientist at Cetus, the company where Mullis had worked when he invented the new technique.

Erlich and the Cetus laboratory focused on the study of individual variation at a particular area on the sixth chromosome. This was the same genetic area studied in the medical field for purposes of tissue matching in transplanting hearts and other organs.

But Erlich and his company did not actually perform the first testing in criminal cases. Instead, Cetus licensed the patent for such use in criminal identification to a California scientist, Dr. Edward Blake.

Most of the early cases using the new technique involved work done by Blake and his laboratory, Forensic Science Associates. Blake was frequently hired by prosecutors and defense attorneys to perform PCR analysis in cases where the more classic form of DNA analysis could not be used.

The new technology had some definite advantages over the more classic form of DNA analysis, RFLP testing. Most of all there was its ability to get results where the other technology could not, from small samples, say a speck of blood or semen. While the new method was very sensitive, like RFLP, it still only picked up the DNA of humans and a few nonprimate species; there needed to be no concern that the laboratory would analyze a spot of ketchup or cold cream and believe it to be blood or semen.

There were other advantages as well. The new technique was also quicker; it could be performed in days, while the more classic one takes several months. And, unlike the classic technique, it does not require the use of radioactive materials.

But the new method was much slower to make its way to court than the more classic form of DNA analysis, for several reasons. Initially, there was much less impetus to use the new method on the part of police and prosecutors. Before recent refinements, PCR was not an especially definitive technology for implicating the guilty. Where today a PCR match can establish a DNA profile that might occur in one in millions of people, at its inception a PCR match was much less significant.

Besides, at the beginning, PCR was a one-man show. Where several laboratories were performing RFLP analysis, at first only Dr. Blake was using the new technique in the criminal context. While proponents of PCR could point to the many medical laboratories where PCR was used, the use in medicine was somewhat different, and the presence of only one laboratory in the field working on criminal matters raised some eyebrows about the new technology. There were also some red flags raised initially about accuracy. A court case in California suggested that there could be flaws in the new technique.

But the most important reason that PCR moved into court slowly was the care and time the FBI took before endorsing the new technology. The FBI, which had become the dominant force in DNA testing, had fully supported the more classic DNA technology from a very early stage of its development. But the Bureau's scientists were slow to support PCR, insisting on conducting the same rigorous experiments and tests they had performed using RFLP.

After performing numerous studies, the FBI began to do PCR analysis on its own cases. To help ensure reliable PCR testing, a group of independent scientists working in association with the FBI issued standards. And the questions previously raised by the California court about the reliability of PCR receded as scientific techniques improved.

Soon a dramatic case involving this second generation of DNA technology brought this new form of testing to the forefront. The crime was one of the most heinous in American history, portending new threats to the nation itself, and it commanded attention in legal and political circles across the country.

ON FEBRUARY 26, 1993, A BOMB WENT OFF in the underground parking garage at the World Trade Center in New York City. It was the first major act of international terrorism carried out on American soil.

The explosion tore a 200-foot hole through four floors of the World Trade Center. Six people were killed, and over a thousand injured. Hours after the explosion, ten people were found trapped in an elevator, unconscious and near death. Thousands of office workers walked down endless stairways in darkness and smoke.

Then, on March 1, 1993, an anonymous letter arrived at *The New York Times* claiming responsibility for the trade center blast. This action, said the letter, was taken in response to American political, economic, and military support for Israel. An end was demanded to U.S. diplomatic relations with and aid to Israel, and future missions were threatened against military and civilian targets in and out of the United States, including nuclear targets.

In the weeks following the bombing, the two key figures arrested were Mohammed Salameh and Nidal Ayyad. Outwardly, the two could not have been more different. Salameh was an unemployed sometime construction worker. Ayyad, by contrast, was a chemical engineer for Allied Signal Corporation. He was a Rutgers University graduate who lived with his pregnant wife in suburban Maplewood, New Jersey. Both men, however, had roots in Israel's West Bank. The families of both had left the West Bank of the Jordan River at the time of the 1967 Six-Day War between Israel and its then Arab enemies.

Salameh's family had moved to Jordan, Ayyad's to Kuwait. Ayyad, a naturalized American citizen born in Kuwait, had come to the United States eight years before the blast. The two men had met in 1992 at a mosque in Passaic, New Jersey, and had become close friends.

It was Salameh, a devotee of the blind Muslim cleric Sheik Omar Abdel Rahman, who rented a yellow Ford Econoline van at a Ryder Truck Rental in New Jersey and drove that van, containing a 1,200- to 1,500-pound bomb produced from chemicals and fertilizers widely available from chemical supply houses and gardening centers, into the trade center's underground parking garage. Salameh left the van parked in the garage, rigged to a timing device, set to explode.

On February 26, when the bomb went off, Salameh must have believed that the van was in a thousand pieces. It was, after all, at the very center of the explosion. It seemed certain that the van, along with all evidence that it had ever existed, was gone.

Salameh had a flight scheduled to depart for Germany on March 5. If only he did not call attention to himself, it did not seem possible that investigators would make their way to him in just one week. Yet he went back to the rental agency and reported the van stolen.

Conjecture as to why Salameh did this narrows to two possibilities. The first was that he had made a $400 deposit on the van and did not want to leave the country without it. Yet it must have seemed risky indeed, considering the crime he had just committed, to demand the return of $400. His future freedom would surely have been worth the sacrifice of his deposit. The other explanation is that Salameh felt it necessary that he behave in a totally reasonable and innocent way until his flight, in a way that would not bring suspicion on him. An innocent man whose rented van had been stolen would most certainly have returned to the agency and gotten his deposit back.

For whichever reason, he went back to the Ryder Truck rental agency in New Jersey on March 4 and sought the return of his deposit. It was there that a surprised Salameh was arrested.

How had the authorities made their way to Salameh? Using a simple principle of explosives, that damage lessens in all directions as distance from the center of the explosion increases, investigators had quickly located the center of the explosion and marked that as the place where the bomb had been.

Radiating from the center of that explosion were pieces of a yellow van. In fact, of the many vehicles damaged in the parking garage, the van was the only one whose pieces were distributed outward in a circle of 360 degrees. This told investigators that this was the vehicle that had housed the bomb.

But how could these scraps of metal lead to the Ryder agency? Contrary to Salameh's likely expectations, many pieces of the van remained. Among these were the driver's side door, the front compartment, the front bumper, two wheels, and the left front frame. It was the left front frame that led to Salameh, for it bore the indelible vehicle identification number carried by every vehicle in the United States. License plates may be switched or altered, but the vehicle identification number is specifically designed and located to resist tampering. Using this number, the police can trace the ownership of any car in the country.

In this case, the number led the authorities to the Ryder dealer and to the person who had rented that particular vehicle. Salameh was already being followed by investigators when he walked into the dealership to get back his deposit. A federal agent posing as a Ryder employee made the refund. Salameh was then followed by other agents to a Jersey City bus stop, where he was arrested.

The case against Salameh quickly mounted. The telephone number listed on the truck rental agreement led investigators to his Jersey City home, and a search of that apartment revealed it to be a bomb factory. The walls and ceilings were splattered and corroded with identifiable bomb-making chemicals—urea nitrate and nitroglycerin—from the boiling caldron used to cook the bomb. Surgical masks, used to protect the bomb makers from the noxious and dangerous chemicals that produced the bomb, were also found in the apartment.

In addition, the investigators found hundreds of pounds of bomb-making chemicals in a Jersey City storage shed rented to Salameh. Hydrogen tanks, which increase the intensity of an explosion, had been delivered to the shed, and witnesses said that Salameh had picked them up the night before the bombing, in the Ryder truck.

Six days after Salameh's arrest, his friend Ayyad was also arrested. While the evidence against Salameh was bold and dramatic—he was the man who had rented the truck, the apartment, and the storage shed for the bomb-making chemicals—the evidence gathered against Ayyad had to be put together from a number of small, less direct clues.

What were those elements that constituted the case against Ayyad? Ayyad shared a joint bank account with Salameh. Telephone records showed that, in the two months before the bombing, he made eighty-four calls to the bomb factory in Salameh's apartment. He personally placed orders for chemicals and hydrogen tanks to be delivered to the storage shed. A search of his home recovered a timing device suitable for use in a bomb. And the piece of evidence that completed Ayyad's identification as a conspirator was the PCR analysis of the saliva on the envelope flap delivered to the *New York Times*. The DNA in the saliva of the person who licked the envelope was consistent with Ayyad's. The statistical significance of this DNA match, as with most matches in the early PCR cases, was extremely limited. One in fifty people could be expected to have these DNA characteristics.

Still, when combined with the other evidence against him, this was powerful evidence against Ayyad. It made sense that this most Westernized member of the conspiracy would be its spokesperson, the man selected to convey its demands to the Western media. The saliva evidence was, in the words of the prosecutor, Gil Childers, a significant part of the "whole picture." In that context, this additional evidence had a power beyond that carried by the numbers. It was the power of logic, and it is the logic and believability of a case that lead juries to convict, as they did Nidal Ayyad. In the trade center case, PCR evidence had been convincing in the context of other evidence against a criminal defendant.

Quickly, the new technique became much more powerful, as scientific breakthroughs dramatically increased the numerical significance of a PCR match. New tests were developed allowing the analysis of other genetic locations on additional chromosomes. The initial PCR test, known as the DQ alpha test, was first marketed commercially in 1990. It was followed over the next several years by a series of additional tests, each of which relied on copying different genetic material through PCR and then analyzing it. These were known as the D1S80 test, the polymarker test, and the STR test. Depending on the amount of bodily material recovered from a crime scene, more than one of these tests may be used on a sample. When the DQ alpha test, the D1S80 test, and the polymarker test are all used on a single sample, a DNA match may reflect a set of genetic characteristics that would be found randomly in one of millions of people. The STR test alone has a power comparable in many cases to that of RFLP technology.

No longer was a PCR match simply a matter of one in fifty or one in a hundred people having those particular genetic characteristics. Now, a PCR match could have a power in the millions, even when based on the most minute of samples. This breakthrough to a more powerful PCR technology was almost as important as the initial development of PCR; it provided PCR with tremendous definitive power.

It was this newfound power of PCR that resolved the question of whether a European celebrity, an ex-convict turned prizewinning author, was a notorious serial killer, with victims in Prague, Vienna, and Los Angeles.

JACK UNTEWEGER LIKED TO TRAVEL, and wherever Jack Unteweger traveled, women died.

This could, of course, have been coincidence. There certainly were those who desperately hoped that the correspondence between Unteweger's travel and a series of murders by a distinctive serial killer was mere coincidence. Among these were the Viennese intellectuals who in 1990 had championed Unteweger's early release from a prison term he was serving for a 1976 murder conviction.

In December 1974, when he was twenty-four years old, Unteweger had kidnapped and murdered eighteen-year-old Margret Schafer, strangling her with her own bra. In 1976, he was convicted of Schafer's murder and sentenced to life imprisonment. The murder had not been Unteweger's first crime. Since 1966, he had been convicted of fifteen crimes, including attempted rape.

While he was in jail, Unteweger learned to read and write. His writings, frequently autobiographical, were filled with fury, and they drew both critical acclaim and popular success. After Unteweger's novel *Purgatory* became a best-seller and was made into a movie, prominent Viennese writers, as well as the literary organization PEN, championed his early release from prison.

"Unteweger represented the great hope of intellectuals that, through the verbalization of problems, you could somehow come to grips with them," said Peter Huemer, an Austrian writer. "We wanted to believe him very badly."

The consensus that Unteweger had been reformed and redeemed went beyond Vienna's literati. It was supported by a psychiatrist who examined him, and even by the warden of his prison. On Unteweger's release date, May 23, 1990, the warden concluded: "We will never find a prisoner so well prepared for freedom."

When he was young, Unteweger had been a criminal and a killer. Now he was thirty-nine years old and, people believed, a changed man. After his release, Unteweger became the toast of Vienna. He appeared at readings of his literary works and on television talk shows. He was charming, witty, polished. His double-breasted suits were stylish, his grooming immaculate.

It was about four months later that the killings started, two weeks after Unteweger's fortieth birthday.

Blanka Bockova, a prostitute, was last seen alive at Wenzelplace in Prague on midnight, September 14, 1990. The next day, her body was found partially submerged in a water-filled trench outside the city limits. She was naked except for a pair of socks. She had been strangled with some form of cloth, but the cloth itself was not found. On the day she was strangled, Unteweger was in Prague, working on an article on the city's prostitutes.

In the next six months, seven prostitutes were murdered in Austria. The victims were Brunhilde Masser, age thirty-nine; Heidemarie Hammerer, thirty-one; Elfriedee Schrempf, thirty-five; Silvia Zagler, twenty-three; Sabine Moitzi, twenty-five; Regina Prem, thirty-two; and Karin Eroglu, twenty-five. The bodies of the seven women were all found in wooded areas. They had been reported missing between 16 and 353 days prior to the discoveries of their bodies. Five women were killed by strangulation using a piece of their own clothing. Some had been strangled with their bras. In two cases, the bodies were decomposed too badly to determine the cause of the women's deaths.

The killer had been remarkably careful. There were no eyewitnesses to any of the murders, no fingerprints, no trail of blood.

In May 1991, a retired homicide detective reminded the Austrian police that, seventeen years before, Jack Unteweger had strangled Margret Schafer with her own bra. But there was nothing more specific to tie Unteweger to these killings.

On June 10, 1991, Unteweger flew to Los Angeles. Upon his arrival, he contacted the Los Angeles Police Department. Unteweger told the LAPD that he was in their city to write newspaper articles about prostitution and wanted to see where the prostitutes worked. The accommodating Los Angeles Police Department promptly arranged a tour for Unteweger of the spots in the city where prostitution flourished. Then, prostitutes began to die in Los Angeles.

During Unteweger's seven-week visit to L.A., three prostitutes were murdered. They were Shannon Exley, age thirty-five, Irene Rodriguez, thirty-three; and Peggy Jean Booth, twenty-six. Each was strangled to death with her own bra. Unteweger returned to Vienna on July 16, 1991, and the Los Angeles killings stopped.

At first, the Austrian authorities knew nothing of the American or the Czech murders. They did know they had a serial murder to contend with, and they contacted Interpol for information about unsolved cases that fit the same pattern. The Czech police informed the Austrians of the Prague murder. And, in September 1991, the Austrians learned of the California murders.

Unteweger's traveling schedule, both inside and outside Austria, read like a tour of murder locales. The police could establish that Unteweger had been in Austrian cities when murders took place in those cities. In some instances, they could place Unteweger in hotels near the locations from which the murdered prostitutes worked. So, for several months, Unteweger was under observation, until he decided it was a good time to absent himself from Austria.

Unteweger left for Switzerland and then flew to Miami on February 15, 1992. He was arrested in Miami on February 27 and extradited to Austria for trial.

As the trial was set to begin, the prosecution faced two huge hurdles. For starters, there was the question of whether one person in fact committed all eleven murders.

To answer that question, the Austrian authorities turned to the Behavioral Science Unit of the FBI, the cadre whose agents analyze, interview, and help apprehend the Hannibal Lecters of the world. The Austrians sent two of their investigators, with their case files, to the FBI facility in the woods of Quantico, Virginia. There, they met with Special Agent Gregg McCrary of the Behavioral Science Unit.

After that initial meeting, McCrary spent months working on

the serial murders; eventually he went to Austria to testify at the trial. McCrary concluded that the murders were so similar that all eleven women were probably murdered by the same person.

If any one person murdered one of the women, said McCrary, then he murdered all eleven women; and if he didn't murder any one of those that fit the pattern, he didn't murder any of the others. Each murder, said McCrary, was a "signature" crime, with distinctive characteristics reflecting the criminal's peculiar psychopathology. The steps taken by the criminal were not simply a distinctive modus operandi, such as wearing a mask, undertaken to avoid being caught or to scare a victim into submission. Instead, the killer took the steps he took obsessively, because he had to in order to gratify his twisted needs. In killing the way he did, he left behind the mark of his personality. Others might commit similar crimes, but nobody other than this killer would leave this signature.

In Czechoslovakia, Austria, and the United States, said McCrary, the signature was the same, and it consisted of the aspects that united all the crimes: The victims had all been women. Each had been a street prostitute, last seen alive working at her usual location. Each had been strangled with an article of clothing. Each had been led to the scene of the crime by the perpetrator. The dead body of each had been transported from the scene of the crime naked or half naked. These aspects were so distinctive, said McCrary, that, since the three Los Angeles murders, there had been no other murders in the United States sharing all these characteristics.

But proof that one person committed all the murders was only one-half the battle. The prosecution still had to prove that Unteweger was that one person.

In preparing for trial, the prosecution had developed some additional evidence beyond Unteweger's itinerary, his focus on the sex trade, and his prior conviction of a murder by strangulation. There were threads on the clothing of Heidemarie Hammerer, one of the Austrian victims, that were consistent with clothing owned by Unteweger. And there was an eyewitness who claimed to have seen Unteweger's white Mustang, with its distinctive license plate, "W JACK 1," near Hammerer's street corner the night she disappeared. All in all, this was an emotionally compelling but hardly airtight case against Unteweger.

So the police continued to look for evidence. Their search yielded the car seats from the BMW that Unteweger had driven in 1990, at the time the Prague murder victim, Blanka Bockova, had been killed. The car itself had been scrapped, but the seat had been removed and had been sitting in a garage for eighteen months. Criminalists examined the seats and recovered several head hairs. These were sent to the Scientific Police Institute in Zurich, Switzerland, along with hair that had been removed from Bockova's scalp and stored in paper envelopes at the time of her autopsy.

At the time, Unteweger's lawyer, Hans-Juergen Lehofer, told his client, "If they can conduct the DNA test, then the Devil's going to catch you."

The Zurich laboratory was able to extract DNA from only one of the car seat hairs submitted, but that hair had enough DNA to run several PCR tests. The tests, conducted by Dr. Manfred Hochmeister, included the new PCR tests that simultaneously copy several genetic locations, dramatically increasing the statistical significance of a PCR match. The tests showed that the DNA from the hair on Unteweger's car seat was consistent with Bockova's, and that this particular set of genetic characteristics could be expected to occur in one in every 2.1 million women.

Unteweger's trial commenced in April 1994. He was charged with all eleven murders, including those in California; under Austrian law, an Austrian citizen may be tried for murders he commits anywhere in the world. The heart of the case against Unteweger was his travel schedule, the similarities between the murders, and the PCR evidence.

Significantly, Unteweger lacked an alibi for any of the eleven murders. Still, he told the court that he was innocent: "I was a rat, a primitive criminal who grunted rather than talked, an inveterate liar. The prosecutor is right; I consumed women rather than loved them. But I'm counting on my acquittal because I'm not the culprit. Your decision will affect not only me but the real murderer, because he's laughing up his sleeve."

On June 24, 1994, DNA and the Devil found Jack Unteweger. He was convicted of nine murders. A majority is sufficient for a verdict under Austrian law, and six jurors voted for conviction, two for acquittal. Unteweger was acquitted outright in the deaths of the two victims whose remains were too decomposed to determine the cause of death.

That same night, at 9:00 P.M., Unteweger was sentenced to life imprisonment. The next morning, at 3:00 A.M., during a routine cell check, a guard saw Unteweger lying quietly on his cot. Forty minutes later, he was found dead, hanging by shoelaces he had knotted into a noose. Unteweger left no suicide note, no clue to the reasons he chose death, just as he had left virtually no physical clues to his crimes.

His suicide inspired varied reactions: "It was his best murder," said one Austrian politician. "The jury said he was guilty. And I believe it was a fair trial," said Unteweger's lawyer. "Maybe on the night he killed himself he saw his victims coming at him. But now I've said too much."

Special Agent McCrary, now retired from the FBI, told me that he was disappointed when Unteweger committed suicide. I was surprised and intrigued to find an FBI agent whose compassion extended to one so evil. It was a comment that I would have expected from a minister, not a former FBI agent. But the spell was quickly broken when I learned that McCrary's reaction was based not on compassion but on his spirit of scientific inquiry. "I wanted to talk to him," McCrary told me. In other words, he had wanted a chance to interview his Hannibal Lecter, done in by DNA, to see what more could be learned about the mind of a signature killer.

Now that chance was gone. Jack Unteweger's entire future, as well as those of other women he would likely have strangled had he been acquitted by that Austrian jury, had hung by a single hair.

THE NEW TRUTH MACHINE WAS ALSO A TIME MACHINE. It made it possible to look into the past, to reveal the truth about events that took place years ago.

On Friday, June 22, 1984, a nineteen-year-old Newport News woman and her twenty-two-year-old boyfriend had driven to Virginia's Blue Ridge Parkway for a camping trip. But they could not find their campground. Lost in rural Virginia, they pulled into a scenic overlook and fell asleep in their car.

The knock on their car window came at 3:00 A.M. as they were sleeping. A large, heavy man wearing camouflage fatigues shined a flashlight into their car and said that he was a police officer. The couple stepped out of the car, pleased at their rescue. The man asked for the car keys, and the woman gave them to him.

But suddenly, the man pulled a gun. He ordered the boyfriend to run into the brush or be shot. The boyfriend ran, stopped, and looked back; the man shined a flashlight in his face and told him to keep running.

The man held his gun to the woman's back and forced her into his truck. He then drove her several miles, parking the truck beside a deserted cabin. He told her to do everything he told her, and do it well.

Over four hours, the man, who wore a silver cross, repeatedly raped and sodomized the woman. Between sexual episodes, he smoked marijuana, drank whiskey, and rambled "completely off the wall" about his experiences as a soldier in Vietnam, particularly about a "Lieutenant Kolacky."

Despite telling her that he would have to kill her because she could identify him, the rapist did not kill the woman. Instead, he drove her away from the cabin and gave her directions back to her car, which she followed. After she found it, her boyfriend also returned to the car, with a local deputy.

The woman was taken to a local hospital. A vaginal swab was taken. The woman and her boyfriend were interviewed by the police, and police sketches were prepared based on their descriptions of the rapist.

Months went by, and nothing happened. But then the police got their "lucky" break. In nearby Roanoke County, an elderly woman, the victim of an assault, told the police that her assailant looked like a man who used to live nearby, Edward Honaker. Honaker maintained that he had nothing to do with the assault and passed a lie detector test. No charges were filed against him. But during the investigation of that crime the police had taken a Polaroid photograph of Honaker.

When a Roanoke County police officer saw the sketches from the earlier Blue Ridge rape, he thought of Honaker. The Roanoke County police sent the Polaroid to the Nelson County police, who were investigating the rape. They showed it to the victim as one of six photographs and asked her if she recognized anyone. The nineteen-year-old woman promptly identified Honaker as the man who had raped her.

Honaker was arrested on October 25, 1984, four months after the rape. The police arrested him at Roanoke Memorial Hospital, where he was being treated for depression following the breakup of his marriage to the mother of his three children.

Honaker, then thirty-four years old, was no Boy Scout. The large, beefy, blue-collar Virginian had a history of encounters with the law that included several bar fights and quarrels with his wife. During high school, Honaker had spent five months in reform school for stealing cash from local stores. As a young man, he was dishonorably discharged after deserting from his Kentucky army base. And, in 1984, Honaker was arrested for and convicted of burglary. His criminal record did not suggest rape, but nothing about his past precluded it. Given his identification by the victim, he seemed a reasonable suspect. It would be up to a jury to decide whether he was in fact the rapist.

The trial took place in Lovingston, Virginia, a small town near Charlottesville. The heart of the prosecution's case was the testimony of the nineteen-year-old woman and her boyfriend.

"This man is in my head all the time," said the woman. "I know that's him."

Is there any doubt in your mind, asked the prosecutor, that Honaker is the man?

"No, sir, no," she answered. "This is the man right here. There is no doubt."

The boyfriend was just as certain.

"There is no mistake in identity and there is no reservation," he testified. "This is the man."

Besides the eyewitness identifications, which would alone have supported a conviction, there was testimony by an expert from the state crime laboratory. The expert had examined a hair found on the woman's shorts and compared it with Honaker's hair. "It is unlikely that that hair would match anyone other than the defendant, but it is possible," he testified.

Finally, the woman had been abducted and assaulted in a Chevy Blazer, the same type of truck owned and driven by Honaker. And Honaker's personal possessions, seized by the police, included camouflage fatigues and a silver cross.

Honaker's defense could offer no evidence powerful enough to overcome this testimony. He testified to his innocence and offered an alibi supported by his family and friends, claiming that he was sleeping at his mother's house eighty miles away. But the alibi was unpersuasive. To the jury, it seemed that Honaker was lying, and that his family and friends were inventing facts to support him.

True, there were some loose ends, some inconsistencies.

Honaker had a vasectomy in 1977, but the vaginal swab recovered intact sperm, inconsistent with Honaker's aspermic state. The victim had last had sex with her fiancé Tuesday or Wednesday; it was unclear whether this could still be the fiancé's sperm, several days later. The rapist spoke obsessively about Vietnam; Honaker had never been there. Both the victim and her fiancé were sure that the rapist held the gun in his left hand, and Honaker was right-handed.

But, given the strength of the government's case, the jury decided to overlook these inconsistencies. The defense counsel was an extremely able attorney, and worked hard on the case, but it took the jury only two hours to convict Honaker.

The prosecution recommended that the maximum sentence be imposed, and Honaker was given three life sentences plus thirty-four years.

Years went by. During this time people married and divorced, including the Newport News rape victim and her boyfriend. In Honaker's words, "The days just kept piling up and piling up." And, all along, Honaker maintained his innocence of this crime. Such assertions of innocence often impress newspaper writers and political activists. But such protestations, by themselves, are of little value. It is rare to meet a man in prison who acknowledges his guilt.

Honaker protested his innocence to Centurion Ministries, a Princeton, New Jersey–based organization dedicated to reviewing claims of innocence made by convicted felons and identifying and pursuing those that may have merit. They investigated his case and were troubled by the loose ends.

There was no question that the state hair expert had overstated the distinctiveness of the hair recovered from the victim's shorts in his trial testimony. There was the lingering question of Honaker's vasectomy, which the state had overcome at trial by suggesting that the vasectomy might have failed. And the review of the case file by Centurion Ministries revealed yet another potential issue: The victim had undergone hypnosis to help her recall events pertaining to the case, but the trial transcript contained no mention of hypnosis.

Centurion Ministries agreed to pay for a DNA test. The new local prosecutor, Nelson County Commonwealth Attorney Philip Payne, agreed to the test. "My expectations were that [Honaker] would be further nailed down as the culprit," Payne said later.

The only semen left was one-half of a vaginal swab; the other half had been consumed in conventional, serological testing. This was not enough DNA for the classic RFLP test, so a PCR test was run by Dr. Edward Blake of Forensic Science Associates.

The test showed that neither Honaker nor the victim's boyfriend was the source of the semen from the vaginal swab taken from the victim after the rape. The state crime laboratory then ran the same tests previously performed by Dr. Blake, and they confirmed the findings of the defense expert and ruled out Honaker. A hair expert retained by the defense also questioned the conclusion of the state's hair expert at Honaker's trial that the hair recovered from the victim's shorts matched Honaker's hair.

Honaker's attorney, New York lawyer Barry Scheck, submitted a clemency petition to Virginia Governor George F. Allen. Scheck had come to Honaker's case as co-director, with Peter Neufeld, of the Innocence Project, a program based at Yeshiva University's Cardozo School of Law that uses DNA results many years after the fact to clear convicts wrongly convicted of crimes.

The Innocence Project is a noble endeavor. Eight of the fifteen to twenty convicts who have been cleared through post-trial testing owe their freedom to it. Many cases challenging old convictions have employed PCR analysis, since it is ideally suited for use on DNA samples from old cases where little DNA may be left either because time has caused the DNA that was present to break down or because much of the evidence has already been used up in traditional serological testing.

On June 22, 1994, prosecutor Payne announced that he would join in the request for clemency to Governor Allen. "What was very critical to me," said Payne, "was that in Virginia we are willing to execute [people] where DNA plays a very, very large role in the prosecution. We ought to be able to consider exoneration on the same grounds."

The director of Virginia's Division of Forensic Science, Paul Ferrara, also supported clemency. "No matter how hard we try, there's going to be a situation where a person is wrongfully convicted," he told the Washington Post. "You know, they make great movies about people that get framed either purposefully or just happen to be in the wrong place at the wrong time. The system isn't perfect."

But before Governor Allen would grant clemency, he sent the state police to talk to the victim, who had maintained that her fiancé was the only person with whom she had had consensual sex. The governor wanted to make sure that the victim had not had consensual sexual relations with any other man besides her fiancé near the time of the rape. If she had, then that man, rather than Honaker or her fiancé, might have been the source of the semen that was tested, and Honaker might still be a guilty man. Governor Allen wanted to have the gravity of the matter communicated to the victim by the state police who would interview her.

The rape victim told the state police that there *had* been a second man in her life at the same time that she was seeing her boyfriend. She did not, however, specifically say that she had had sex with the second man in the days preceding the rape, and she had been dating her boyfriend for years.

The Virginia State crime laboratory took a blood sample from the second man and determined his DNA profile. All of a sudden, the complexion of the case changed. Honaker was no longer entirely in the clear. The results showed that the DNA from the vaginal swab could have been a combination of Honaker's and that of the second man. Honaker might be the rapist, but he might not.

At this point, the results from the PCR test were inconclusive. If they remained inconclusive, Honaker might not get clemency, and would remain in prison. But the matter did not end there.

The first test performed by the scientists was the PCR test used in all the early cases employing this technique. It was the same test used in the World Trade Center case, a test known as the DQ alpha test, that focuses on the sixth chromosome.

The prosecution and the defense agreed that each side's experts would test the semen from the vaginal swab using one of the new, more definitive forms of PCR analysis. Each then tested the semen from the vaginal swab using the polymarker test, which allows the simultaneous copying and analysis of several genetic locations instead of simply one genetic location, and so provides more definitive results. When that testing was done, it cleared Edward Honaker.

The DNA in the semen on the vaginal swab was not that of Honaker, the fiancé, or the second man. It was apparently that of an unidentified rapist. Unfortunately, this man was never identified nor apprehended.

On October 21, 1994, Governor George F. Allen signed a pardon, citing the DNA tests and concluding that Honaker could not have been the rapist. That afternoon, Honaker was released from Nottaway Prison after ten years of imprisonment.

Honaker's release was entirely due to the availability of DNA testing and the confidence in the technique shared by those with the power to bring about his release. As prosecutor Philip Payne said: "Absent the development of DNA testing, it would probably be the same conclusion were the case tried today."

Two breakthroughs—the development of PCR, and the development of new, more powerful techniques of PCR analysis— freed Edward Honaker, an innocent man, from prison. And, but for the new power of PCR, Jack Unteweger, a talented, charming, and compulsively violent man, would likely still be at large, preying on unsuspecting females.

The development of more powerful forms of PCR analysis also has enormous implications for the use of DNA data banking to solve unsolved crimes. The new tests may be used to find previously identified criminals through DNA data banks, such as the rapist for whom Edward Honaker took the fall. Even more important, the particular PCR test known as the STR technique is uniquely adaptable to high-volume analysis of DNA samples and could help make routine processing of tests on all unsolved crimes the norm within the next few years.

But, data banking aside, the power of DNA to free the innocent and to protect society from the violently dangerous now extended to evidence that was small, old, and broken down, to evidence that, only a short time before, would have been effectively useless. It has been a triumph of technology, in which humankind has reached into the smallest, most degraded material to learn answers that make the difference between exoneration and conviction, freedom and imprisonment, justice and injustice. The new techniques would figure dramatically in what has been called the "trial of the century," that of O. J. Simpson, the former football player and later actor and television personality, for the murders of his former wife, Nicole Brown, and her friend Ronald Goldman.

9 O. J. SIMPSON: WHAT THE BLOOD REALLY SHOWED

THE MOST FORMIDABLE challenge facing O. J. Simpson's defense lawyers at his double murder trial was the trail of blood evidence implicating the former football star in the murders of his former wife, Nicole Brown, and Ronald Goldman. Even before DNA testing became available, any person in such a spot would have been hard-pressed to explain the presence of blood in his car and at his home immediately following the crime. DNA technology took Simpson's problem to a new level; it was now possible to establish to a scientific certainty that the blood was that of the victims.

When the results of the DNA testing were reported, the defense team had to face the worst. Blood with DNA that matched Simpson's was found at Nicole Brown's home. Blood spots in Simpson's car contained DNA matching Brown's, Ronald Goldman's, and Simpson's. Blood at Simpson's home contained DNA that matched Nicole Brown's and Ronald Goldman's.

To those familiar with the capabilities of this new technology, the case against Simpson seemed airtight, and to many observers the matter ended right there. DNA had sealed Simpson's fate; his guilt had been proven conclusively. He would be sent to prison for the rest of his life.

While the defense lawyers were not expected to throw up their hands in surrender, the sheer quantity of DNA evidence against Simpson made less promising the most frequent avenue of attack on DNA evidence—an assault on the mathematical calculations that had established the meaning of the DNA matches. There were so many bloodstains, in so many places, all identified as having come from Simpson or the victims, and astronomical numbers. What difference would challenging the calculations make when so many of the numbers were so high? Even a successful attempt to knock them down a notch would likely have left them high enough to persuade any reasonable juror that coincidence could not have accounted for the matches. And even if the numbers quoted for certain of the blood drops could have been very much reduced, how about those for all the other drops?

Yet O. J. Simpson's trial lawyers did win his acquittal. How did they do so? What were the specifics of the DNA evidence against Simpson, how did his defense attorneys contest that powerful evidence, and how genuine were the issues they raised in doing so?

The answers to these questions begin with the broad themes used by the defense to explain away the DNA results. The best criminal defense attorneys are often distinguished from the lesser lights by their focus on broad themes and their ability to marshal facts to support those themes. A less qualified lawyer will simply quibble with the prosecution's case, nitpicking every small inconsistency or contradiction, reminding the jury at every opportunity that the burden of proof is on the prosecution, that the defense has to prove nothing; when the case is done, the lawyer takes his bows for a good try, and the client is led off to jail.

But the best defense lawyers, from the celebrated to the obscure, know that no matter what the law says about who bears the burden of proof, they must pose a theory or theories that the jury will see as supporting the client's innocence and then develop facts that support this theory. Through cross-examination of the prosecution's witnesses and by calling their own witnesses, they lay the groundwork for a final summation that will package this evidence in such a way that the jury will find the exculpatory scenario if not as plausible as the prosecution's at least reasonably plausible.

This is not to say that the burdens on each side are the same, for they are not. Though both sides must develop facts throughout the trial that can finally be brought together to support their own version of what likely occurred, all the defense needs for a win is a tie. The prosecution must convince the jury their scenario is the *only* reasonable one; the defense must prove that their scenario, one that leaves the defendant innocent, is also a reasonable scenario. If it is plausible, by definition it subjects the prosecution's scenario to reasonable doubt, leading to a jury responsibility to acquit. Still, creating such an alternative scenario is much harder to do than it is to say, for there must be facts to support it, not mere conjecture, and the majority of criminal trials end in convictions.

Criminal lawyers, both prosecutors and defense attorneys, frequently note the relatively limited universe of standard defenses available in criminal trials. Most trials, criminal or civil, indeed most disputes, are about, among other things, the credibility of the accuser and the witnesses, as well as the alleged actions of the accused, and so revolve about the honesty of the victim and the accuracy of the witnesses' perception and recall. In certain cases, though, there is no living victim, and the accuser is most often a police officer or governmental agent. This is particularly common in homicide, narcotics, gun, and organized crime cases, where the person bearing witness against the defendant is frequently a detective or police officer. Since the accusers in these cases are witnesses who work for the government, the defense may seek to put the government on trial, attacking the impartiality, competence, or even honesty of the police who gathered the evidence.

In the O. J. Simpson case, this is precisely what the defense chose to do—put the government on trial. Those in the dock were the police and criminalists who had found and gathered the evidence and the DNA laboratory that first handled it. It became a matter of trust, or lack of trust. Could the jury trust those who had gathered evidence from the crime scene, Simpson's car, and Simpson's home? Could they trust the police department's DNA laboratory? These were the twin questions animating the defense claim that everything the prosecution did—including what they claimed the DNA proved—should be looked at with a jaundiced eye. Making this approach particularly alluring for the defense team was the fact that the case was being tried before a largely minority group jury in a city where the police had a well-established reputation for abuse of minority men.

The campaign to undermine the DNA evidence began not with an assault on those who had done the testing but with Mark Fuhrman, the Los Angeles Police Department detective who claimed to have found a bloody glove on the grounds of Simpson's estate. This glove was laden with blood containing Simpson's, Nicole Brown's, and Ronald Goldman's DNA. But as conclusive as this evidence promised to be, it was soon eroded as witnesses offered evidence that undermined Fuhrman's character as well as his credibility.

Among the most important building blocks in the scenario that defense lawyers would ask the jury to accept as plausible were audiotapes of Fuhrman using a racial epithet which he swore to the jury that he had not used in the past ten years. In addition, besides his general animus to African Americans, Fuhrman arguably had a grudge specifically against Simpson; as a patrolman, he had first encountered Simpson and a sobbing Nicole Brown in 1985 when he responded to a domestic incident at Simpson's home after Simpson smashed the windshield of his wife's Mercedes-Benz with a baseball bat, an incident which Fuhrman later recalled was "indelibly pressed" in his memory.

He had bragged of stopping interracial couples for no good reason; Simpson and Nicole Brown were an interracial couple. Fuhrman had spoken of his desire to put black people in a pile and burn them. He had told would-be screenwriter Laura Hart McKinny that he was against having women on the police force because they would not engage in cover-ups. And the prosecution inadvertently helped the defense when they presented Fuhrman as a fully trustworthy witness wronged by false accusations of racism. If anyone had the motive, means, and opportunity to frame Simpson and cover it up, certainly it was this man.

Of course, a one-man conspiracy is not much of a conspiracy. The defense's candidate for co-conspirator was Detective Philip Vannatter. Vannatter's vulnerability began with the detectives' testimony about the reasons they had entered Simpson's home without a warrant. To explain why they had not waited for a warrant, the detectives focused on the risk that there was another victim. Although Fuhrman had known about the 1985 incident involving Simpson and Nicole Brown, and the detectives had seen a spot of blood on Simpson's Bronco, Vannatter denied that Simpson was a suspect at that time, and, in a bit of hyperbole, told defense attorney Robert Shapiro on cross-examination that Simpson was initially no more a suspect than Shapiro.

So here was another question the defense lawyers would ask the jurors to consider. Had Vannatter lied about the reason for the detectives' entry into Simpson's home so that the evidence seized (including the bloody glove) would not be suppressed before trial as the unconstitutional fruit of an unlawful search and seizure? And if he had lied about that, what else might he be lying about? Vannatter had serious credibility problems.

More significant, Vannatter, unlike Fuhrman, had access to the blood of both Simpson and the victims. The murders took place on the night of June 12, 1994. Vannatter was given Simpson's liquid blood sample by the nurse who drew it on June 13; he then carried it around town with him rather than logging it in, as police procedures required, saying that he knew the lead criminalist was at Simpson's home, and he wanted to get the blood to him for analysis. But Vannatter could not remember any other case where he had taken that unusual step. His testimony was almost guaranteed to raise some ugly questions.

And Vannatter had also handled Nicole Brown's and Ronald Goldman's blood. He had picked up their blood samples at the coroner's office on June 15, and delivered them to the Los Angeles Police Department's DNA lab that day.

The innuendo that Simpson's blood had been planted was immeasurably strengthened by evidence that there was a quantity of blood missing from the sample taken from Simpson. The nurse who drew Simpson's blood, Thano Peratis, testified before trial that he had drawn between 7.9 and 8.1 milliliters of blood on June 13, 1994. The DNA analyst at the LAPD, Collin Yamauchi, testified that he had used one milliliter of Simpson's blood for DNA testing on June 14. The police department's toxicology unit measured the remaining blood in the vial at 5.5 milliliters on June 21. This meant that 1.5 milliliters of blood was missing. How would the prosecution account for the missing blood, which could have been enough to account for Simpson's blood found at the crime scene?

Members of the prosecution team went to Peratis, now too ill to come to court, and made a video in which he took back his earlier sworn testimony. He claimed that he had been mistaken in his first estimate of the amount of blood taken and asserted that, months later, he could now provide a more accurate assessment. This was a strange story as a substantive matter, but even worse, Peratis did not deliver this new story under oath. Prosecutors took his statement at his home, without providing notice to the defense that might have given them an opportunity to object to it or at least demand the right to be present and ask questions too. With just a video to deal with in court, the defense was deprived of an opportunity to cross-examine the witness in a situation cross-examining attorneys love—in which the witness is changing former, sworn testimony. Matters were getting more and more problematic for the prosecution as facts were offered to support the defense's claim that there had been a frame and a "cover-up."

The defense attorneys included the prosecuting attorneys as after-the-fact accomplices in the plot against Simpson, referring repeatedly to a "cover-up." It is not unusual for defense attorneys to make such allegations when they place the government on trial, and while these allegations are usually mostly bark, in the Simpson case they had some bite. When a prosecutor brings a witness to the stand, he or she in essence endorses that witness. Not only had the lead prosecutor, Marcia Clark, called Fuhrman but she had coddled him during his testimony and brought out denials by him of specific allegations about his use of racial slurs. As the truth came out about Fuhrman, Clark's earlier considerate treatment of him brought her own judgment into question. A jury could well ask, fairly or unfairly: If Marcia Clark did not know or care to learn the truth about this man, how could she know or care to learn the truth about anything else? How, and why, could they rely on her?

And so, fairly or unfairly, the trust issue extended not just to the police but to the lead prosecutor. This was a potentially deadly turn of events, for it was the lead prosecutor who would have the primary responsibility for leading the jury through a complex review of the evidence at summation time. If they did not trust her, they would not likely trust her scenario.

The theme of trust also animated the defense's critique of the Los Angeles Police Department DNA laboratory, the first DNA laboratory to handle much of the evidence against Simpson. Here the issue was not venality but the laboratory's competence in using the second generation of DNA tests, the PCR technique. The claim was that the laboratory's procedures created a risk that evidence from the crime had been contaminated with Simpson's own blood sample to the point where its PCR tests and any subsequent PCR tests by other laboratories would be meaningless.

Significantly, the defense did not attack the more classic form of DNA testing, the RFLP technique, with one notable exception to be treated later. For the most part, they essentially conceded the reliability of the RFLP evidence in the Simpson case but urged that it had been planted. In other words, the RFLP techniques could prove that the blood at the scene was the former football star's, and that some of the blood in Simpson's vehicle and home belonged to the victims, but could say nothing about how any blood got anywhere. Perhaps the jury might be willing to accept even the ugliest of answers to this question.

But first, as part of an attempt to paint the prosecution's whole process of blood testing as a comedy of errors, the defense team were merciless in their critique of the PCR evidence. They sought to take the very strength of PCR analysis, its extraordinary ability to detect small quantities of DNA, and use it to impeach the technology. PCR, they argued, is exquisitely sensitive and can copy and analyze the most minute quantities of DNA. So, they argued, in the circumstances of this case, it was possible that Simpson's blood sample had gotten into the evidence being analyzed through laboratory error, and that it was just such contamination with Simpson's own blood that had produced the DNA results matching the crime scene evidence with the blood taken from the defendant's arm. The defense never contested that any of the DNA determined to be Simpson's was not his. Instead, they argued that it was introduced through planting of blood drops taken from his arm or through contamination made possible by lab personnel's incomplete understanding of the risks of such contamination.

Contamination, defined as the presence of DNA that did not originate in the crime-scene sample, is probably the most significant issue faced by PCR laboratories. There are many forms of contamination. It may take place before evidence is brought to the laboratory; this can happen if a police investigator picks up two

different pieces of evidence using the same pair of tweezers or if
two pieces of evidence, say a blanket and a shirt, are packaged
together in the same evidence bag. Or there may be contamination because two pieces of DNA are intermingled in the laboratory through sloppy handling or a failure to maintain sterile
conditions. This latter form of contamination is the kind alleged to
have taken place in the Simpson case.

There were several avenues available to the prosecution to
answer the defense's allegations of contamination. For one thing,
there was the prospect that a planting defense and a contamination defense could be made to seem mutually antagonistic. After
all, a successful planting conspiracy relies on DNA tests that will
function properly, while a contamination theory is premised on
failures in the DNA lab.

Instead of choosing between the two theories, the defense
had offered both. In many circumstances this approach would be
risky; the prosecution could claim that the defendant had to be
the unluckiest man in the world. First, he was framed, then the
planted evidence was subjected to laboratory work that was
faulty, but not so faulty that it failed to find the "right" DNA in the
dishonest evidence.

But only at its own peril could the prosecution have ridiculed
the defense in these circumstances. Besides, the two theories
were unified by an insistence on Simpson's innocence and a purportedly innocent explanation for the presence of his DNA. The
defense could claim that they did not know exactly what happened; they were not present when the crime took place or in the
LAPD laboratory at the time of the DNA testing. All they knew
was that Simpson was innocent. By claiming contamination with
Simpson's own blood sample, the defense could claim consistency in arguing a frame defense and a contamination defense,
for both allegedly explained the innocent presence of Simpson's
own DNA.

There was a second formidable hurdle involved in asserting a
contamination defense. Before the trial began, the prosecution
had taken a seemingly ingenious step to ward off any claims of
contamination.

Three years before, the report on DNA of the National
Academy of Sciences had suggested that one of the best safeguards against contamination of PCR test materials is to have

PCR typing performed in two laboratories and see if the results match. The Simpson prosecutors had done the report one better. They had DNA testing performed in three laboratories—at the Los Angeles Police Department DNA laboratory, the California Department of Justice laboratory, and Cellmark, a private laboratory. Many of the same items of evidence were tested by all three laboratories, and the DNA tests in all three implicated Simpson.

But the defense found a way to leap this hurdle too, countering the prosecution's ingenious stroke with a brilliant move of its own. They focused on the passage of most of the DNA evidence through the Los Angeles Police Department laboratory; the claim was that much of the evidence had been handled, opened, and contaminated in the LAPD lab before it was packed up and sent to the other laboratories. The results in the other labs, no matter how impressive those laboratories might be, would reflect contamination that took place in the LAPD laboratory. "You could do a hundred tests," Barry Scheck told the jury on his summation, but it would not matter, since the evidence had already been contaminated in the LAPD.

The focus on the LAPD lab was a highly effective strategy. "If you have a common source of the evidence, you have one target," Simpson defense lawyer Peter Neufeld told the *Washington Post.* "It is much more difficult to cut off tentacles. It is easier to cut off the head and kill the beast. In this case, the beast was the LAPD crime laboratory." It was especially important that the defense neutralize the impact of subsequent testing by Cellmark and the California Department of Justice laboratory, since the witnesses from those labs, Robin Cotton and Gary Sims, were both extraordinarily impressive.

To show the jury that the LAPD's DNA laboratory could not be trusted, and that it might have contaminated the PCR evidence, the defense called Dr. John Gerdes, a Denver biologist who runs a tissue typing lab. Gerdes occupies an unusual niche among scientists who testify regularly in DNA cases; he believes that PCR tests are so sensitive and vulnerable to contamination that they should not be allowed in court, either to clear defendants or to implicate them. Generally, he has no quarrel with RFLP analysis. Gerdes was one of two PCR critics on the defense witness list.

In a strange twist of fate, the second critic listed was Kary Mullis, the man who invented PCR on a California night ride. But the defense did not ultimately call him. Although Mullis had won the Nobel Prize for his discovery of PCR, he was a free spirit, perhaps too much so to be relied on in a murder trial. Mullis had told his college alumni magazine that he uses LSD from time to time because it keeps his mind "from getting really old." Contrary to virtually all informed scientific opinion, he does not believe that the HIV virus causes AIDS. He has freely talked about how much of his life since his discovery of PCR has focused on surfing and the pursuit of women. "As a father, he's more like Jim Morrison than Fred MacMurray," his son once told an interviewer. And, when the television camera focused on Mullis as he sat in court for Gerdes' testimony, Mullis made faces at the camera. Who knew what impact he might have had on a jury? Besides, the defense got most of what they needed from Gerdes.

Gerdes, in contrast to Mullis, presented an extremely solid, middle American image. He looked and spoke like the family doctor. He was blond haired and bespectacled, and gave the appearance of being exceedingly careful; he took the witness stand carrying three loose-leaf binders. He was a purist and an idealist, living on that line where idealism sometimes meets rigidity. In presenting Gerdes to the jury, the defense did not simply rely on Gerdes's somewhat unusual opinion that as a general rule PCR is too sensitive to be used to implicate or exonerate criminal suspects. Instead, they skillfully developed facts to support their claim that the PCR evidence could have been contaminated in *this* case.

Gerdes's testimony was the key to the defense's overcoming the largest hurdle that they faced in asserting their contamination theory. Since PCR is an extremely sensitive technology, laboratories practicing the technique generally take extraordinary measures to prevent contamination in the laboratory. Various controls are built into the process to detect contamination in the laboratory should it occur. In urging the jury to accept the PCR results, the prosecution's most simple and yet strongest argument was that the controls reflected the absence of substantial contamination in this case, despite the analysis of numerous samples that all pointed to Simpson's guilt.

But Gerdes's testimony allowed the defense to neutralize that very simple and powerful fact. Gerdes testified that he had performed a study of contamination in the LAPD crime lab by reviewing test materials (mostly from mock cases) analyzed from May 29, 1993, through August 25, 1994—before and during the time that testing was conducted in the Simpson case. He claimed that the controls on those tests showed a pattern of widespread contamination in the laboratory's PCR tests. Gerdes described the nature and scope of that contamination in the most sweeping terms. He said that he had studied a number of crime labs, and the contamination in the LAPD was the worst he had ever seen. It was "extremely serious." A medical laboratory with a comparable level of contamination would have been shut down. The laboratory should have detected contamination and taken remedial measures to eradicate it. But, said Gerdes, it had not done so.

And Gerdes criticized more than a pattern of contamination in other cases. He squarely challenged the continuing practices of the lab in PCR testing, saying that they posed a risk of contamination in this case. He attacked the laboratory's practice of testing blood samples from the accused and samples from the crime scene in the same room at the same general time. He also claimed that the LAPD analysts did not change gloves, papers, and solutions or bleach down their laboratory with sufficient frequency.

Gerdes was specifically critical of the practices in this case of the LAPD criminalist who prepared evidence for PCR testing. On June 14, 1994, Collin Yamauchi had prepared various items for DNA analysis, pipetting blood from Simpson's sample onto a card, leaving it to dry on a table, cutting samples from the bloody glove Fuhrman claimed to have found, then removing samples for testing from the blood drops from Nicole Brown's home and finally from the card itself. Yamauchi did this "sampling" in one room in one session. He asserted that he had not violated the rule against working with evidence items at the "same time." The card with Simpson's blood on it was left to dry on the table while Yamauchi went on to work with evidence from the crime, but no two items of evidence from the crime were open at the same time, and Yamauchi kept and took samples from the card, glove, and blood drops in different parts of the room. Gerdes criticized Yamauchi's moving from handling a blood sample to handling the glove found at Simpson's estate. He also asserted that there should be a separation time of twenty to thirty minutes between handling a suspect's sample and handling evidence from a crime scene, and that an analyst must totally clean and bleach an area and allow a period of time to go by before moving on to handling the evidence.

Nor was that the end of Gerdes's criticism of the analyst's practices. Yamauchi had testified that some of Simpson's blood got on his gloves when he opened the vacuum tube in which it was contained, soaking through the tissue that he held over the cap as a protective measure. He had then thrown out the tissue and the gloves, and put on a new pair of laboratory gloves. Gerdes claimed that this was an inadequate response. Yamauchi should have stopped everything, cleaned the entire laboratory, and waited for a period of time before moving on to handling items of evidence. At this point, said Gerdes, there's "blood on the table"—meaning the drying card with Simpson's blood—and an "aerosol in the air."

The extent to which the events that took place in the evidence processing room on June 14 posed any genuine danger of contamination was a subject of sharp dispute. The DNA from Simpson's blood sample would have to have been introduced into the evidence from the crime to have contaminated that evidence. Yamauchi testified that he had changed laboratory gloves at each crucial step of the process—after he got blood on his laboratory gloves, after he processed Simpson's blood sample, and after he handled the glove found at Simpson's home. What was the risk that Yamauchi's handling of the evidence had somehow contaminated it?

These risks of laboratory contamination were addressed by expert witnesses for the prosecution. Dr. Robin Cotton, Cellmark's DNA expert, testified that contamination would require physical contact, touching. Another DNA scientist, Gary Sims, from the California state lab, was questioned by prosecutor Rockne Harmon on this issue. Harmon, one of the country's top DNA prosecutors, was on loan from the Oakland District Attorney's Office for the trial. He is known for his fight and his biting wit, and he did not disappoint.

"Can DNA fly?" asked Harmon. The witness's answer was in the negative. It was a crucial point, for it was indeed hard to see how Simpson's DNA would have been introduced into item after item of evidence based on Yamauchi's conduct in the laboratory.

But this telling point was undercut by Gerdes's criticism of

Yamauchi's laboratory practices and by his assertions about rampant contamination in the LAPD laboratory. The defense denied that they were asserting a defense based on "flying DNA," instead seeking to argue that the laboratory and Yamauchi had created an unacceptable risk of contamination, and that the results could reflect contamination even though the controls failed to show it.

To support the argument that contamination may have taken place despite clean controls, Gerdes relied in part on the report of the National Academy of Sciences. The 1992 report had noted that contamination in one experiment "indicates a potential problem not just for that experiment, but for any experiment performed at about the same time." It had stated that controls are useful for monitoring general contamination in a laboratory, not the accuracy of a particular experiment. The blue-ribbon panel had noted that controls do not necessarily become contaminated on every occasion though contamination may actually be present in a laboratory. It also made the broad statement that errors take place "even in the best laboratories and even when the analyst is certain that every precaution against error was taken." These statements were used by the defense to argue that there could have been contamination as a result of Yamauchi's alleged mishandling of evidence even though controls designed to test for contamination indicated its absence.

The National Academy of Sciences report was also used to damage the prosecution's case in one more significant respect. The report had recommended the implementation in the long term of a regulatory program for DNA laboratories, including a procedure in which the labs would regularly be subjected to testing on mock cases they believed to be genuine. Such testing is known as external blind proficiency testing, because it is administered by an outside (external) testing agency that measures a laboratory's proficiency without the lab's knowledge (or on a "blind" basis).

Although the National Academy report had been issued in 1992 and the Simpson trial took place in 1995, external blind proficiency testing had not yet been implemented in any DNA laboratory. The debate over its practicality is ongoing. The advocates of external blind proficiency testing argue that it is the norm in checking the quality of medical labs and should also be utilized in crime laboratories. But forensic scientists argue that there are better means to protect against laboratory error and that medical labs deal with liquid blood samples, which can be easily gathered, while the crime scene evidence forensic experts analyze would be unwieldy and impractical to mock up.

In 1994, Congress stepped into the debate over external blind proficiency testing when it passed the DNA Identification Act of 1994. The act provided funding for DNA laboratories across the United States, and it required the director of the FBI to issue laboratory standards that will supplant the standards set by the group of independent scientists working in association with the FBI. It charged the National Institute of Justice to develop a program for external blind proficiency testing or to certify that "it is not feasible to have blind external testing for DNA forensic analyses." In June 1995, a representative of the National Institute of Justice reported that it was leaning toward a conclusion that it is not feasible to have external blind proficiency testing, but as of the Simpson trial no final decision had been made.

So, while this issue was still undecided as a policy matter on a national level, the Simpson defense lawyers could still compare the National Academy's recommendation that there be external blind proficiency testing with the absence of such testing by the DNA laboratories in this case. And they did, arguing that, in the absence of such testing, it was impossible to know whether laboratories were performing DNA analysis with the accuracy merited by its consequences. On his summation, defense attorney Barry Scheck noted the absence of external blind proficiency testing, which, he said, "You know is what you need." Scheck also pointed out that Cellmark had made errors years before in nonblind proficiency tests when it was starting up its DNA analysis program, just as the LAPD lab was now starting its program. The argument that there may have been multiple errors was, of course, something of a stretch. The sheer number of DNA results that typed to Simpson was a compelling argument against accepting the possibility of some laboratory error as fatal to the prosecution's case. Still, this was one more factor the defense could point to, and they certainly did.

The supposed risk of error was further highlighted by Gerdes's claim that he found five "typing errors" in his study of the LAPD's DNA testing. Cross-examination by George "Woody"

Clarke, a leading DNA prosecutor on loan to the Simpson prosecution team from the San Diego District Attorney's Office, demonstrated this claim to be highly dubious. Two "typing errors" were tests that the analyst herself decided to run again, two more were tests that Gerdes admitted on cross-examination were not called wrong, and the fifth was an instance where Gerdes called a result an error because it detected contamination that was actually present. Gerdes's claimed "typing errors" faded away under cross-examination, but there was no question that this was highly complex material, difficult for a jury to sort out, and the courtroom had been filled with days of testimony about contamination and laboratory error.

The twin themes of planting and laboratory error through contamination were firmly in place. But that was only one-half of the defense's dismantling of the DNA. Elaborating on those themes with specific facts, they challenged each drop on the trail of blood, from Nicole Brown's home to the Bronco and then to O. J. Simpson's home.

THERE WERE FIVE BLOOD DROPS AT NICOLE BROWN'S home containing DNA that matched Simpson's. Four were located on the walkway; a fifth was in the driveway. The blood drops on the walkway began near the murder victims, to the left of bloody footprints leading away from Nicole Brown's home, and they continued past her rear gate and into her driveway. Their location indicated that they were shed by the killer, as he left the scene of the crime.

These blood drops were numbered Los Angeles Police Department evidence items 47, 48, 49, 50, and 52. The blood drop found in the driveway, LAPD evidence item 52, produced a one in 170 million RFLP match to Simpson. There was a one in 240,000 PCR match to Simpson on four of the blood drops, and a one in 5,200 match on a fifth. DNA analysis was conducted by the LAPD, Cellmark, and the California Department of Justice; the PCR tests used included not just the DQ alpha test but also the polymarker and D1S80 tests, two of the newer PCR tests that had dramatically increased the numerical significance of a PCR match.

These five blood drops were the most powerful evidence against Simpson, because they represented the DNA evidence least persuasively contested by the defense. They were collected by criminalists on June 13, the same day that Simpson voluntarily provided the police with a sample of his own blood, but before Simpson's blood was drawn. This meant that any police tampering would have involved not simply the placement but the substitution of evidence and would have had to have taken place while the drops were in the custody of police criminalists. Just as significant, that substitution would most likely have had to take place between the collection of the blood drops on June 13 and Collin Yamauchi's analysis of them on June 14, since his PCR analysis showed a match to Simpson.

To meet this evidence, the defense offered testimony designed to show that tampering may indeed have taken place and within that brief window. Their main witness to support this point was Dr. Henry Lee, chief criminalist of the state of Connecticut, a man frequently described as the "world's foremost criminalist." His testimony related to suspicions raised by the packaging of one of the blood drops. All the drops had been collected on "swatches," very small pieces of cotton. Some blood drops yielded only one swatch; some were large enough to produce multiple swatches. The swatches or multiple swatches from each blood drop were stored together in a folded piece of paper; the swatches from each drop were stored separately from those from the other blood drops. Dr. Lee testified that there were blood smudges on the packaging of one of the five blood drops (LAPD evidence item 47). This, said Dr. Lee, indicated that the swatches on which that blood drop had been collected were wet when placed inside the folded piece of paper. The swatches, left to dry on June 13, had more than adequate time to dry before they were placed in the paper packaging on June 14, so stains from wet material raised a question. "Who did it, what happened, I don't know," testified Lee. Asked his opinion of the significance of the existence of these stains, Lee said that the "only opinion I can give under this circumstance" is that there is "something wrong." He then rejected several potentially innocent explanations for the presence of these smudges.

Defense lawyer Barry Scheck, never shy, took up Lee's implication that the swatches might have been switched. As usual, he provided facts purporting to support his claim. A criminalist had given testimony that she had placed her initials on the packaging containing the swatches, but no initials were found. Besides,

claimed Scheck, swatches like those on which the blood was collected are distributed to detectives for purposes of evidence collection, so that a detective intent on switching swatches would
have had material to work with, swatches to wet with blood.

There were significant problems with this argument that
swatches had been switched, even beyond the audacity of the
conduct alleged. The DNA found in the blood drops was heavily
degraded, and there was no reason why swatches dabbed in O. J.
Simpson's pristine blood sample, with a preservative in it, would
have been degraded. And why would rogue police officers,
who according to the defense's own theory truly believed that
Simpson was guilty, have removed evidence that they would
have thought would point directly to him? Besides, switching
swatches would have required not simply substituting five
planted swatches for the five drops collected, but many more
than five swatches, since some of the blood drops were sufficiently large that they were collected on several swatches,
later tested by DNA analysis. The jump from the statement
that there was "something wrong" to the conclusion that multiple swatches had been switched between June 13 and June
14 was a great leap, with little basis in logic, reason, or evidence.

But the defense relied not just on the insinuation that evidence
had been deliberately removed and replaced but also on their
contamination theory, maintaining that Collin Yamauchi had contaminated the blood drops when he prepared them for DNA
analysis on June 14 after getting blood from Simpson's voluntarily
given sample on his laboratory gloves. There were various weaknesses in this argument, but one in particular stood out.

Had the blood drops from the walkway been infected with
Simpson's own DNA by laboratory error, they would have shown
not just his DNA profile but also that of the real killer. But there
was only one DNA profile, and that was Simpson's.

So the defense constructed a scenario to explain the absence
of a second DNA profile, that of the real killer. And they skillfully
offered facts to support their theory. They began with genuine
scientific evidence that the DNA from the blood drops was
heavily degraded—that it had broken down into smaller pieces.

It was hardly surprising that the blood drops had degraded.
They had been stored for seven hours in plastic bags in a hot

truck, an environment conducive to degradation. But degradation itself does not change a person's DNA type. So the defense had to go one better than heavy degradation and argue that the DNA in all five blood drops had totally degraded, broken down to the point where it had literally disappeared for purposes of DNA analysis, and that this was why finding any profile besides Simpson's had been impossible. Then, they argued, Simpson's blood had inadvertently been introduced into the blood drops through laboratory contamination.

This scenario required a highly unlikely series of events. Degradation would have had to have been so severe that the DNA disappeared entirely in each of five separate blood drops. Next, a transfer would have had to take place in which the blood present in Simpson's own sample made its way into each of the blood drops themselves—five separate drops, collected and stored on numerous swatches, each swatch infected, contaminating result after result. Finally, there would have had to have been a failure in five controls, each designed to determine whether contamination had taken place on an individual blood drop. In each instance, contamination would have had to have jumped onto the blood drop being tested but declined to jump onto a control that would have revealed its presence. In an alternative explanation for this third eventuality, Barry Scheck argued to the jury that there was no reason to assume that the controls were handled properly in a laboratory that was a "cesspool of contamination," although Yamauchi testified in detail to his proper use of the controls.

No one of these three events—total degradation, a transfer of DNA, and failure of five controls—was a strong possibility. The defense had built factual support for their case by bringing out statements from the prosecution's witnesses establishing that each of these occurrences was a theoretical possibility. It was unlikely that any one of these possibilities had actually occurred; there was something less than a chance that all three had coincided.

Beyond the practical improbability of these events having taken place, there was objective scientific evidence to suggest that actual contamination did not take place. To begin with, the evidence linking Simpson to the blood drops on the walkway of Nicole Brown's home (LAPD evidence item 52) using the more classic RFLP technology included a DNA match to Simpson of one in 170 million.

While Dr. Gerdes's critique was premised on the sensitivity of PCR technology, he also offered the opinion that this one RFLP result could not be relied upon. Because of the low amount of DNA contained in the stain, the lowest amount in any RFLP stain in the case, this stain too could have been contaminated, said Gerdes.

In this unlikely scenario, the underlying DNA actually present in that blood drop would have had to degrade so dramatically that none of it could be detected using the most sensitive DNA technology, while a visible contaminant was introduced that was large enough to be detected using the least sensitive DNA technology. It was not a rationally appealing hypothesis. While the defense assault had been geared to show that the risk of contamination was too great to trust the DNA laboratory, this result tended to show that, risk or no risk, contamination had not actually taken place.

The defense's contention that the walkway blood drops were contaminated was further undercut by conventional blood tests that predate DNA testing. These tests require more blood than that used in DNA testing. As a result, they are much less susceptible to contamination. A trace contaminant simply will not register with these tests. Contamination in these tests would have required not some inadvertent transfer of microscopic amounts of biological material but the introduction of a visible amount of blood into the materials tested, even more than that necessary for the RFLP test.

The conventional blood tests were used to analyze a second drop from the walkway (LAPD evidence item 49). This blood drop had been typed using PCR and shown a one in 5,200 person PCR match to Simpson. The conventional blood tests also showed the blood in item 49 to be consistent with O. J. Simpson's; the characteristics analyzed through that test could be expected to occur in one in every 200 people. This was significant evidence that the blood drops on the walkway had not been contaminated. Like the RFLP test on LAPD evidence item 52, conventional blood tests of evidence item 49 indicated the likely absence of contamination.

The significance of the blood tests in confirming the PCR results was explored by Woody Clarke, who, with Rockne Harmon, filled out the prosecution's DNA team. Clarke shares Harmon's high intelligence, and he is as courtly as Harmon is combative. Clarke noticed that the defense lawyers had not asked Gerdes about the conventional blood tests. This seemed odd, so during his cross-examination the prosecutor asked Gerdes if he was aware that conventional serological (blood) techniques had also been used in this case?

Yes, said Gerdes.

The prosecutor then asked if Gerdes had examined those conventional techniques.

No, he said, he had not.

Did you believe they were important? asked Clarke.

"No," said Gerdes. "My function was to look simply at the science involved and the data involved in PCR."

"Did any member of the defense team ever discuss with you the existence of serological tests in this case?" asked the prosecutor.

"No," said Gerdes.

Would that factor have any effect on your opinions? asked Clarke.

"No," said Gerdes. "My opinions are to the scientific reliability of PCR-based testing and the chance of error due to cross-contamination."

Clarke bored in on Gerdes, asking him whether contamination would "necessarily never" be detected by serology.

"I think it highly unlikely," said Gerdes, "because PCR is the most sensitive method possible and those items would have very little amount of material."

As a scientist, asked Clarke, wouldn't you want to know all the scientific results on a given bloodstain?

"It is not my job," said Gerdes, "to look at this entire case."

Gerdes then disclaimed any expertise in serology, saying it should be left to an expert in that area; he had not discussed the serological tests with anyone and had heard about them on television.

These professions of ignorance could have had a substantial impact on the jury. Here was a man of science who ignored evidence that could go beyond the alleged risks and "chance" of contamination and begin to shed light on whether contamination had actually taken place. Gerdes claimed that PCR could not be relied upon because it was subject to contamination; he then admitted on Clarke's cross-examination that serological tests do not share that vulnerability, but disclaimed any interest in learning the results of serological tests. And those serological tests had typed to Simpson, reflecting a one-in–200-person match to the former football player, and indicating that contamination had not in fact taken place. It was a powerful point, but it was a subtle one, and could easily have been missed or discounted by a jury over-whelmed and troubled by extensive and complex scientific testi-mony about contamination.

SIMPSON WAS NEXT IMPLICATED IN THE DOUBLE HOMICIDE by three sep-arate bloodstains on the rear gate of Nicole Brown's home. The largest stain (LAPD evidence item 117) produced a one in 57 bil-lion RFLP match to Simpson. Two smaller stains (LAPD evidence items 115 and 116) matched Simpson using PCR analysis, each producing a one in 520–person match. These stains were ana-lyzed by the California Department of Justice.

In challenging the significance of these bloodstains, the defense abandoned their double-barreled approach and relied on a claim that the stains had been planted. Again, they offered facts to support their view.

There was, first of all, the matter of opportunity. The blood-stains on the gate were not collected by police criminalists until July 3, three weeks after the murders. This was one of several instances in which blood was collected or found weeks or months after the crime. The innocent view of such late collec-tion recognizes limited resources and the human tendency to miss certain things initially. Such late detection and collection can, however, be problematic in a criminal case, raising ques-tions about the integrity of the evidence for those who view the world through a more sinister lens. Here, it allowed the defense to pose a devastating question: Who knew what rogue police officers might have visited the crime scene in the interim between the crime and collection, and what they might have done?

But the defense's proof of planting went beyond opportunity. A defense expert testified that the blood recovered from the back gate included a preservative, thereby suggesting that it had come from Simpson's "missing blood." The defense also focused on the condition of the bloodstains on the gate relative to that of the stains on the walkway, noting that those that had supposedly been on the rear gate, exposed to the elements for weeks, were in better condition and contained more DNA than the stains that had been collected immediately.

The prosecution sharply challenged the defense expert who asserted that the blood on the rear gate contained a preservative, and an FBI expert said that he had found no preservative. The prosecution also offered explanations for the relative condition of the blood on the gate. The painted surface of the gate was less absorbent than that upon which the other stains had been deposited, and there was no testimony that the rear gate stains had been placed in a hot truck for seven hours, as had the other, more degraded stains.

Most compelling, though, was the testimony by two police officers that they had seen bloodstains on the rear gate on the night of the murders. But, here too, the defense lawyers had an argument. The gate was rusty, argued the defense, and had imperfections and discolorations. The defense did not question the veracity of these officers but claimed that they were mistaken, that they thought they saw blood when in fact they saw rust or berry stains. That, argued the defense, was the reason that the LAPD criminalists had not collected blood from the rear gate on June 13. It was not yet there.

To raise questions and have them hang in the air could be a path to a defense victory in a case where so many other questions had already been raised.

THE TRAIL OF DNA CONTINUED INTO SIMPSON'S CAR, the Bronco, found parked askew at his home on the morning following the murders. Both RFLP and PCR results placed O. J. Simpson's, Nicole Brown's, and Ronald Goldman's blood in Simpson's car.

A first set of bloodstains was collected from the Bronco on June 14, and they were all analyzed with the PCR technique. Bloodstains containing Simpson's DNA had been found at five locations: the instrument panel, the driver's side carpet fiber, the steering wheel, the center console, and the driver's side wall (LAPD evidence items 24, 25, 28, 30, and 34, respectively). Nicole Brown's DNA was found in a partial bloody footprint on the driver's side (LAPD evidence item 293). A stain containing a mixture of Simpson's and Ronald Goldman's DNA was found on the center console (LAPD evidence item 31).

But that was not to be the end of the DNA evidence against Simpson from the Bronco. Collected at a later date, on August 26, 1994, were bloodstains containing a mixture of the DNA of Simpson, Nicole Brown, and Ronald Goldman (LAPD evidence items 303, 304, and 305). Most of the stains, those collected on both June 14 and August 26, were analyzed by the California Department of Justice.

Here again, the double-barreled defense was back in full force, though with some twists. The bloodstains in the Bronco that typed to Simpson alone were left mostly uncontested. The defense noted Simpson's statement to Dr. Michael Baden, the former chief medical examiner of the City of New York and an expert witness for the defense, that he had somehow cut himself while retrieving his cellular phone from the Bronco before leaving for Chicago on June 12. In his summation, Barry Scheck said that the initial deposits of blood in the Bronco were made by Simpson.

This left two bloodstains for the defense to account for from the initial June 14 collection. There was the stain analyzed through PCR allegedly containing a mixture of Simpson's and Ronald Goldman's DNA. Dr. Gerdes neutralized the impact of that stain for the defense, testifying that the controls failed in the analysis of that blood drop, LAPD evidence item 31.

That left one more potentially damning bloodstain among this group, the partial bloody footprint containing the blood of Nicole Brown. According to the prosecution's theory, Simpson had left this footprint in the car after committing the murders.

The defense offered an alternative explanation, claiming that it was Detective Mark Fuhrman who had left this footprint on the morning after the murders. He had, they argued, stepped in the blood at the crime scene, then, after the blood on his shoe had dried, stepped in the Bronco after walking in the morning dew at Simpson's estate. Fuhrman denied having been in the Bronco at all, but the defense alleged that he was lying. They claimed that Fuhrman had described seeing blood patterns in the Bronco that could only be seen with the door open. The defense also relied on a supposed slip of the tongue, which they characterized as Freudian, in which Fuhrman made reference to having seen blood in the Bronco; Fuhrman said he had simply misspoken.

As the trial proceeded, the prosecution developed more DNA

proof against Simpson relating to the Bronco. In the second evidence collection, on August 26, criminalists had gathered three more bloodstains from the Bronco console. PCR analysis showed that the blood from the console contained DNA matching the profiles of Simpson, Brown, and Goldman, but initially there was only PCR analysis from the Bronco. So, as the trial proceeded, the California Department of Justice laboratory combined the three stains, producing enough blood to analyze using RFLP analysis. That brew also showed a match to Simpson, Brown, and Goldman.

These stains, however, were subjected to the frame defense. They had, after all, not been collected until more than two months after the murder. This allowed the defense to raise the question of what blood might have been planted in the parked car between the crime and the collection. A theft from the Bronco while it was in police custody reinforced the view that the vehicle would hardly have been secure from LAPD detectives who chose to enter it. And a detective investigating the theft had not noticed any blood in the Bronco, although, she said, she had not specifically been looking for blood. Once again, the defense had been able to raise some doubt about every drop of blood.

O. J. SIMPSON'S BLOOD WAS ALSO FOUND at his own estate, in his driveway, foyer, and master bathroom. A blood drop in his foyer (LAPD evidence item 12) produced a one in 170 million RFLP match and a one in 5,200 PCR match. Two blood drops in the driveway (LAPD evidence items 6 and 7) each produced a PCR match to Simpson. The blood drop from the master bathroom (LAPD evidence item 14) also produced a PCR match to Simpson. The tests on the bloodstains were conducted variously by Cellmark and the California Department of Justice.

But Simpson's claim that he had cut himself while retrieving his cell phone from the Bronco before leaving for Chicago was before the jury and was essentially uncontested. There was certainly room for skepticism about this claim; after all, Simpson also claimed to have cut himself more seriously in a Chicago hotel room later the next morning upon hearing of Nicole Brown's murder. As prosecutor Christopher Darden asked in his summation, How many times can one man cut himself in one night in how many states?

But the dismissal of a claim like Simpson's may well trouble a jury. Juries take very seriously the requirement that proof be established beyond a reasonable doubt. It was difficult for government to prove its case through the presence of Simpson's blood in his own home, especially when there was "evidence," namely his say-so, that he had cut himself in an innocent manner that evening.

Much more damning was the presence of Nicole Brown's and O. J. Simpson's blood on the socks allegedly found at the foot of Simpson's bed. DNA testing produced a one in 57 billion RFLP match to Simpson and a one in 7.7 billion match to Brown. The socks were analyzed by both Cellmark and the California state DNA laboratory.

The defense did not attack the accuracy of the DNA results on the socks. Instead, they relied on a claim that the socks had been planted at the foot of Simpson's bed and that blood had later been planted on the socks.

To establish the first part of their claim, the defense team relied on a police department videotape showing the foot of Simpson's bed and no socks. The timer on the videotape indicated that it was taken at 4:13 P.M., and the socks were collected between 4:30 and 4:40 P.M. on June 13. However, the police department employee who took the videotape said he had been told to take the videotape of the room only after it had been searched. The purpose of the tape was not to videotape evidence but to record Simpson's possessions and protect the police department against any claims of theft by its officers and employees. The employee had not, according to the prosecution, checked or adjusted the timer on the video.

The evidence that blood had been planted on the socks was more compelling. The socks had been collected on June 13, but no one had noticed the bloodstains on them and arranged for their analysis until August 4, 1994. An LAPD criminalist, Dennis Fung, had not noticed stains on the socks when he collected them on June 13. Defense experts had not noticed any blood when they looked at the socks on June 22. On June 29, an LAPD criminalist had conducted an inventory review of the evidence and noted that no blood was obvious on the socks.

In addition, the defense expert who testified to the presence of a preservative in the blood on the rear gate also testified that there was preservative in the blood on the socks. Another defense expert testified to his conclusion that one of the stains came from the other side of the sock when wet, and that such a stain could not have been transferred that way if there had been a foot in the sock at the time.

The prosecution countered these claims with an argument in substance asserting that it would have made no sense for a rogue police officer to have planted socks without any blood on them. After all, why plant socks and then plant blood at a later time? In a world of conspiracy and intrigue, however, anything becomes possible.

The prosecution explained that the stains were not noticed earlier because they were dark stains on dark socks, not readily visible without high-intensity lighting. They asserted that the June 29 review of the socks had simply been an "inventory" review, not a detailed examination. The FBI agent who said that there was no preservative in the blood on the rear gate also found no preservative in the blood on the socks. Marcia Clark offered the jury several possible explanations in her summation for the transfer of the stain from one side of the sock to the other, including the way the socks lay on the floor. However, most of her explanations had been anticipated by the defense, posed to Dr. Henry Lee during his testimony, and rejected by him as highly unlikely.

The socks were among the prosecution's most powerful evidence. But they also aided the defense contention that something was rotten in Denmark. After all, even if the jury were inclined to credit other items of evidence, how many troubling issues could the prosecution explain away? On his summation, Barry Scheck argued that the jury could not trust any other evidence in the case if the police had manufactured evidence on the socks. That is reasonable doubt, said Scheck, and the end of the case. It was an argument that did not lack for power. Johnnie Cochran, the defense's lead counsel, carried this theme further: "If you can't trust the messenger," he told the jury, "you can't trust the message."

BESIDES THE SOCKS, THERE WAS A BLOODY GLOVE allegedly found on the grounds at O. J. Simpson's home, the glove that Simpson tried on at the trial, the the glove that purportedly "did not fit." It was a right-handed glove, the mate to a bloody glove found at Nicole Brown's home, which had contained only the blood of the murder victims. The glove was packed with bloodstains and DNA. These were analyzed by the LAPD laboratory and Cellmark. Fifteen bloodstains were identified on the glove. Most contained the DNA of more than one person, and those people, in various combinations, were Simpson, Brown, and Goldman. DNA consistent with Simpson's was found at four areas on the glove through PCR analysis. All four were near the wrist area; three were outside and one inside the glove.

But the person who claimed that he had found this glove at Simpson's home was Detective Mark Fuhrman. Besides their generalized critique of Fuhrman, the defense also argued that there were facts to support their contention that Fuhrman had planted the glove. Most of all, Fuhrman had described the glove as "moist and sticky" when he found it, although, said the defense, it should have already dried if he had found it at Simpson's home. Moreover, Judge Lance Ito had told the jury that they could choose to conclude that a person who had per- jured himself in one respect had perjured himself in all respects, and the jury knew that Fuhrman had lied on the stand about his racial animus.

So the impact of the glove as evidence of guilt may have been virtually eliminated even before Simpson tried it on in court. This could explain prosecutor Christopher Darden's apparent blunder in having Simpson try on the glove while standing before a jury. It is axiomatic that trial lawyers should never ask a question to which they do not know the answer, nor propose a demonstra- tion whose results are uncertain, but there will always be situa- tions in which a lawyer has no other choice. This may have been such a case, a desperation play to save a piece of evidence other- wise sullied.

By the end of the trial, some commentators criticized the prosecution for even arguing the significance of the glove to the jury during their summation. This was, however, hard evidence to let go. Most of all, there was the power of the DNA evidence on the glove. And, on the emotional side, the jury could even see a photograph that seemed to show Simpson wearing both gloves, or at least very similar gloves. Richard Rubin, a former executive of Aris Isotoner, testified that the Aris gloves found at

Brown's and Simpson's homes appeared identical to the gloves Simpson wore in a photograph taken at a Cincinnati Bengals–Houston Oilers football game in January 1991. But the defense claimed that Rubin's testimony should be discounted because he made only a limited search for other manufacturers of similar gloves, and they urged that Rubin had revealed favoritism toward the prosecution when he wrote them a letter concluding with the words "Maybe I can make it to the victory party."

Still, there was additional evidence, also separate from Fuhrman's testimony, which seemed to show that the glove had not been planted. The defense theory was that Fuhrman had picked up the bloody glove at Nicole Brown's home and then planted it at Simpson's home. But several police officers had responded to Brown's home before Fuhrman, and they had seen only one glove. Besides, there were blue-black fibers on the glove matching fibers found on the socks and on Ronald Goldman's shirt. The implication argued by the prosecution was that these fibers had all rubbed off the dark sweatsuit that Simpson was seen wearing earlier that evening by Brian "Kato" Kaelin.

And there was still another indication that the glove had not been planted. If Fuhrman had taken the glove from the murder scene and planted it at Simpson's home while he was still in Chicago, why would Simpson's DNA have been on the glove? The presence of Simpson's DNA on the glove not only implicated him in the crime but also undercut the claim that the glove had been planted.

The defense's principal answer to this argument once again lay in the interplay of the frame defense and the contamination defense. In the defense scenario, the glove was "found" at Simpson's home because it was planted there. Then, they claimed, the glove was contaminated by Collin Yamauchi when he worked with it in the evidence processing room on June 14. This scenario was not quite as far-fetched as the defense's claim of contamination regarding the blood drops at Nicole Brown's home, since contamination in this instance would not have required any disappearing DNA. Still, it would have necessitated laboratory error involving the introduction by Yamauchi of spots of Simpson's blood sufficient to contaminate four PCR results from the glove. In this version of reality, it was not that the evidence was planted *or* contaminated but that it was both planted *and* contaminated.

The defense also suggested another scenario to account for the presence of Simpson's DNA on the glove. What if Fuhrman had the glove in the Bronco, and the glove had come into contact with the side of the console, where Simpson had earlier left blood when he retrieved his cell phone? That, the defense argued, could account for the small transfer of blood to the glove—although it was hard to understand how that could have explained four results implicating Simpson on both the inside and the outside of the glove. It was not a realistic scenario, but it was one more argument for the jury to consider, one more defense claim of doubt.

WHEN THE JURY RECEIVED THE CASE FOR DELIBERATION, they had been told by the judge that their decision must be governed by the law applicable in a "circumstantial evidence" case. After all, there were no eyewitnesses who saw Simpson commit murder, no knife found in his pocket, no confession of guilt. The prosecution argued that guilt could be inferred from all the circumstances, including the blood and DNA evidence.

Circumstantial evidence cases are governed by special legal rules that can be extremely exacting. Juries may not simply consider the totality of the evidence and derive from it a cumulative and commonsense belief that the prosecution has proven the defendant's guilt beyond a reasonable doubt. Instead, juries are told that each essential fact must be proven beyond a reasonable doubt. Where two reasonable inferences are possible from a circumstantial fact, the jury must provide the defendant the inference consistent with innocence. To convict, the jury had to take into account only those items of circumstantial evidence that could not be reconciled with any rational conclusion but guilt. What we do in daily life, determine in a commonsense manner what is true from a series of facts that each alone might not persuade us, is not allowed in a case relying on circumstantial evidence.

As a legal matter, it was an issue not of whether the prosecution's or the defense's inferences were more reasonable but of whether the interpretations urged by the defense were reasonable at all. The defense team had provided the jury with inferences which it argued were consistent with innocence for virtually every piece of blood evidence implicating Simpson.

By this route the defense was able to neutralize the impact of the six sets of DNA stains that all pointed to Simpson, and even the two sets of stains—the blood drops at Nicole Brown's home and the bloody glove—for which the defense's explanations were least convincing. Those two sets of stains (and most of all the blood drops at Nicole Brown's home) formed a irreducible core of evidence that strongly indicated Simpson's guilt. Although the defense challenged those results vigorously and elaborately, its arguments regarding those stains, when carefully scrutinized, finally had little support in logic or reason. Still, in a case where the government was on trial, its conduct so strongly questioned, so many doubts raised, and the evidence so complex, even the compelling impact of those two sets of stains was blunted. On October 3, 1995, Simpson was acquitted, despite some DNA findings that were on their face and at their core as strongly indicative of guilt as the prosecution could have wished.

WHAT ARE THE IMPLICATIONS OF THE SIMPSON CASE for the future of DNA in the courtroom?

The question of whether PCR is simply too vulnerable to contamination for reliable use in criminal cases was raised at the Simpson trial, but the view that this is so is very much a minority view among knowledgeable scientists. The claim that the PCR evidence was contaminated in this case apparently had more to do with appearances than with reality. DNA analysis using the RFLP technique and traditional blood tests confirmed the PCR findings in a crucial set of evidence. Despite storage in plastic bags in a hot truck, despite heavy degradation, despite laboratory practices that were less than ideal, PCR analysis seems to have worked. This would indicate that DNA is far more robust, and less subject to contamination, than the defense suggested.

All the same, the questions raised in this case reflect issues which prosecutors and crime labs will now ignore at their peril. Throughout the United States—throughout the world—criminal defense lawyers will study the Simpson case as a road map to challenging PCR. They will want to know: How sure can the jury be that this very small sample was deposited during the course of the crime by the criminal or victim? What steps were taken in the collection and packaging of evidence to maintain its integrity by separating one item of evidence from another? Was the evidence stored in a manner conducive to degradation? Is the laboratory that performed the DNA testing accredited? What are the training and experience of its personnel? What steps were taken in the lab and what controls were in place to protect against contamination by a suspect's blood sample and by other items of evidence from this and other cases?

In trying to provide answers to these questions that will be useful to their own sides, defense lawyers and prosecutors will look to the standards DNA laboratories must meet. These will include, most significantly, the standards issued by the independent scientists working in association with the FBI and those issued by the director of the FBI, which will supplant them pursuant to federal law. Defense attacks on DNA, when made, will likely revolve about claims that the laboratory violated established standards and will focus on the violations alleged and their significance.

The courtroom review of DNA testing may be useful, but it certainly has its limits. Few criminal defendants will have the resources of O. J. Simpson; few defense attorneys will have the expertise or ingenuity of his attorneys. Nor should every trial be turned into an exploration of a laboratory's past and present testing program. A far more appropriate and useful means of promoting and checking good laboratory practices would be the participation of DNA laboratories in accreditation programs. Many major DNA laboratories already do so. (The LAPD DNA laboratory did not.) The importance of accreditation will increase as state and local crime laboratories develop the capacity to perform DNA testing and the FBI turns over the responsibility for testing to those new laboratories. Then, accreditation can begin to provide the confidence that those start-up laboratories are operating at a highly professional level.

On the whole, though, it is most significant that the Simpson defense did not rely solely or even predominantly on a challenge to the DNA. Each of six sets of DNA bloodstains—the blood drops at Nicole Brown's home, the rear gate stains, the Bronco stains, the stains at Simpson's home, the stains on the socks, and the stains on the bloody glove found on the grounds of Simpson's home—implicated O. J. Simpson in the murders. The defense team essentially admitted the accuracy of four of those six sets of results, not challenging scientifically the RFLP results that implicated Simpson on the rear gate stains, the Bronco stains, the stains at Simpson's home, and the stains on the socks. These stains were all explained by alleged planting or by Simpson's having bled at a location for reasons unrelated to the crime. The two sets of stains explained through alleged contamination, the blood drops at Nicole Brown's home and the stains on the glove, were alternatively accounted for through a planting theory.

In this regard, the Simpson trial was not the first in which the defense for the most part admitted the accuracy of DNA tests. The tactic: Admit the DNA is yours and find other ways to explain its presence in terms consistent with innocence. The precedent can be found in previous cases; the approach has been used in defending both the innocent and the guilty. Most notable was the case of a doctor charged with rape.

10 THE POWER OF DNA

D R. MORTEZA MOHIT, a fifty-five-year-old gynecologist in Westchester County, New York, was accused of raping a twenty-seven-year-old female patient during a physical examination. The woman told the jury that she had gone to the doctor's office for a pregnancy test.

"When I got on the scale he slapped me on the right hip and said I needed to lose some fat," she testified. The patient then got on the examining table with her legs in stirrups. Dr. Mohit began to caress her "like he was trying to stimulate me," she said, and told her that she had a "good body."

Then, during the examination, she said, the doctor pushed himself against her and raped her. "He kept staring at me," she testified, "a cold, hard stare. I was scared. He reached up as if he was going to grab my throat. . . but he grabbed my breasts." According to the woman, Dr. Mohit then went to his desk, wrote out a prescription, and told her to get dressed.

The woman reported the incident to the police. When the police interviewed Dr. Mohit, he denied having had sexual intercourse with his patient. But DNA results using the RFLP method indicated that it was Mohit's semen found on a vaginal swab taken from the woman at the hospital several hours after her visit to his office. His lawyer challenged the DNA in a pretrial hearing but was unable to keep the judge from ruling that the results would be admitted at trial.

So, at the trial, Dr. Mohit's lawyer took a different tack,

urging that the doctor and his patient had had consensual sex. During cross-examination by the defense lawyer, the woman admitted to being an alcoholic, having a history of drug use, and having received counseling for troubled relationships.

The defense rested without calling Dr. Mohit or any other witnesses in his defense, relying for the most part on impugning the credibility of his accuser, hoping that the jury would not send a medical doctor to prison on the say-so of someone who had been forced to seek help for emotional problems. The Westchester jury acquitted Mohit.

Though Dr. Mohit was thus spared from a prison sentence, this was not the end of the matter. Soon thereafter, the state began civil proceedings to revoke his medical license. After hearing testimony from the patient and Dr. Mohit, the state found that the sexual intercourse between the two had not been consensual and revoked his license to practice medicine.

Had the consent defense worked? It had prevailed in the criminal trial, where the standard of proof was guilt beyond a reasonable doubt, but been rejected in the civil proceeding, where a lesser standard of proof applied. Dr. Mohit had maintained his liberty but lost his license to practice medicine.

A defense based on consent is the one most likely to be asserted in rape cases where DNA testing confirms that intercourse has taken place. As it did in the Mohit case, DNA testing can make virtually indefensible the claim that the suspect did not have sex with his accuser, and the defense must switch to the claim that the sex took place but was consensual. In many cases, that claim will be based on truth. In many others, it will not. But that is not a point DNA can settle.

Oddly, the "frame" defense utilized in the O. J. Simpson trial is in certain legal respects a distant cousin to the "consent" defense in a rape trial. In both cases, a suspect acknowledges the presence of his blood or semen but offers a theory for where it was found that allows for his innocence. The focus shifts from whether it is the defendant's blood or semen at the crime scene to how it got there. Rather than challenging the accuracy of DNA laboratories, this may be the way defense attorneys will deal with the fact that DNA test findings put their client at the scene of the crime. Some of these defenses are a tribute to the ingenuity of defense lawyers, but in the first instance they are a tribute to the power of DNA. It is only because the scientific validity of this means of identification cannot for the most part be directly challenged that realistic defense lawyers have accepted that, if their client is to go home rather than prison after the trial, what is required is an end run around the DNA.

No matter how powerful any new tool, there will always be limits, some never imagined until a bizarre case makes them apparent.

When fifteen-year-old Amanda Hall was raped and murdered in suburban Maryland, it looked like the perfect crime. True, there were witnesses who could link the Page twins to Hall shortly before her murder. The twins had expressed interest in the beautiful runaway, who had been sleeping on the steps of the local recreation center. On the evening that she was murdered, they asked a man who had been talking with her if he was her boyfriend. Later that night, around midnight, they told a clerk at the 7-Eleven across the street that they wanted to buy a hot chocolate for her and were last seen walking toward the recreation center. But there were no witnesses to the rape, or to Amanda Hall's strangulation.

Semen and DNA were recovered from the rape, but that did not resolve the case. The DNA matched both Jerome Page and Tyrone Page. The two are identical twins, and while identical twins do not have identical fingerprints, they do have identical DNA. This left the police stymied. Guilt in the United States is of course an individual matter. A jury cannot convict two brothers because it knows that at least one of the two committed the crime. Since all the DNA evidence could say was that someone with a certain DNA had raped Amanda Hall, and the twins each had that DNA, it alone was insufficient to charge or convict either brother.

But there was a twist to the case, and it lay in one of the ways that identical twins may be different from each other. While identical twins usually have identical hair, the characteristics of their hair can vary if they have had substantially different diets, or if only one has a history of drug or alcohol abuse.

Hall's body had been found the next morning, in a wooded area by some old railroad tracks, two miles from the recreation center. Her body was wrapped in the blanket in which she had slept. Within that blanket, there were pubic hairs that were not

Amanda Hall's and were not identical to each other. The FBI analyzed those hairs, comparing them with Jerome Page's and
Tyrone Page's. The two brothers' hairs were different from each
other, and the hairs of each matched hairs found in the blanket.

One of the twins had previously spent time in jail, doubtless
eating a diet substantially different from his brother's. That difference in diet could reasonably have accounted for the difference in the characteristics of the twins' hairs. Whatever the
reason, the difference was a fact, and the pubic hairs found on
the blanket in which Hall's body was wrapped indicated that both
twins had had intimate contact with Hall near the time of her
death.

Both brothers were convicted of murder and rape and were
sentenced to life in prison without parole. Without DNA, there
would have been no case against either twin, since pubic hairs,
on their own, are not sufficiently distinctive to form the basis for
a criminal conviction. DNA alone was not sufficient to make a
case against either brother, because it could not determine if only
one or both had done the crime. If the state decided to settle for
half a loaf and proceed on the basis of one brother's having done
the crime, how could anyone know if it was trying the right
brother? The jury verdict that both brothers had participated
came out of the totality of the evidence.

The case of the Page brothers, while hardly typical, points out
dramatically that DNA does not exist in a vacuum. Other evidence must be contended with. In the Matias Reyes case, the
Minnesota data-banking case, and the O. J. Simpson case, there
was other evidence, and other issues, that had to be considered
alongside the fact of a DNA match. And, in the Central Park
jogger case, it was the sum of the evidence that explained the
absence of the defendants' DNA.

In most of those cases where there is DNA and some additional evidence against a defendant, that person will choose to
plead guilty. This means that victims will be spared the trauma of
testimony at trial and that society will be spared the expense and
uncertainty of trying guilty people.

But in those cases where a defendant chooses to exercise his
right to go to trial, a jury will assess the meaning of the DNA, or
the absence of DNA, along with all the other evidence favorable
and unfavorable to the person charged with a crime. A person

K= 96665.C4P

Lang H. (1996), AND THE BEANS CROSSED OUT. 'KOUBEK.'
BASZCBOOKS.

TWORS HAVE ZDEPUTZCUS DUA P6 191

charged with a crime on the basis of DNA tests may have a valid defense based on consent to sex, the planting of evidence, or problems in the collection or handling of the evidence. DNA is a powerful tool for determining identity, but it must always be considered in the context of the individual criminal case.

THE FUTURE OF DNA ANALYSIS REMAINS STRONG. Scientifically, its capacity to identify the guilty has grown year by year. Over time the RFLP technique has been refined so that it can in many cases analyze more genetic locations than was possible when the technology was introduced. In those cases, it has become more and more like the "fingerprint" it was initially supposed to be, uniquely identifying an individual. This trend can only be expected to continue.

And the underlying soundness of DNA testing was underscored in the aftermath of the Simpson trial when the National Research Council of the National Academy of Sciences issued its long-awaited second report on DNA evidence on May 2, 1996. This second panel had been formed to reconsider the first committee's proposal for limiting DNA numbers, but its report ranged beyond that original mission. The new committee was composed of scientists and law professors mostly different than those who authored the controversial 1992 report. Its essential conclusion: DNA technology and statistics "have progressed to the point where the admissibility of properly collected and analyzed DNA should not be in doubt."

While never mentioning the Simpson case by name, the new report seemed to limit some key avenues of attack that his defense lawyers had happily strolled in challenging the DNA. The new panel expressed views sharply at odds with certain aspects of its predecessor's comments which had proved useful to DNA defense lawyers, although in most instances it did not specifically point out these divergences. Where the previous panel raised the possibility that contamination might not be detected through laboratory controls, the second panel noted that "appropriate safeguards and controls can be built into the analytical system to protect against contamination and to detect it when it does occur." The new committee urged that laboratories "make every effort to be accredited" but, unlike the previous panel, made no suggestion that accreditation be an absolute requirement, now or in the future, for the admissibility or acceptance of work performed by a DNA laboratory. And the new committee scorned the very suggestion (embraced by the first panel) that blind proficiency testing should be used to measure error rates and the implication that such testing should at some future point be mandatory. The proper use of blind proficiency testing, it wrote, is not to measure error rates but to identify problems which need to be corrected and improve laboratory performance, and its utility for even that limited purpose is under review by the National Institute of Justice. The use of such testing to determine error rates would be outlandishly expensive and disruptive, a badly misplaced effort consuming resources much better spent in other ways, such as improving laboratory standards. A more useful protection against laboratory error would be early separation, into two portions, of crime scene evidence, with one reserved for retesting.

Significantly, there were also substantive implications arising from a major shift in tone in the second report. The National Research Council's first report had used sweeping language about its long-range proposals. It could not have gone unnoticed by the new panel that the critics of DNA testing had seized upon that language to argue that the failure to meet those aspirations had rendered DNA testing invalid and inadmissible. So the new panel used more modest words, separated its "recommendations" from its "suggestions," and made specifically clear that it was not making formal recommendations to the effect that its views of matters of legal policy should be prerequisites to the acceptance of DNA evidence. Aware of the potential power of its own words, the committee chose to tread carefully and minimize the risk that its policy preferences might undercut the acceptance of DNA evidence in court.

The new panel also addressed the diminished but once vitriolic controversy over the impact of race and ethnicity on stating the significance of a DNA match, renouncing its predecessor's much-criticized proposal for limiting DNA numbers on practical and statistical grounds, and because there is "no scientific justification for its use." This time, the panel embraced the position advocated by the supporters of DNA testing and endorsed the use of broad racial groupings in stating a DNA match. Where the race of the person who left the evidence is known, a number should be given for that race; where it is unknown, statistics for whites, blacks, Hispanics, and East Asians should be provided. The conclusion that broad racial groupings are acceptable was supported by the new committee's important finding on a previously disputed issue: that "differences between races are considerably larger than those between subgroups within races." According to the panel, there was now "new data" that allowed numerical estimates to be made with greater confidence than before. The frequency of a DNA profile may vary among ethnic groups within broad racial groups as much as ten times in either direction, but this variation simply provides a guide to the level of uncertainty, with the true value estimated to lie between the upper and the lower boundary.

It was clear from the new report that the nation's leading scientists continue to hold the view that DNA testing is fundamentally sound, although issues regarding the collection and analysis of evidence may still arise in individual cases.

The popular view of DNA is another matter. It is certainly possible that a popular misperception that the Simpson trial somehow discredited DNA will lead to the outright acquittal of some defendants squarely implicated by it. But any such effect will surely be short-lived, for DNA is overwhelming evidence of identity, and, in most cases, the courtroom is an empire of reason, where fully credible evidence will continue to have influence.

To the extent that defense lawyers attack the reliability of DNA outright, rather than focus on contextual issues—such as consent, planting, or specific problems in the field or laboratory—they will likely fail. They will be like King Canute, ordering the waters to recede. It simply will not happen.

Still, there is a substantial danger that the Simpson case may pose a setback to DNA outside the courtroom that will reverberate ominously throughout the criminal justice system. That will happen if the case results in an increased reluctance on the part of prosecutors to request DNA tests because of a misbegotten belief that such tests are so complex and their explanations so difficult to deliver that they will inevitably confuse jurors and create a fertile field for the planting of reasonable doubt.

Analysis of DNA was relatively infrequent even before the Simpson case. Prosecutors and crime laboratories do not routinely arrange for DNA analysis in all cases where it can be used.

The tests are expensive, and many prosecutors' offices and crime laboratories are not well enough funded to allow such broad application of this tool.

Besides, many individual prosecutors are wary of the new world of criminal justice DNA threatens to create. They would prefer to continue doing things the same old comfortable and familiar way they have always done things, relying on the conventional triad of criminal proof and leaving science to those of their college classmates who attended medical school or graduate school in the sciences. Lawyers like to be in charge, and in a courtroom, as in any intellectual arena, the lawyer who has the knowledge has the power. What lawyer would relish getting involved in either an extended hearing or battle at trial about scientific material so complex and esoteric that the lawyer comes off as poorly versed compared with the witnesses he or she must examine?

In this regard as well the Simpson trial may exacerbate the reluctance of prosecutors to introduce DNA experts into their private preserve. Here the experts brought in were so well informed, and of such high repute, that to examine and confront them the prosecution had to borrow better-qualified prosecutors from other jurisdictions. This is not a picture the average prosecutor wants to use as a model.

Often criminal defense lawyers are just as hesitant, if not more hesitant, to push for DNA testing. Hardened by long exposure to career criminals, many defense lawyers start off believing that their clients are guilty, regardless of their clients' protestations that they were not within miles of the scene of the crime on the day in question. As a consequence, many criminal defense attorneys are wary of ordering a test in each individual case that may force them to face that their client has been lying to them— and that could potentially be admitted at trial to prove their client's guilt. This presents the criminal defense attorney with a difficult choice: Forgo DNA testing, and risk the conviction of an innocent person, or request such testing and possibly aid the conviction of the lawyer's own client.

So, if the criminal justice system is to deserve its name, prosecutors, crime laboratories, and those who fund their efforts must develop the will, and expend the funds, for routine DNA testing of high quality, for here is a tool that can provide the most accurate information possible on at least one of the issues which dominate criminal trials, namely identification. Developments since the advent of DNA testing have suggested that human inadequacies in discerning innocence and guilt may run deeper than previously thought. It is often said that eyewitness testimony is the most faulty aspect of the criminal justice system, and as long as there are strong-willed police and weak-minded suspects, there will be false confessions. But DNA evidence is virtually unchallengeable on the issue of identity. Unlike eyewitness testimony and confessions, it provides objective evidence of the source of bodily material, which may clear or implicate the accused.

Consider the cases of Colin Pitchfork, Gregory Ritter, and Edward Honaker. In these instances, DNA testing demonstrated once again that human beings do not always know what they think they know. That realization has been underscored by the results of the FBI's DNA-testing program, which has excluded suspects as the sources of samples submitted to it in one-quarter of its cases. This fact is sufficiently noteworthy to bear repetition: In one-quarter of the cases handled by the FBI, the samples tested do not match a suspect's DNA. This does not necessarily mean that one-quarter of criminal suspects are innocent. There may be explanations for many of these test results consistent with guilt. A rape suspect, for example, may not have ejaculated, and the source of semen found in the victim may have been a husband or boyfriend with whom she had consensual sex near the time of a rape. Still, the statistic must give pause, especially when we look at all those cases where DNA testing is not performed.

Few aspects of DNA analysis have been so moving as its use to free people who have spent years in prison after their wrongful conviction of crimes that they did not commit. Yet the number of people so cleared, fewer than twenty overall, is small compared with the number of people routinely cleared before trial by genetic testing. The greatest friend of the falsely accused is DNA testing at the beginning of a criminal investigation; it clears far more people than post-conviction tests. Early genetic testing can spare suspects months and years spent in jail and under suspicion by their communities.

Besides, the days of post-conviction testing are surely numbered. Because DNA testing was not available until recently, legal requests for post-conviction testing were frequently granted on the ground that DNA was newly discovered evidence not available to the defense at the time of the trial. Judges often had no choice but to order the testing of evidence stored for years in police property rooms. By contrast, it is difficult to imagine judges ordering the testing of evidence in cases arising years after the advent of DNA testing, giving convicts who could have requested testing during their first trial but did not a second bite at the apple of an acquittal. Further, justice is best served when the DNA evidence is introduced at the time of the trial, when a rape victim can better remember if there were consensual sexual partners immediately prior to the crime, or what a particular stain in her bedroom might reflect. Timeliness is also a factor when exploring issues that might arise regarding integrity and competence in the collection and storage of evidence.

An expanded commitment to DNA testing should include steps to ensure that new laboratories do not introduce another source of potential error into our criminal justice system. Accreditation or other guarantees of laboratory quality will become even more important as DNA analysis increasingly devolves from the FBI to state and local crime laboratories. Of course, a laboratory may perform good quality work without accreditation. But since many defendants lack money and many defense attorneys lack the expertise to pose a challenge to genetic testing in each case, accreditation, rather than the adversary system, is probably the best way to protect quality for all, rich or poor. It is one thing to set standards but another to make sure they are met, and accreditation is one means to that end.

Because of the enormous weight given to DNA findings, it is important that the laboratories supplying the test results be fully funded, sophisticated facilities, with appropriate outside monitoring. This is of course above all a matter of proper funding and training, but, to protect quality, laboratories should ideally participate in accreditation programs for both RFLP and PCR testing. Today, many do not. The critics of DNA analysis deserve plaudits for highlighting these concerns; measures to ensure the quality of DNA analysis are an important part of promoting the future of the technique.

Analysis of DNA, first used in a criminal case in 1987, is still relatively new. But it is well established as a science. No one maintains that it is "junk science." Questions concerning the fundamental soundness of DNA testing concerning the congressional Office of Technology Assessment are in the words of the, "red herrings" and a "public disservice." Obviously, DNA analysis must be done scrupulously; power, including scientific power, must always be exercised with care, and the greater the power, the greater the care that must accompany its use. An insistence that things be done right hardly renders this powerful technology invalid.

The objective information provided by DNA is among the most reliable evidence available to those seeking truth in our criminal justice system. Criminal convictions and acquittals result from a subjective weighing of evidence presented, and subjectivity is a necessary and proper part of the criminal justice system. But the reliability of the verdicts jurors reach depends on the quality of the evidence to which they are exposed.

There is no question that under the current system the guilty are sometimes set free and the innocent convicted. DNA testing cannot change the system into one where a verdict of guilty or not guilty is preordained by the presence or absence of DNA, for DNA must always be considered in the context of all the evidence. But it can avoid many miscarriages of justice that might occur without it, in a world where the truth is often hidden and elusive. And the use of data banks to solve unsolved crimes can identify repeat offenders guilty of new rapes and help incarcerate them for appropriate periods of time, and so limit their opportunities to inflict more harm and violence on innocent women.

And so, at long last, thousands of years after Cain killed Abel, science has provided the means to hear blood cry out the names of those who have brought violence on others. It is a technology that must be nurtured and protected, for a society that treasures justice cannot afford to turn away from the piercing sound of truth.

ACKNOWLEDGMENTS

S EVERAL PEOPLE were kind enough to read and comment on a draft of this entire book: John Ballantyne, Jonathan Dorfman, Cindy Klein Roche, and Robert Shaler. I am grateful to each of them for their time as well as their detailed and excellent advice. The scientists among them, John Ballantyne and Robert Shaler, spent a substantial amount of time engaged in telephone conversations with me when they had better things to do, as did Paul Ferrara, another scientist to whom I am indebted.

No two people were more helpful to me in getting this book launched than Laura Goldin and Charles Danziger, and I am very thankful to each. Along the way, many people generously provided interviews and materials: Scott Shellenberger, Risa Sugarman, Peter Coddington, George Clarke, Rockne Harmon, Elizabeth Lederer, Manfred Hochmeister, Gil Childers, and Lori Yoffe stand out.

As a lawyer, I was new to the world of publishing. My agents, Georges Borchardt and Cindy Klein Roche, and my editors, Susan Rabiner and Steven Fraser, guided me through that realm with the utmost of professionalism. I could not have been in better hands.

This work draws heavily on experiences had and expertise developed during my years in the Manhattan District Attorney's Office. During that time, my work in the new field of DNA analysis had the full support of the District Attorney, Robert M. Morgenthau, and my bureau chief, Allen Frazer, and I am extremely thankful to them both.

Finally, I am grateful to my parents, Herbert Monte Levy and Marilyn Wohl Levy, and my siblings, Matthew Levy and Alison Levy, for the support and encouragement only family can provide.

NOTES AND SOURCES

CHAPTER 1: GETTING TO HOMICIDE

This chapter is based primarily on my experience as co-counsel on the Matias Reyes case. I have also drawn heavily from court records and police reports. Of course, my eight years of experience prosecuting criminal cases figures heavily in the perspective on the criminal justice system and DNA offered in this and other chapters.

The lawyers originally responsible for prosecution of the Reyes case were Assistant District Attorneys Peter Casolaro and Richard Girgenti, two of the most senior and talented trial lawyers in the Manhattan District Attorney's Office. I was initially brought into the case to advise Richard Girgenti about the DNA results and to aid him in preparation for the pretrial hearing on the admissibility of the DNA evidence. When Girgenti left the District Attorney's Office to become New York State commissioner of criminal justice, Peter Casolaro asked me to assume the role of co-counsel on the Reyes case, and I did.

CHAPTER 2: BREAKTHROUGH

My account of the story of Cain and Abel and the quotation upon which the title of this book is based are drawn from *Tanakh: The Holy Scriptures* (Philadelphia and Jerusalem: The Jewish Publication Society, 1985).

———

Most scientific discussions of DNA testing, in both court decisions and scientific articles, explain it by laying out the separate components of the scientific process that result in a DNA print. These "explanations" are usually unintelligible to a layperson, who has no familiarity with the various scientific techniques described. Instead of reciting these highly technical steps in the text, I have sought to explain the science of DNA testing in broad terms that capture its drama and its genuine scientific meaning. I have not found any source besides this book that explains the meaning of a DNA match in such terms and places DNA testing in its proper context among the great breakthroughs in biotechnology of our time. I hope that this book will make a contribution in these areas.

204   NOTES AND SOURCES

Three books were particularly helpful in educating me about the broader scientific developments in human genetics that laid the foundation for the use of DNA testing in criminal cases. I have drawn factual details regarding the modern revolution in human genetics underlying DNA testing from Jerry E. Bishop and Michael Waldholz's *Genome* (New York: Simon and Schuster, 1990) and Robert Shapiro's *The Human Blueprint* (New York: St. Martin's, 1991). I also found helpful James D. Watson's inside account of the discovery of the structure of DNA in *The Double Helix* (New York: Atheneum, 1968).

While I have declined to recite the scientific techniques underlying DNA analysis in the main text, no work on DNA would be complete without an explanation of them. The technical process that produces a DNA print has seven steps: (1) DNA is extracted from the various biological samples to be tested, for instance, the victim's DNA, the crime-scene DNA, the suspect's DNA. (2) DNA from each sample is broken (digested) into a precise number of fragments through the application of a restriction enzyme, a chemical scissors that cuts the DNA at specific known sites. (3) The fragments are placed in a gel, loaded at the top, with the fragments from each separate DNA sample (i.e., the crime scene DNA, the suspect's DNA) placed in a separate lane in that gel. An electrical charge is applied to separate the fragments within each lane by length, a process known as electrophoresis. (4) The DNA molecule is separated into two strands (denaturation). (5) The single strands are transferred from the malleable surface of a gel to the firm surface of a nylon membrane. (6) Radioactive single strands of DNA known as probes locate specific complementary strands of DNA on the membrane and bind with those strands in a process known as hybridization. (7) The membrane is placed on an X-ray film and exposed to produce a piece of film known as an autoradiograph. The locations of the fragments that have hybridized are seen as bands on the autoradiograph. Usually, there are two bands in each lane, one contributed to an individual's DNA by that person's father and one contributed by that person's mother. When the bands in the suspect's lane and the crime-scene lane are in alignment on a piece of film, there is a DNA "match" at the particular genetic location that has been probed. After removal of the bound radioactive probe from the membrane, steps 6 and 7 are repeated, using additional probes to produce additional autoradiographs. Each autoradiograph represents an analysis of DNA fragment lengths at a different genetic location.

The phrase "raw graphic power" to describe the impact of DNA autoradiographs is drawn from Rockne Harmon's article "Legal Criticisms of DNA Typing: Where's the Beef," 84 *Journal of Criminal Law and Criminology* 175 (Spring 1993).

The account of the discovery of DNA analysis by Dr. Alec Jeffreys and of the use of DNA testing to solve the murders of Lynda Mann and Dawn

Ashworth is drawn from Joseph Wambaugh's *The Blooding* (New York: William Morrow, 1989). Wambaugh's account of Jeffreys's discovery and of the investigation of the Narborough village murders is detailed and compelling.

———

Alec Jeffreys himself published several scientific papers relating to his seminal discovery: A. J. Jeffreys, V. Wilson, and S. L. Thein, "Hypervariable 'Minisatellite' Regions in Human DNA," 314 *Nature* 67 (1985); A. J. Jeffreys, V. Wilson, and S. L. Thein, "Individual-Specific 'Fingerprints' of Human DNA," 316 *Nature* 76 (1985); and P. Gil, A. J. Jeffreys, and D. J. Werrett, "Forensic Application of DNA Fingerprints," 318 *Nature* 577 (1985).

CHAPTER 3: THE TROUBLE WITH DNA

My account of the Castro case is based heavily on my review of transcripts, court records, and police reports, and interviews with the prosecutors, Risa Sugarman and Peter Coddington. A transcript of Dr. Eric Lander's initial encounter with Dr. Michael Baird at the Banbury Conference can be found in J. Ballantyne, G. Sensabaugh, and J. Witkowski, *DNA Technology and Forensic Science,* Banbury Report 32 (Cold Spring Harbor Laboratory Press, 1989), at 183–90. The discussion also draws extensively on four articles relating to the Castro case, listed here in chronological order: Roger Lewin, "DNA Typing on the Witness Stand," 244 *Science* 1033, June 2, 1989; Eric Lander, "DNA Fingerprinting on Trial," 339 *Nature* 501, June 15, 1989; Roger Parloff, "How Barry Scheck and Peter Neufeld Tripped Up the DNA Experts," *American Lawyer,* December 1989, at 50; and Rorie Sherman, "DNA Tests Unravel?" *National Law Journal,* December 18, 1989, at 1.

———

Judge Gerald Sheindlin's decision in *People v. Castro* can be found at 144 Misc. 2d 956 (Sup. Ct. Bx. Co. 1989). The joint statement of the Castro experts, which weighed so heavily in that decision, was signed by four experts (Richard Roberts, Eric Lander, Carl Dobkin, and Lorraine Flaherty) on May 11, 1989.

———

The scientific standards for DNA testing developed by a group of independent scientists working under the auspices of the FBI are known as the TWGDAM standards because these "Guidelines for a Quality Assurance Program for DNA Restriction Fragment Length Polymorphism Analysis" were promulgated by the Technical Working Group on DNA Analysis Methods. The standards were initially published in *Crime Laboratory Digest,* April–July 1989, at 40–59. A revised version was next published in the April 1991 issue of *Crime Laboratory Digest,* at 44–75. The current version of these guidelines may be found in the April 1995 edition of *Crime Laboratory Digest,* at 21–43.

———

The FBI's environmental insult studies, which assessed the impact of various contaminants on RFLP testing, were summarized in a paper by Dwight E. Adams, "Validation of the FBI Procedure for DNA Analysis: A Summary," in *Crime Laboratory Digest*, October 1988, at 106–8.

———

This chapter includes quotations from a number of publications, as follows:

Page
46   "I quickly became rather concerned" and "none of this lawyerly talk," Lewin, "DNA Typing," at 1034.
47   "a ten-foot-wide butterfly net," Lander, "DNA Fingerprinting," at 504.
50   "Some Scientists Doubt the Value of 'Genetic Fingerprint' Evidence," Gina Kolata, *New York Times*, January 29, 1990, at A1.
50   "excellent agreement," unpublished letter to the editor of *New York Times*, February 9, 1990, by C. Thomas Caskey; co-signers listed are Daniel D. Garner, James W. Geyer, Thomas Marr, and Raymond White.
51   "There is a great danger," Lewin, "DNA Typing," at 1035.
56   "red herrings that do the courts and the public a disservice," U.S. Congress, Office of Technology Assessment, *Genetic Witness: Forensic Uses of DNA Tests* (Washington, D.C.: U.S. Government Printing Office, July 1990), at 8.

CHAPTER 4: INSIDE THE CENTRAL PARK JOGGER TRIAL

This chapter draws on my personal involvement in the Central Park jogger case, on transcripts of the court proceedings, and on the defendants' own statements, both videotaped and written.

I have also drawn some factual details from Timothy Sullivan's *Unequal Verdicts: The Central Park Jogger Trials* (New York: Simon and Schuster, 1992).

CHAPTER 5: THE TRIUMPH OF DNA

This chapter is based primarily on my extensive interview of Scott Shellenberger, the former Baltimore County prosecutor responsible for the investigation and prosecution of the Ritter case, and our visit to the crime scene. I also interviewed Terry Woodhouse, the detective assigned to this investigation. I have relied heavily on my review of the case files of the Baltimore County District Attorney's Office.

The statements made at the time of Ritter's sentence (by Scott Shellenberger, Detective Woodhouse, and the rape victim) were quoted in an April 27, 1992, Associated Press report by John Roll, "DNA Evidence Frees Man, Convicts Another in Rape Case."

CHAPTER 6: VITRIOL

My summary of the arguments of the critics and proponents of DNA testing is drawn directly from R. C. Lewontin and Daniel L. Hartl, "Population Genetics in Forensic DNA Typing," 254 *Science* 1745–50, December 20, 1991, and Ranajit Chakraborty and Kenneth Kidd, "Utility of DNA Typing in Forensic Work," 254 *Science* 1735–39, December 20, 1991.

———

The report that Dr. Hartl's office was the source of the leak of the *Science* article was published by Leslie Roberts in "Science in Court: A Culture Clash," 257 *Science* 732, August 7, 1992, at 735.

———

For a discussion of the DNA case law that preceded publication of the Lewontin and Hartl article, see my article "DNA: Race, Ethnicity, and Statistical Evidence," *New York Law Journal*, July 25, 1991, Outside Counsel Column, at 1.

———

The Ohio case referred to in the text was *United States v. Bonds,* 12 F. 3d 540 (6th Cir. 1993), affirming 134 F.R.D. 161 (N.D. Ohio 1991). That case was more widely known by those who follow legal developments relating to DNA as *United States v. Yee,* under which it was reported in the federal district court.

———

The quotations in this chapter are from the following sources:

Page
106 "45 percent of those arrested," Fox Butterfield, "More Blacks in Their Twenties Have Trouble with the Law," *New York Times,* October 5, 1995, at A18.
107 "terribly misleading" and "unjustifiable," Lewontin and Hartl, "Population Genetics," at 1749, 1750.
108 "melting pot," Chakraborty and Kidd, "Utility of DNA Typing," at 1737.
109 "I'm a statistician," comment by Bruce Weir, author's personal notes made at general session of Second International Symposium on the Forensic Aspects of DNA Analysis, Federal Bureau of Investigation, Quantico, VA, March 29–April 2, 1993.
109 "general acceptance," *Frye v. United States,* 293 F. 1013, 1014 (D.C. Cir. 1923).
113 "barnacles on the walls of society" and the "discrepancy," Affidavit of James R. Wooley, February 19, 1992, on Government's Response to Motion for New Trial, in *United States v. Yee.*
114 "I told him that," Leslie Roberts, "Fight Erupts over DNA Fingerprinting," 254 *Science* 1721, December 20, 1991, at 1722.
114 "political consequences," Christopher Anderson, "DNA Fingerprinting Discord," 354 *Nature* 500, December 19/26, 1991, at 500.

Page

114 "very serious breach," Letter from R. C. Lewontin, Professor, Harvard University, to James R. Wooley, U.S Department of Justice, October 16, 1991.

115 "I felt publishing the article" and "I thought that there were major scientific points," Roberts, "Fight Erupts," at 1722.

116 "Pure politics"; "I think it is quite extraordinary," ibid.

116 "I did it to give a more balanced view," ibid.

116 "disturbed that the data"; "ask him for revisions," ibid.

116 "would be met with the biggest stink," ibid.

117 "long-awaited Federal report . . . "; "says courts should cease to admit DNA evidence," Gina Kolata, *New York Times,* April 14, 1992, at A1.

117 "Forgive me if I seem to be a little bit out of breath," Opening statement, Victor A. McKusick, Chair, Committee on DNA Technology in Forensic Science, April 14, 1992.

117 "incorrect" and "strong evidence," National Research Council, "Statement Regarding April 14, 1992, article in *New York Times* and New York Times News Service."

119 "ceiling principle," National Research Council, *DNA Technology in Forensic Science* (Washington, DC: National Academy Press, 1992).

120 "common ground," *People v. Barney and Howard,* 8 Cal. App. 4th 798, 10 Cal. Rptr. 2d 731 (Ct. App. 1992).

120 "incompetent," author's personal notes, Second International Symposium on the Forensic Aspects of DNA Analysis. Newton Morton's comment regarding Galileo's time was made at the same conference and is also reflected in my personal notes. Both comments were made in general session.

120 "illogical," Peter Aldhous, "Geneticists Attack NRC Report as Scientifically Flawed," 259 *Science* 755, February 5, 1993, at 755.

120 "If I were asked if there is any scientific justification," ibid.

121 "persistence of disputes threatens," *People v. Wallace,* 14 Cal. App. 4th 651, 17 Cal. Rptr. 2d 721 (Ct. App. 1993).

122 "austere standard," *Daubert v. Merrell Dow Pharmaceuticals, Inc.,* 113 Sup. Ct. Rptr. 2786, 2794 (1993). The case law interpreting *Daubert* as supporting a liberal standard for the admissibility of DNA evidence is discussed (and criticized) in B. Scheck, "DNA and Daubert," 15 *Cardozo Law Review* 1959 (April 1994).

123 "has been resolved" and "time to move on," Bruce Budowle and Eric Lander, "DNA Fingerprinting Dispute Laid to Rest," 371 *Nature* 735, October 27, 1994.

CHAPTER 7: MANHUNT

The account of the Jean Ann Broderick case is based on my interview of the Hennepin County prosecutor, Steve Redding, as well as press reports regarding the case. These reports include: "DNA Identifies Suspect in

Slaying," *Saint Paul Pioneer Press,* December 20, 1991, at 1B; "Jury Find
Perez Guilty of First-Degree Murder; Life Sentence Imposed," *Saint Paul
Pioneer Press,* April 23, 1993, at 2B; and "Rapists Have It Easy," *Our
Town,* May 4, 1994, at 18.

———

The quotation from Redding is from "Rapists Have It Easy." The count of
the number of states with DNA data banking laws by 1993 is based on a
survey conducted that year by the Office of the Chief Medical Examiner
of the City of New York. The details of the Stuyvesant Town case are
based primarily on court records and police reports. The quotation
describing Michelle Munagas ("She was terribly upset") and certain factual details regarding the case are from a news article, "Prosecutor's
Duty and a Sister's Dilemma," *New York Times,* April 10, 1994, at 41. The
quotations from Richard Girgenti and a Manhattan prosecutor (the
author) are from "Rapists Have It Easy."

———

The ruling from New York State's highest court endorsing DNA testing was
People v. Wesley, 83 N.Y. 2d 417, 611 N.Y.S. 2d 97, 633 N.E. 2d 451 (1994).

———

The states that had enacted data banking laws by the beginning of 1996
were Alabama (Ala. Code 36–18–20 and materials following); Alaska
(Alaska Stat. 22.20 and 44.41.035); Arizona (Ariz. Rev. Stat. Ann. 31–281
and 13–4438); Arkansas (House Bill No. 1560); California (Cal. Penal Code
290.2); Colorado (Colo. Rev. Stat. 17–2–201 [5][g][I]); Connecticut (Conn.
Gen. Stat. 54–102g–54–1021); Delaware (Del. Code Ann. title 29, sec.
4713); Florida (Fla. Stat. Ann. 943.325); Georgia (Ga. Code Ann. 24–4–60);
Hawaii (Haw. Rev. Stat. 706–603); Illinois (Ill. Rev. Stat. chap. 730, para.
5–4–3); Iowa (Iowa Code Ann. 13.10 and 61–8.1[13] and materials following); Kansas (Kan. Stat. Ann. 21–2511); Kentucky (Ky. Rev. Stat. Ann.
17:170 and 17:175); Louisiana (La. Rev. Stat. Ann. 15:535); Maine (Me.
Rev. Stat. Ann. title 25, at 1571, and materials following); Maryland (Md.
Ann. Code, art. 88B, at 12A); Michigan (Michigan Comp. Laws Ann. sec.
750.520[m] and 791.233d); Minnesota (Minn. Stat. Ann., at 609.3461 and
299C.155); Mississippi (Miss. Code Ann. 45–33–15); Missouri (Mo. Ann.
Stat. 650.050 and 650.055); Montana (Mont. Code Ann. 41–5–604);
Nevada (Nev. Rev. Stat. 176.111); New Jersey (N.J. Stat. Ann 53:1–20.17
and materials following); New York (Laws of N.Y. chap. 737, art. 49-B,
sec. 995-C); North Carolina (N.C. Gen. Stat. 15A–266.1 and materials following); North Dakota (N.D. Cent. Code 31–13–01 and materials following); Ohio (Ohio Rev. Code 2901.07); Oklahoma (Okla. Stat. Ann.
57.584 and 74 sec. 150.27a); Oregon (Oregon Rev. Stat. 181.085 and
137.076); Pennsylvania (18 Pa. Cons. Stat. 9209); South Carolina (S.C.
Code Ann. 23–3–600 and materials following); South Dakota (S.D. Codi-
fied Laws Ann. 23–5–14 and materials following); Tennessee (Tenn. Code
Ann. 38–6–113, 40–35–321, and Senate Bill No. 1144); Texas (Tex. Code
Ann. 411.141 and materials following); Utah (Utah Code Ann. 53.5–212.1
and materials following); Virginia (Va. Code Ann. 19.2–310.2); Wash-

ington (Wash. Rev. Code 43.43.752 and 43.43.754); West Virginia (W. Va. Code 15–2B–6); and Wisconsin (Wis. Stat. Ann. 973.047, 165.76, 165.77). The source of this compilation is the American Prosecutors Research Institute, Alexandria, Virginia.

CHAPTER 8: SUDDEN INSIGHT: THE WORLD TRADE CENTER BOMBING AND BEYOND

The account of Kary Mullis's invention of PCR is drawn from his article "The Unusual Origin of the Polymerase Chain Reaction," 262 *Scientific American,* April 1990, 56, 65. Mullis's California night ride, during which he conceived the PCR process, took place in 1983. Mullis left Cetus in 1986.

———

Mullis was a coauthor of two scientific articles regarding PCR: R. K. Saiki, T. L. Bugawan, G. T. Horn, K. B. Mullis, and H. A. Erlich, "Analysis of Enzymatically Amplified Beta-Globin and HLA-DQ-Alpha DNA with Allele-Specific Oligonucleotide Probes," 324 *Nature* 163 (1986); and R. K. Saiki, D. H. Gelfand, S. Stoffel, S. J. Scharf, R. Higuchi, G. T. Horn, K. B. Mullis, and H. A. Erlich, "Primer-Directed Enzymatic Amplification of DNA with a Thermostable DNA Polymerase," 239 *Science* 487 (1988).

———

The use of PCR to analyze the DNA of a woolly mammoth was discussed in Jean L. Marx, "Multiplying Genes by Leaps and Bounds," 240 *Science* 1408 (June 10, 1988), at 1408.

———

Mullis's animus toward Henry Erlich is recounted in Robert Shapiro, *The Human Blueprint* (New York: St. Martin's Press, 1991), at 249.

———

The early court case from California indicating that PCR analysis could falsely exculpate criminal defendants was discussed extensively in my article "DNA Evidence in Criminal Cases: Legal Developments," *New York Law Journal,* April 25, 1990, Outside Counsel Column, at 1.

———

The tests performed by the FBI in determining the readiness of PCR testing for forensic use included studies focusing particularly on the susceptibility of PCR to contamination. These included Catherine Comey and Bruce Budowle, "Validation Studies on the Analysis of the HLA DQ alpha Locus Using the Polymerase Chain Reaction," 36 *Journal of Forensic Sciences* 1633–48, November 1991.

———

In 1991, the independent scientists who had previously promulgated laboratory standards for RFLP analysis (the TWGDAM group) issued revised standards applying to both RFLP and PCR analysis. Revised standards also applicable to both RFLP and PCR were issued in 1995 (see note, *supra*).

The discussion of the World Trade Center bombing case is based primarily on transcripts of that trial. Some facts are drawn from my interview of the prosecutor, Gil Childers, and on excellent coverage of the bombing itself by the *New York Times*. The quotation from Gil Childers is from his remarks to the jury on his rebuttal in closing arguments.

The PCR test first used in criminal cases was the DQ alpha test. It discriminates among twenty-one genetic types a person can have on the DQ alpha region of his or her sixth chromosome. The DQ alpha test was first marketed by Cetus in 1990. Subsequently, the PCR division of Cetus was acquired by Hoffmann La-Roche, the New Jersey–based pharmaceutical company. The DQ alpha test is today marketed by Perkin-Elmer under license from Roche Molecular Systems.

Like the DQ alpha test, the D1S80 test analyzes variation at one genetic location (here a location on the first chromosome). The D1S80 test analyzes variation in DNA fragment lengths and provides greater individuation than the DQ alpha test. The D1S80 kit is owned by Roche Molecular Systems and was first marketed by Perkin-Elmer in 1991.

Two more PCR tests, the polymarker or "PM" test and the STR test, both allow analysis of several genetic locations. These tests provide far greater individuation than the DQ alpha test.

The polymarker test, like the DQ alpha test, analyzes specific genetic types rather than variations in DNA length. It is owned by Roche Molecular Systems and was first marketed by Perkin-Elmer in 1993. In 1995, Perkin-Elmer issued a revised version of the polymarker kit, which also performs the DQ alpha test. As a scientific technique, it poses some issues relating to its utility for analyzing mixtures of fluids from different sources.

The STR test, based on work first published in 1991 by Dr. Thomas Caskey, analyzes the number of copies of short, repetitive sequences (known as short tandem repeats) on numerous chromosomes, accordingly analyzing characteristics more like those analyzed by the RFLP and the D1S80 tests than those analyzed by the DQ alpha or polymarker tests. It was marketed by Promega in 1994, and primer sets for STR analysis are also sold by Perkin-Elmer. An STR match has a statistical significance comparable to that of a RFLP match at four genetic locations.

Depending on sample size, several PCR tests (the DQ alpha test, the D1S80 test, and the polymarker test) may be run on one biological sample. The greater the number of PCR tests that match a suspect, the greater the significance of the PCR match.

My account of the Jack Unteweger case is based in part on my interviews of Dr. Manfred Hochmeister of the University of Bern, Switzerland, and former FBI agent Gregg McCrary. Dr. Hochmeister kindly provided me with an advance copy of his forthcoming article about the Unteweger case from the *Journal of Forensic Science*, coauthored with Bruce Budowle,

Arthur Eisenberg, and Richard Dinhofer, "Using Multiplex PCR Amplification and Typing Kits for the Analysis of DNA Evidence in a Serial Killer Case." That manuscript contained facts regarding both the crimes and the scientific evidence from the Unteweger case that I used in preparing this chapter. Gregg McCrary provided me with a variety of materials relating to the case. The description of the "signature" aspect of Unteweger's crimes is based both on my interview of Gregg McCrary and on the account of his courtroom testimony contained in the article "Motive der Serienmorder: Macht uber Leben und Tod," *Neue Kronen Zeitung,* June 9, 1994, at 20, translated for me from the German by Berlin attorney Esther Caspary.

––––––

The discussion of the Honaker case draws in part on my interviews of Philip Payne, Commonwealth Attorney, Nelson County, Virginia, Paul Ferrara, Director of the Virginia Division of Forensic Science, and Kate Germond of Centurion Ministries. I have also drawn on scientific reports prepared in connection with that case and on the clemency plea submitted to Virginia Governor George F. Allen on behalf of Edward Honaker.

––––––

My discussion of the Unteweger and Honaker cases also draws facts from the following media sources and uses quotations from them as follows:

Page
145 "Unteweger represented," Rick Atkinson, "Killer Prose," *Washington Post,* August 3, 1994, B1, at B9.
146 "We will never find," ibid.
149 "If they can conduct the DNA test," ibid.
149 "I was a rat," ibid., at B1.
150 "It was his best murder," ibid., at B9.
150 "The jury said he was guilty," ibid., at B1.
151 "Lieutenant Kolacky," Tom Dunkel, "Reasonable Doubt?" *Washington Post,* June 26, 1994, F1, at F4.
152 "This man," ibid.
152 "No, sir, no," "DNA," *60 Minutes,* October 23, 1994, Transcript produced by Burelle's Information Services, at 11.
152 "There is no mistake," Dunkel, "Reasonable Doubt?" at F4.
152 "It is unlikely," ibid.
153 "The days just kept," ibid., at F1.
153 "My expectations," "No Higher Calling," *Los Angeles Times,* January 2, 1995, at E4.
154 "What was very critical to me," Dunkel, "Reasonable Doubt?," at F1.
154 "No matter how hard we try," ibid., at F1.
156 "Absent the development," ibid.

––––––

My discussion of the likely role of STRs in the future draws particularly on conversations with John Hicks, former chief of the Laboratory Division of the FBI, and Paul Ferrara. John Hicks also provided me with information about the FBI's original involvement in the field of DNA testing.

CHAPTER 9: O. J. SIMPSON:
WHAT THE BLOOD REALLY SHOWED

This chapter is based primarily on my analysis of the testimony from the O. J. Simpson trial, drawing heavily on my review of court transcripts and exhibits. Simpson trial DNA prosecutors George "Woody" Clarke and Rockne "Rock" Harmon were both extraordinarily generous with their time in discussing the issues posed by the DNA evidence in the trial. I have drawn some factual details from David Margolick's and Kenneth R. Noble's excellent reporting of the Simpson trial in *The New York Times*. My analysis of the defects in the prosecution's case draws in part on insights from Scott Turow's fine article "Simpson Prosecutors Pay for Their Blunders," *New York Times*, October 4, 1995, at A21. The statement that the National Institute of Justice was likely to conclude that external blind proficiency testing is "not feasible" was drawn from the minutes of the June 22, 1995, meeting of the DNA Advisory Board established pursuant to the DNA Identification Act of 1994.

———

This chapter includes quotations from court testimony and from the following media sources:

Page
165 "If you have a common source," Lorraine Adams and Serge F. Kovaleski, "The Best Defense Money Could Buy; Well-Heeled Simpson Legal Team Seemed One Step Ahead All Along," *Washington Post*, October 8, 1995, at A1
166 "From getting really old," Kenneth R. Noble, "Tempers Flare over Simpson DNA Expert's Drug Use," *New York Times*, March 31, 1995, at A27.
166 "As a father," David Margolick, "Simpson Defense Lawyers Decide, for Now, Not to Present Testimony by DNA Expert," *New York Times*, August 9, 1995, at A20 (quoting *Esquire* magazine).

CHAPTER 10: THE POWER OF DNA

I first became aware of the Mohit case from a presentation regarding that case by the presiding judge, Donald Silverman, at the Second International Symposium on the Forensic Aspects of DNA Analysis, held at the FBI Academy, Quantico, Virginia, March 29–April 2, 1993. My account of the case draws on that presentation, on Judge Silverman's decision in *People v. Morteza Mohit*, 153 Misc. 2d 22, 579 N.Y.S. 2d 990

(Sup. Ct. Westchester Co. 1992), and on the decision of the New York State Administrative Review Board for Professional Medical Conduct, *In the Matter of Morteza Mohit, M.D.* (March 11, 1992). I have also drawn some factual details regarding the Mohit trial from a series of articles in the *Gannett Westchester Newspapers,* as follows: "Doctor Pleads Innocent to Rape," October 20, 1990; "DNA Evidence OK'd for Rape Case," July 30, 1991, at A10; "Defense: Doctor's Sex with Patient 'Wrong,'" July 31, 1991, at A13; "Jury Due to Get Case of Doctor Charged with Rape," August 6, 1991, at A10; "Doctor Acquitted of Rape," August 7, 1991, at A1; "State to Review Mohit's Conduct," August 8, 1991, at A19; "Woman Maintains Doctor, Despite Acquittal, Raped Her," August 9, 1991, at A1; "Doctor Ruled Unfit by State Conduct Board," February 7, 1992, at A12; "Doctor Found Innocent to Appeal State Fitness Ruling," March 6, 1992, at 6; and "Doctor's Sex with Patient Brings License Revocation," June 6, 1993, at A6.

My discussion of the Page case is based on my conversations with former Baltimore County prosecutor Scott Shellenberger, who was responsible for the prosecution of the Page brothers.

The account of the contents of the National Research Counsel's second report is based on a pre-publication copy of *The Evaluation of Forensic DNA Evidence* (Washington, D.C.: National Academy Press, 1996).

The popular mistrust of DNA testing following the O. J. Simpson trial is discussed in William Glaberson, "Rematch for DNA in a Rape Case," *New York Times,* April 10, 1996, at B5.

INDEX

Allen, George F., 154–56
Ashworth, Dawn, 27–29
"Austere standard" concept, 122
Autoradiographs
  in Castro murder trial, 44
  defined, 204
Ayyad, Nidal, 141–44

Baird, Michael, 43, 45, 47
Blake, Edward, 139–40, 154
Blood evidence
  for DNA analysis in Reyes case, 12
  Ponce-Rivera murders, 41
  in Ritter case, 95, 99–101
Blood evidence, Simpson trial
  challenged by defense, 171–85
  conventional serological tests of, 175–77
  detection of Goldman's blood, 178–79, 183
  detection of Nicole Brown's blood, 178–79, 181, 183
  DNA matches, 157–64
  implicating Simpson, 186–88
  RFLP analysis, 165, 171–88
Blooding, The (Wambaugh), 31
Blood samples
  for DNA data banks, 128–29
  for DNA testing, 99–100
  Narborough murders, 29–30

Stuyvesant Town rapes, 133
Broderick, Jean Ann, 125–26
Budowle, Bruce, 53–55, 123

Caskey, Thomas, 13–14, 54, 111, 113, 115
Castro, Joseph
  admission by, 49
  identification of, 37–40
  as suspect in Ponce-Rivera murders, 33–35
Central Park jogger
  assault on, 4
  discovery, hospitalization, and identification of, 69–70
  facts about, 64–65
Central Park rampage, Central Park jogger case, 61–68
Cellmark laboratory
  role in development of DNA testing by, 52
  RFLP system for analysis, 54
  use of DNA for criminal identification, 53–54
Cetus Corporation, 138–39
Chakraborty, Ranajit, 116
Childers, Gil, 144
Chin, Ming, 121
Chromosomes
  composition and role of, 23
  DNA match at, 25, 118–19
Clark, Marcia, 162

215

Clarke, George "Woody,"
  170–71, 175–76
Colon, Carlos, 68–69
Confession
  as evidence, 10
  legal limits to obtaining,
    21
  by suspect, 1–3
Conneally, Michael, 13–14
Contamination
  effect on DNA print, 54
  in second NRC report (1996),
    194
Contamination theory,
    Simpson trial
  blood evidence in Simpson
    trial, 175–77
  of planted glove, 184–85
  strategy of defense related
    to, 163–67, 173–74
  strategy of prosecution
    related to, 164–65
Cotton, Robin, 165, 168
Court system
  admission of DNA evidence,
    123
  decision in California based
    on NRC DNA report,
    120–21
  DNA admissibility standards
    in California, 120
  evidence using PCR tech-
    nique, 140–41
  Supreme Court decision in
    Daubert, 122–23
  use of PCR technique, 140
Criminal cases
  analysis of repeat DNA pat-
    terns, 24–25
  conference on use of DNA
    in, 43–44
  DNA testing for identifica-
    tion, 196–97
  kind of evidence in, 10
  signature crimes, 148
Criminal identification

commercial laboratory use
    of DNA for, 53
  using PCR technique, 139–40
Cuomo, Mario, 134

Darden, Christopher, 180, 183
Data banks. See DNA data
    banks
Daubert v. Merrell Dow Phar-
    maceuticals, Inc. (1993),
    122–23
Davis, John
  arrest and release of, 94–96
  identification as rapist,
    92–94
  relationship with Carole
    Sanders, 88–90
Davis, Katherine, 5–6
Dean, Patricia, 63–64
Defense case
  based on consent in Mohit
    rape trial, 190
  Castro trial, 44–48
  raising reasonable doubt,
    11–12
  Simpson trial, 158–86, 190
Denaturation, 204
Detectives
  strategies to elicit confes-
    sions, 1–11
  strategy in Central Park
    jogger case, 71–8
Diaz, Antonio, 63–64
DNA
  copying through PCR tech-
    nique, 138–39
  in human cells, 22–23
  as identifying tool, 25–26
  as markers to find specific
    genes, 23–24
  popular view of, 195
  technical process to produce
    print, 204
DNA analysis
  of blood evidence in
    Simpson trial, 171–85

differences in patterns, 107
as established science,
    198–99
FBI research and training in,
    53
first use to solve homicide,
    26–31
frequency of, 195–96
of hairs of identical twins,
    191–92
power of, 24, 191
probes, 54, 204
role of, 18, 20
in Sanders rape investiga-
    tion, 95–96, 99–101
scientific guidelines for, 55,
    205
threats to admissibility in
    court, 111–15
of watchband blood in
    Ponce-Rivera murders, 41.
    See also PCR technique;
    RFLP analysis
DNA autoradiographs, 44, 204
DNA data banks
Perez profile in Minneapolis,
    126–27
proposed New York State
    legislation for, 134–35
state-level data banking
    laws, 209–10
as tool, 126–29, 156
DNA evidence
admissibility linked to race
    and ethnicity, 105–24
admissibility of, 13–15,
    42–49, 109–12
in case against Martin Perez,
    126–28
in Central Park jogger case,
    59–60, 78–81, 85
defense criticism of PCR evi-
    dence, 163
in determination of truth, 21
in dismissal of case against
    Davis, 96

hair of identical twins, 191
hair in prostitute murders,
    149
influence of Daubert deci-
    sion on introduction of,
    122–23
on issue of identity, 197
judicial support for relia-
    bility of, 134–35
in Monagas rape cases, 133
power of, 25–26, 105, 156,
    191
rejection by judge in Castro
    trial, 44–49
Reyes pretrial hearing,
    13–15
Science article critical of FBI
    approach, 111–14
Simpson attorneys strategy
    to undermine, 159–86
in World Trade Center
    bombing, 144. See also
    Blood evidence; Hair evi-
    dence; Saliva evidence;
    Semen evidence
DNA Identification Act (1994),
    170
DNA laboratories
accreditation of, 187, 198
external blind proficiency
    testing for, 169–70, 194-95
standards in aftermath of
    Simpson trial, 187. See
    also Cellmark laboratory;
    Federal Bureau of
    Investigation (FBI); Life-
    codes laboratory; Los
    Angeles Police Depart-
    ment DNA laboratory
DNA match
ceiling principle and NRC
    reports, 119–22, 193
described, 24–26
in DNA analysis, 204
factors in determination of,
    24–25, 204

DNA match (*cont.*)
  FBI guidelines and statistical
    methods, 54–55
  matching of chromosomes,
    118
  power of, 105–6
  race and ethnicity in stating
    significance of, 106–7
  saliva in World Trade Center
    bombing, 144
  statistics and, 25–26
  using PCR tests, 144
DNA technology
  FBI exploration of, 54
  invention of PCR technique,
    138–39
  NRC report endorsement,
    118
DNA testing
  development in United
    States, 52
  Office of Technology
    Assessment report (1990),
    56
  post-Castro case acceptance
    of, 55–56
  post-Castro trial debates
    over, 49–52
  post-conviction, 197–98
  questions of reliability
    (1989), 52
  scientific standards for, 205.
    See also DNA analysis;
    External blind proficiency
    testing
DQ alpha test. *See* PCR tests
D1S80 test. *See* PCR tests

Electrophoresis, 204
Erlich, Henry, 139
Ethnic groups
  differences within racial
    groups, 14, 107–9
  interpretation of DNA
    match, 93-94, 106, 119,
    193–94

Evidence
  in case against Honaker, 153
  in criminal cases, 10
  fingerprints, 7
  identification as, 10
  legal limits to obtaining, 21
  physical, 10
  in Ponce-Rivera murders,
    40–41
  in Unteweger trial, 149
  in World Trade Center
    bombing, 142–44. *See also*
    Blood evidence; Blood evi-
    dence, Simpson
    trial; DNA data bank; DNA
    evidence; Hair
    evidence; Saliva evidence;
    Scientific evidence;
    Semen evidence
Expert witnesses
  for DNA in Castro murder
    trial, 44–47
  Frye hearing testimony of,
    112
  in pretrial hearing, 13–14
  Simpson trial, 165–72,
    175–77, 182
External blind proficiency
    testing
  arguments for and against,
    169–70
  NRC recommendation for,
    169–70
  provisions in DNA Identifi-
    cation Act for, 170
  in second NRC DNA report
    (1996), 194–95

Fairstein, Linda, 79
Federal Bureau of Investiga-
    tion (FBI)
  Behavioral Science Unit, 147
  choice of statistical methods
    in DNA match, 54–55
  DNA analysis of Reyes's
    blood, 12

DNA analysis unit, 52
DNA matching approach,
    118–19, 121–22
endorsement of single-locus
    probe analysis, 54
and guidelines for DNA
    analysis, 55
research and training in
    DNA testing, 53–55
Science article critical of
    DNA approach, 111–14
scientific support for DNA
    matching approach, 120
standards for PCR analysis,
    140–41
Ferrara, Paul, 154
"Flexible standard," 122
Forensic Science Associates,
    139, 154
Francisi, Bruno, 3–6
Frye standard
for admissibility of scientific
    evidence, 109–10
discussion in *Daubert*,
    122–23
review of testimony in pre-
    trial hearing, 112
Fuhrman, Mark, 160, 162, 179,
    183–85
Fung, Dennis, 181

Garner, Robert, 66
Garrett, Patrick, 70
"General acceptance" stan-
    dard, 122
Genes
markers to find specific,
    23–24
role of, 23
Genetic characteristics
of DNA in Reyes case, 12–13
of ethnic groups within
    racial groups, 107–8,
    193–94
from PCR test, 144–45,
    149

Genetic diseases
analysis of DNA patterns to
    diagnose, 24
detection using PCR tech-
    nique, 139
Genetic fingerprinting tech-
    nique, 26, 193. *See also*
    RFLP analysis
Gerdes, John, 165–71, 176–77
Girgenti, Richard, 134
Good, David, 66

Hair evidence
of identical twins, 191–92
in murders of prostitutes,
    149
Hall, Amanda, 191
Harmon, Rockne, 168, 175–76
Hartl, Daniel, 111–15
Hildebrandt, Harry, 72–73
Homicide trials
evidence in, 41–42
presentation of DNA evi-
    dence in Castro trial,
    42–43
Honaker, Edward
case against, 151–53
clemency for, 154–56
proof of mistaken identity,
    197
verdict and sentencing of,
    153
Huemer, Peter, 145–47
Hybridization, 204

Innocence Project, 154
Ito, Lance, 183

Jeffreys, Alec, 26–31, 54
Jury
judge's instructions in
    Simpson trial to, 183,185
raising reasonable doubt
    with, 11–12
response to testimony of
    defendant, 81–84

Jury *(cont.)*
  use of evidence by, 10–11
  verdict in Central Park
    jogger case, 85
  verdict in Honaker case,
    152–53
  weight given to DNA match,
    123–24
  willingness to convict, 84

Kaelin, Brian "Kato," 184
Kidd, Kenneth, 54, 115–16
Kolata, Gina, 50, 117–18
Koshland, Daniel, 116

Laboratories, commercial. *See*
    Cellmark laboratory;
  Lifecodes laboratory
Lander, Eric, 43–47, 56, 123
Lansing, James, 62
Lederer, Elizabeth, 59, 73, 75,
    79–85
Lee, Henry, 172
Lewis, David, 65–66
Lewontin, Richard, 111–15
Lifecodes laboratory
  DNA analysis of blood in
    Ponce-Rivera murders, 41,
    44–47
  DNA testing in Castro case,
    41, 43–47, 49, 51
  RFLP system for analysis, 54
  role in development of DNA
    testing, 52
  use of DNA for criminal
    identification, 53–54
Los Angeles Police Depart-
    ment DNA laboratory
  criticism by defense in
    Simpson trial, 162–63,
    165–66
  defense claim of contamina-
    tion in, 165–69
  defense claim of DNA typing
    errors, 170–71
Loughlin, John, 67, 78

McCrary, Gregg, 147–48,
    150
McCray, Antron, 68, 72–75, 80,
    84–85
McKenna, Thomas, 76–77,
    82
McKinny, Laura Hart, 160
McKusick, Victor, 117
Malone, Gerald, 63–64
Mann, Lynda, 27, 29
Mohit, Morteza, 189–90
Monagas, Anthony, 132–33
Monagas, Michelle L.,
    131–32
Moore, Vinicio, 68–69
Morgenthau, Robert M., 19
Morton, Newton, 120
Mullis, Kary, 138–39, 165–66

Narborough murders, 26–31
National Academy of Sciences
  ceiling principle in DNA
    matching, 118–23, 193
  first report on DNA testing
    (1990), 56, 116–17
  scientific criticism of first
    DNA report, 120–21
  second report on DNA
    testing (1996), 193–95
  use of first DNA report in
    Simpson trial, 169
Nature
  article (1994) on DNA testi-
    mony, 123
  Jeffrey's genetic finger-
    printing article (1985), 26
Neufeld, Peter, 56, 165
  actions in Honaker case,
    154
  Castro's lawyer in DNA
    hearing, 44–45, 48
  challenge to DNA popula-
    tion statistics, 113
New York Times, the
  mistaken reporting of NRC
    DNA report, 117–18

post-Castro trial reporting
on DNA testing, 50, 52

Office of Technology Assessment (OTA) DNA report,
56, 199

Payne, Philip, 153–54, 156
PCR technique
advantages over RFLP
analysis, 140
discovery of, 138–39
handling criticised by
defense in Simpson trial,
163
matching, 144–45
for organ tissue matching,
139
uses for, 139–40
PCR tests
of blood evidence in
Simpson trial, 171–85
DQ alpha test, 144, 155, 211
D1S80 test, 144, 211
of hair in prostitute murders, 149
polymarker test, 144, 155,
211
in reopened Honaker case,
154–56
saliva in World Trade Center
bombing, 144
STR test, 144–45, 156, 211,
212
World Trade Center
bombing case, 144
Peratis, Thano, 161–62
Perez, Martin, 126–27
Pitchfork, Colin, 30–31, 197
Plea bargaining, 33
Polymarker test. See PCR
tests
Polymerase chain reaction
(PCR) technique. See PCR
technique
Powers, Robert, 67–68

Presley, Larry, 52–53
Pretrial hearing
Castro trial, 42– 49
Frye standard, 112
Reyes case, 13–15, 111
role of scientific experts in,
109
Probes
defined, 204
multi- and single-locus, 54
Prosecutors
basis for case against Central Park teenagers, 78,
84–85
role and responsibilities of,
19–20
Prosecutors, Simpson trial
counterarguments of, 182
criticism of, 183–84
DNA testing and proof in,
163–65, 179–80

Race
differences in frequency of
DNA patterns by, 107
FBI racial classification,
107–9, 111–13
in interpretation of DNA
match, 106, 119
NRC use of broad racial
groupings (1996), 193. See
also Ethnic groups
Rahman, Omar Abdel (sheik),
142
Reasonable doubt criterion,
11
Redding, Steve, 128
Reyes, Matias
blood sample for DNA
analysis, 12
confession to murder,
9–12
confession to serial rapes,
1–7
evidence in murder case
against, 10–11

Reyes, Matias (*cont.*)
  probability of specific DNA
    profile, 107
  trial and sentencing of,
    15–16
Reynolds, Elizabeth, 4
Reynolds, Eric, 67–68
RFLP analysis
  of blood evidence in
    Simpson trial, 165, 171–88
  early differences in commer-
    cial laboratory systems, 54
  and genetic fingerprinting
    technique, 26
  measurements of DNA pat-
    terns by, 23–25
  of Mohit semen, 189
RFLP testing
  advantages of PCR tech-
    nique over, 140
  by commercial laboratories
    in United States, 52
  FBI system, 54
  by Lifecodes and Cellmark
    laboratories, 52
Risch, Neil, 120
Ritter, Gregory, 95–103, 197
Rivera, David
  husband and father of
    Ponce-Rivera murder vic-
    tims, 34–38, 40
  identification of murder sus-
    pect, 37–40, 48–49
Roberts, Richard, 42–43,
  46–47
Rubin, Richard, 183–84

Salaam, Yusef, 76–78, 80, 82–85
Salameh, Mohammed,
  141–43
Saliva evidence, 144
Sanders, Carol
  assault and rape of, 90–92
  identification of rapist, 92–94
  relationship with John
    Davis, 88–90

Santana, Raymond, 68, 75–76,
  84–85
Scheck, Barry, 56
  actions in Honaker case,
    154
  Castro's lawyer in DNA
    hearing, 44–45, 48
  challenge to DNA popula-
    tion statistics, 113
  on handling of blood evi-
    dence in Simpson trial,
    174
  implied switching of blood
    swatches in Simpson tial,
    172–73
  summation in Simpson trial,
    170, 182
Science
  acceptance of Lewontin-
    Hartl DNA article,
    111–14
  publication of Lewontin-
    Hartl article and rebuttal
    (1991), 116
Scientific evidence
  "austere standard" of admis-
    sibility, 122
  "flexible standard" of admis-
    sibility, 122
  Frye standard of admissi-
    bility, 109–10
  "general acceptance" stan-
    dard of admissibility,
    109–10, 122
  Supreme Court *Daubert*
    decision, 122–23
Search warrant
  probable cause to get,
    100
  to take blood for DNA
    testing, 99–100
Semen evidence
  Central Park jogger case, 60,
    78, 80
  for DNA analysis in Reyes
    case, 12–13

in Honaker case, 151,
154–55
match to DNA data bank
information, 127–28
Narborough murders, 27,
29, 31
in Ritter case, 92, 96
in Stuyvesant Town rapes,
130–31, 133
Sex offenders, convicted,
128–29
Sheehan, Mike, 1, 7–9, 11–12
Sheindlin, Gerald, 48
Shellenberger, Scott, 94–96,
101–2
Simpson trial
implications for courtroom
use of DNA, 186–88
possible impact of, 195–96
strategy of defense in,
159–86. *See also* Blood evidence, Simpson trial;
Contamination theory,
Simpson trial; Defense
case, Simpson trial;
Prosecutors, Simpson
trial
Sims, Gary, 165, 168
STR test. *See* PCR tests

Stuyvesant Town rapes,
129–35
Sugarman, Risa, 33–34

TWGDAM standards, 205

Unteweger, Jack, 145–46,
148–50, 156

Vanatter, Philip, 160–61
Vigna, Michael, 62, 64

Wade, Nicholas, 118
Walsh, Joseph, 68–69
Walters, Alice, 88, 95, 97
Wambaugh, Joseph, 31
Watson, James, 42
Weir, Bruce, 109
White, Ray, 23, 54–55
Woodhouse, Terry, 94–101
Wooley, James R., 113–15
World Trade Center bombing,
facts about, 141–45
saliva evidence in, 194–95.
See also DNA evidence,
Evidence, World Trade
Center

Yamauchi, Collin, 161, 167–69,
172–74, 184